The Collapse of Apartheid and the Dawn of Democracy in South Africa, 1993

REACTING CONSORTIUM PRESS

This book is a "reacting" game. Reacting games are interactive role-playing games in which you, the student, are responsible for your own learning. They are used at more than 300 colleges and universities in the United States and abroad. Reacting Consortium Press is a publishing program of the Reacting Consortium, the association of schools that use reacting games. For more information, visit http://reactingconsortiumpress.org.

The Collapse of Apartheid and the Dawn of Democracy in South Africa, 1993

JOHN C. EBY AND

FRED MORTON

REACTING
CONSORTIUM PRESS

This game requires use of the
"Collapse of Apartheid" Instructors Manual and Role Sheets.
Participants in this game may play historical characters.
The representation of historical people by individuals
playing this game is a matter of personal interpretation
and should not be considered a thorough or precise
depiction of the character.

The University of North Carolina Press has been a
member of the Green Press Initiative since 2003.

ISBN 978-1-4696-3316-9 (pbk.   )
ISBN 978-1-4696-3317-6 (ebook)

Cover illustration: Frederik de Klerk and Nelson Mandela shake hands at the Annual Meeting of the World Economic Forum held in Davos in January 1992. Copyright © World Economics Forum (www.weforum.org).

Distributed by the
University of North Carolina Press
116 South Boundary Street
Chapel Hill, NC 27514-3808
1-800-848-6224
www.uncpress.unc.edu

Contents

Abbreviations Used in the Text / viii

1. INTRODUCTION / 1

Brief Overview of the Game / 1

Prologue: A Country on the Brink / 2

What Is a Historical Role-Playing Game? / 8

How to Play / 9

Game Setup / 9

Game Play / 9

Game Requirements / 10

Skill Development / 10

Counterfactuals / 10

2. HISTORICAL BACKGROUND / 12

Map / 12

Timeline / 12

1990 / 12

1991 / 14

1992 / 15

1993 / 17

The Struggle for a Democratic South Africa / 17

Toward the Multi-Party Negotiating Process (MPNP) / 17

The Multi-Party Talks (Kempton Park, April 1993) / 20

South Africans All / 21

The Road to the Multi-Party Talks / 29

3. THE GAME / 36

Major Issues for Debate / 37

Rules and Procedures / 38

Roles / 38

Prestige Points / 38

Cards / 39

Objectives and Victory Conditions / 40

Constitutional Working Groups / 40

Assignment / 40

Constitutional Working Groups Online / 40

Guidelines / 41

Assignments / 42

4. ROLES AND FACTIONS / 44

The African National Congress (ANC) / 44

The National Party (NP) / 46

Concerned South African Group (COSAG) / 47

Inkatha Freedom Party (IFP) / 48

Bophuthatswana, Ciskei / 49

Afrikaner Volksunie (AVU) / 49

Conservative Party (CP) / 50

South African Communist Party (SACP) / 50

Pan-Africanist Congress (PAC) / 51

Democratic Party (DP) / 51

Congress of South African Trade Unions (COSATU) / 52

Natal Indian Congress (NIC) / 52

5. CORE TEXTS AND SUPPLEMENTAL READINGS / 54

Core Texts / 54

Universal Declaration of Human Rights (1948) / 54

Hendrik F. Verwoerd: Explaining Apartheid (1950) / 57

The Freedom Charter (1955) / 61

Nelson Mandela: "Verwoerd's Grim Plot" (1959) / 64

Nelson Mandela: "I Am Prepared to Die" (1964) / 70

Steve Biko: "White Racism and Black Consciousness" / 82

Statement by the UDF National Executive Committee (1983) / 87

The Kairos Document: Challenge to the Church (1985) / 90

Supplemental Readings / 104

Constitution of the African National Congress / 104

ANC Policy Guidelines for a Democratic South Africa / 107

AZAPO Constitution (Excerpts) / 108

Address by State President F. W. de Klerk / 109

Joe Slovo: "Has Socialism Failed?" / 116

The Birth of the Inkatha Freedom Party (IFP) / 126

Buthelezi: "The Future of South Africa Should Be Determined by All Its Citizens" / 132

Negotiation Agreements / 133

Nelson Mandela Speeches / 139

Nkosi Sikelel' iAfrika / 146

Violence: The Role of the Security Forces / 147

Founding of COSATU, November 1985 / 151

Constitution of the South African Communist Party / 154

Significance of the African and Indian Joint Struggle / 155

Appendix 1—Homelands, Regions, and Countries / 165

Appendix 2—Pronunciation Glossary / 167

Appendix 3—Constitutional Worksheet / 169

Bibliography / 179

Acknowledgments / 183

Abbreviations Used in the Text

ANC	African National Congress
ANCWW	African National Congress, Women's Wing
ANCYL	African National Congress, Youth League
APLA	Azanian People's Liberation Army
AVU	Afrikaner Volksunie
AZAPO	Azanian People's Organisation
CCB	Civil Co-Operation Bureau
CODESA	Convention for a Democratic South Africa
COMSA	Commonwealth Observer Mission to South Africa
COSAG	Concerned South Africans Group
COSATU	Congress of South African Trade Unions
CP	Conservative Party
DP	Democratic Party
DRC	Dutch Reformed Church
IFP	Inkatha Freedom Party
INC	Indian National Congress
MK	Umkhonto we Sizwe
MPNP	Multi-Party Negotiating Process
NEC	National Executive Committee (ANC)
NIC	Natal Indian Congress
NP	National Party
PAC	Pan-Africanist Party
SACP	South African Communist Party
SADF	South African Defence Force
SAP	South African Police
UDF	United Democratic Front
ZCC	Zionist Christian Church

The Collapse of Apartheid and the Dawn of Democracy in South Africa, 1993

1

Introduction

"The Collapse of Apartheid and the Dawn of Democracy in South Africa" is a reacting role-playing game in which participants assume roles in the 1993 Multi-Party Negotiating Process (MPNP) at the World Trade Centre in Johannesburg. In their roles, participants seek to navigate complex political relationships, a troubling history, and often dissonant goals and concerns to build a constitution for a post-apartheid state.

While the historical setting for this game was deeply shaped by the legacies of European colonialism, years of racist political policy, and systematic injustice and disproportionate privileging of a minority population, this is *not* a game about race. Instead, this game reflects the highly complex interrelationships of "racial" groups in the collaborative effort to create a just society out of one that had been defined by injustice.

The immediate context for the game is a tense sociopolitical atmosphere that is on the verge of erupting into violent civil conflict. In fact, everyone expects things to head in that direction after a series of failed attempts at political negotiation. Only you, the participants in the MPNP, can put a halt to what seems to be an inevitable bloodbath.

You will begin in All-Party sessions in which the assembly meets as a whole to discuss some critical initial issues, mostly importantly whether the constitution drafted by the MPNP will be permanent or temporary. The process will then devolve to smaller Constitutional Working Groups (CWG) that will attempt to hash out details of the constitution in more manageable pieces. Finally, you will all reconvene in All-Party Talks to discuss the constitutional recommendations of each CWG and decide whether they are to be adopted or not.

All the while, skepticism abounds on the streets, and daily, even hourly, news comes to you of events looming over your conference, threatening to disable and destroy this last-ditch effort.

PROLOGUE: A COUNTRY ON THE BRINK

1 April, 1993

"Your first trip to South Africa?" he said to me as we took our seats next to one another on the flight from London to Johannesburg. "Let me guess—American?"

"Yeah. My first trip overseas, all right. I'm from Illinois. What about you?" I had no clue. He looked like he was from India or Pakistan or someplace like that.

"I guessed right about you, so what do you think?" he said, looking at me, amused. "Indian?" I said, in what seemed like a whisper.

"Ha ha," he chuckled. "I'm South African, from Jo'burg, though some of my relatives in Durban came from British India generations ago. Not the answer you expected, eh? Name's Rahim."

"Hi, Rahim. John. John Willmaeker." *What's Jo'burg? Maybe I should get back to my magazine. But I kind of like this guy.*

After takeoff, I told him a bit about where I'm from and that I was headed to South Africa to spend a month or two traveling around the region. After that, I planned to do a semester at the University of Cape Town, starting in August. Rahim was taking a break from Sussex University to see his family and attend his first cousin's wedding, which, from the sound of it, was going to be a big deal.

Then came the meal, a movie, and, surprisingly, sleep. With two hours left before landing, the flight attendants roused us and served up breakfast. The sun was coming up and beaming light into the cabin. I caught my first glimpse of Africa, below.

"So," asked Rahim, "where do you plan to stay after we clear customs and immigration?"

"Well, I've been corresponding with a student at Wits University who says I can always stay with her parents, but I've got to figure out how to phone her after we land."

"Oh, your first acquaintance in South Africa is a female, eh? Are you sure you're here to study?"

Rahim, I could see, was a jokester. "If I don't make contact with Fiona," I told him, "I'll just find

a youth hostel in town and crash there. I've got an address of one in a place called Hillbrow."

"Hillbrow? You're kidding. Not the safest place to be, Johnny, my boy," said Rahim. "How much do you know about South Africa?"

"Oh, I've done a bit of reading," I mumbled. Not much, though. I'd signed up for study abroad in South Africa like I'd done before in Europe—without much prior knowledge. It was more just a way to get out and around, do cool things, and have something to boast about with my bros when I got back. Africa sounded cool: a place to see some animals, see the Victoria Falls, go deep-sea diving off the coast, stuff like that. Something told me I was in for a surprise.

"Johnny," said Rahim. "Mind if I stay with you 'til you've made the call?"

"Sure," I told him. "Okay." He could see I was nervous.

"Hi, may I speak to Fiona?"

Silence. Then, "No one here by that name. They left, sold the place. Must have headed overseas, like all the rest."

"I'm not surprised, Johnny," Rahim said when I told him about the call. "Lots of whites are leaving South Africa these days. Listen, you're welcome to stay at our place until you get yourself squared away. I know you'll like my parents."

"Okay, sure, thanks," I said. *I guess this is where the adventure begins. Our study abroad officer told us* not *to do something like this, but you have to trust someone . . .*

Soon, Rahim's sister Miriam picked us up in a Mercedes, and we headed for his family's home in Lenasia.

"Sit back. Relax. Your journey's not over. This will take a while," said Rahim.

It took almost two hours. Miriam, who told me she worked at a travel agency, drove us through the center of "Jo'burg," as everyone seems to call it. It was much more modern than I was prepared for. Watched too many Hollywood movies about Africa, I guess. As we wove our way through the skyscrapers and streets lined with shops and department stores, I could see that the sidewalks were full of mostly black people, walking fast, in all directions.

"I thought blacks were supposed to be outside the city in . . . whaddaya call 'em . . . 'locations,'" I said, puzzled.

"You mean townships, like Soweto, those segregated areas in and around the cities. Locations are those black-only areas in the countryside," Rahim explained. "Almost all these people you see here in downtown Jo'burg live in townships. Some, like Soweto, are a good hour or two away. They're just here to work or find work, sell something, or just spend the day idling about. By dark, this city will be empty—a ghost town, you might say. These people will all have hopped a bus, a train, or something on wheels to carry them back to the townships."

Miriam chimed in: "Some of these folks live in squatter camps three or four hours away. Some women will leave their kids at home around three A.M. to reach town in time to wash dishes, clean house, and babysit for white people, and won't get back sometimes until 10 or 11 at night. And they're the lucky ones, 'cause they have some income."

"Damn."

"So where is this Lenasia, Rahim? Is it a township, too?"

"It's a township, all right. Just for 'Indians,' created during the 'good old days' when everyone was either white, colored, Indian or 'bantu.' We so-called 'Indians' don't like the name that much. Some of us, like my great grandparents, came from Gujarat—Gandhi's province. But some who had 'Indian' stamped in their passbooks by the government, come from Ceylon, now Sri Lanka, or even Indonesia or the Philippines. We get around this system by using 'Asian,' which is closer to reality."

"But even then," Miriam interjected, "the few Japanese and Chinese you'll see walking around or running a shop or two are classed as 'honorary whites'!"

"This is a crazy, fucked-up place—excuse the expression," muttered Rahim.

Beyond downtown, the buildings began to thin out a bit, and as we headed southwest toward Lenasia, small patches of countryside appeared here and there.

Then, seemingly all of a sudden, we entered a different world. House upon house, some really nice, were bunched together along narrow streets. Shops were scattered here and there, and I saw what appeared to be a school—a pretty big one, actually. I soon spotted a large mosque, and a bit farther on I saw something like a temple with a statue of a fat man with an elephant trunk. "Weird," I thought. And was that a Catholic church? It was not all that big, but there was no mistaking the cross.

"Almost there, Johnny," said Rahim.

We then passed through a gate and Miriam drove up to a large house surrounded by high walls.

These guys like their privacy, it seems.

Miriam honked the horn, and, seconds later, nine or ten people of all ages, from maybe six up to eighty, poured out of the house from different doors and pinned Rahim to the car with hugs, laughter, poking, slaps on the shoulders.

Popular guy, Rahim.

When the hoopla died down, Rahim introduced me as Johnny, his Yankee bodyguard. One man, who I'd say was about fifty to sixty years old, approached me and offered his hand.

"Welcome, John. Rahim has a way of joking, even with the names he pins on people without their permission. My name is Hashim, Rahim's father. You are most welcome at our place. You must be tired. Please come in."

I was given my own room, undoubtedly at the inconvenience of some of the kids. But I heard no complaints (just one of many examples of South African hospitality), so I lay down and was out in seconds.

When I awoke it was late afternoon. After I'd had a nice hot shower and put on fresh clothes, there came a knock on the door.

"Johnny, my boy," called Rahim. "It's time for some real food."

Downstairs, the large table was surrounded by the entire family and heaped with dishes of all types. I confess I had to write it down afterward, so I could report it to the folks back home: two kinds of bread (roti, naan), keema mince, tandoori chicken, chicken masala, lamb baba ganoush, beef biriyani, and basmati rice—all, in loads of combinations, eaten by hand (the right, always the right, I soon learned), and much of it spicy. I decided that Asian food easily outclassed the burgers, pizza, and cafeteria chow I had lived on since moving away from my parents' place. I ate too much, as I discovered the next morning!

It seemed, too, that everyone was talking, laughing, and clearly happy to have Rahim back home. Hashim snatched a pause in the dinner conversation and Rahim's tales of life in England to change the subject.

"John," he said, turning to me. "There's quite an event taking place tomorrow. You and Rahim might be interested in getting a look at it."

"My father runs several businesses," said Miriam, "among them a large catering company that has been contracted to look after the people over near the airport at Kempton Park. There's going to be a big conference. The whole country is watching. It's like everyone believes it's 'do or die' for South Africa, and that's no joke."

I wasn't too keen on another crawl back through Johannesburg, but Rahim said we'd be taking the bypass, which would cut an hour off the driving time.

"I wanted Miriam to drive us through the city," Rahim chimed in, "so you could check out the scene, as you Yanks put it."

"Sure. I would like to go. What's Kempton Park? And what's going on?"

"Oh, of course, excuse me," said Hashim. "Kempton Park is the location of the World Trade Centre."

"Is there an international conference or something?"

"Not really," Hashim said. "We've not had many of those in South Africa for the past few years, what

with our being a pariah state and all. Many countries have limited or stopped altogether their political contact with us. Businesses around the globe have stopped commercial activity here. Banks have pulled away from us. Universities no longer invite our scholars to conferences, and we can't get academics to come here."

"It's putting quite a crimp in our style," chuckled Miriam.

"That's the sanctions and divestment program against apartheid, isn't it?" I asked, relieved to know at least something. "Must be hurting you, I guess"

"It *is* hurting us," Hashim said, "but that is a *good* thing. After many years, it's having an effect. The government has finally caved in to the pressure.

"We were happy when your Congress adopted sanctions against South Africa," he continued, "even though your President Reagan then vetoed it. Seems some in your Republican party bought the apartheid propaganda that South Africa was a democratic state."

This guy knows more about the United States than I do, I thought. I had to say something.

"Reagan was convinced the African National Congress was a puppet of the Soviet Union. He was more concerned about geopolitics than about human rights, I guess."

"He was not alone," Hashim said. "Israel was a staunch supporter of Apartheid South Africa up to the end."

"So what is happening at Kempton Park?" I asked.

"It's a conference about the future of South Africa, now that apartheid is over. Lots of people disagree on what the next government should look like. Delegates from twenty-six parties are showing up there to talk. Whether they can achieve anything is the question."

(*Twenty-six!* I thought in amazement.)

"Seems you have your doubts," I said aloud. "Why—because there are so many parties?"

"No," interjected Miriam. "We're skeptical because the same people have been meeting for the past three years, and each time the talks have broken down. The fact is that the delegates probably have only one last chance to come up with a new constitution that will move our country beyond apartheid."

"So, what are the odds they'll succeed?"

"Maybe fifty-fifty, at best." Hashim's eyes locked on mine. "John, apartheid was an evil system that created bitterness and distrust among people. It is hard to imagine that now, suddenly, these people can even sit in the same room together, let alone find a common solution."

"I guess that's why apartheid means *separateness*, right?"

"Right," he said, nodding. "And separate us it did. It categorized people using arbitrary ideas about race, and then did its best to see that its so-called races led separate lives—not residing next to each other, or marrying each other, or even attending the same schools. Those who controlled the system labeled themselves white or 'European'—and made sure whites got the best jobs, schools, and neighborhoods and lots of government help. It was unfair to the vast majority of South Africans who were not labeled 'white.' That's past now, we hope. But we don't know what's coming next."

"We had racial segregation in America, too, but even now race remains a big problem."

"Any honest scientist will tell you that race is a nonscientific concept," said Rahim, "but once race perceptions take hold, even some educated people continue to believe in this stuff, although they won't admit it," said Rahim. His voice was rising. "It's ridiculous being called 'Indian' in South Africa: my family has been here for nearly one hundred years. I've been to India once." Rahim's tone was no longer playful.

"I am, in fact, African, plain and simple," he continued. "Calling me an 'Indian' or even 'Asian' in this place just means that I have darker skin than the whites. I can't claim to be colored or mixed, and I don't look the same as the bantu—now there's a crazy word for black people. All of us have been in South Africa for generations, even the white Afrikaners, which means 'African' in Afrikaans!

Hey, I'm an African. We *all* are—black, white, brown, spotted, whatever." Rahim chuckled, but I could tell he was pissed just talking about it.

I turned back to Hashim. "So are you part of one of the parties at this conference, then?"

"Actually, yes. I've long been a member of the Natal Indian Congress, the NIC, which has historic ties to the ANC."

"The African National Congress. Mandela's party."

"Yes. I'm in the NIC, but I stay open. Maybe I'll move over to the ANC, maybe not."

"What do you mean? Why don't the NIC and ANC just merge if they're so close?"

"Good question," interjected Rahim. "It seems like residue from the separation of people under apartheid. Well, maybe so. But also we are very proud of the historic connection to Gandhiji."

"You mean Mahatma Gandhi?" I asked.

"Yes. Before he was the Mahatma, he helped to form the NIC."

"It was in South Africa," Miriam added, "that Gandhi developed his idea of *satyagraha*. That's soul-force, the idea that love and nonviolence can defeat injustice. It was here that he developed his techniques of nonviolent resistance and launched collective efforts to resist the evil government without doing harm to others."

"How'd that turn out?" Rahim asked snarkily.

"Hey, let's not go there, okay?" his father replied. "It's complicated. Anyway, back to the idea of separateness. It's odd, you know, but, I've never been out to Soweto myself, though it's not far away. My brother has, though. He is a member of the NIC, the ANC, *and* the Communist Party."

"Imagine his subscription fees," cracked Rahim. The jokester I liked so much was back.

"Wait, how can you be in more than one party at a time?" I asked.

"In this country," Miriam explained, "many people are, because some parties have broad-ranging goals and others focus on specific interests. Part of the reason I have not taken the same path as my brother is that I think it's important to have some diversity in the political process. The ANC has many,

many members. If we get a new constitution, it will win elections handily. We need its leadership, but it might be good to have other voices as well."

"Best to remain NIC," said Hashim, "for the time being, at least."

The Next Day

I'm a late sleeper, but when the sun came up at six, Rahim was hammering at my door.

"Come on, Yankee Doodle. Time to cockle-doodle-do."

Strong coffee and what people around here call "fat cakes" were enough to get me going and out the door with Rahim and his dad by half-six, as they say here. Salim, Rahim's younger brother who never talked, was behind the wheel this time. Within minutes we were on the N12 superhighway (or "dual carriageway," as they call it in this neck of the woods), whizzing along at seventy miles per hour past the massive Soweto township, on to Germiston, then taking another superhighway north toward Kempton Park. All along the way we drive among strings of white van-like taxis (*kombi* is the local term) packed with black people headed into the city.

Rahim turned around from his shotgun seat and pointed in no particular direction. "Here is one of the big jokes on apartheid. It stands for separating the races—even self-determination for each of them—but the system is dependent on the poor blacks taking care of wealthy whites. The rich can't function without the poor, even with apartheid no longer on the law books."

"That's really messed up," I mutter.

Along the way we passed white neighborhoods with dwellings ranging from simple bungalows to classy apartment high-rises and large estates. Plenty of trees and grass were visible, not to mention swimming pools. I don't recall having seen anything of the sort when we passed by Soweto.

Just before eight, we reached Kempton Park and drove up to the World Trade Centre. We got out and stood for a moment, taking in the bright sun as it warmed the morning air, which had an autumn crispness. April in the lower half the world, I thought, feeling suddenly wide awake.

Then I noticed a small crowd of men and women milling about, waiting to enter the Centre. They were all shapes, colors, and sizes, but all of them were wearing black or gray. Others began to arrive, steadily, looking much like those already there. Most were black, or "bantu," as some of the whites say. Everyone was bunched with one group or another; I assumed these must be the delegations. *Is it just me?* I thought. *Seems like they're separated into the so-called racial groups. So much for the end of apartheid.*

Rahim and I were alone now. Hashim had already made his way inside the building with his staff.

"So Rahim," I said, "can you tell me who is who here? What about the different groups of white folks?"

"There are a bunch of them, mostly small splinter groups, except for De Klerk's National Party. What they have in common is that they're all afraid." He chuckled. "It's their turn to feel the heat, I'd say."

I gave him a quizzical look.

"I'm not saying they deserve payback," he continued. "Whichever white group we're talking about, for them the issue is what they will lose—government positions, livelihoods, standard of living, even personal safety. A few here, like the Conservatives and the Afrikaner *Volksunie*, are diehards who want to keep white control of at least a part of South Africa. But most Afrikaners and the English whites know that apartheid is a dead duck and that change must come. Some, perhaps a majority, pray that good things will come of it."

"So the whites are divided, then. And the others?"

"This, Johnny boy, is a divided country, no matter how you slice it. We are all Africans, but we are so accustomed to dealing with one another using these silly racial categories—white, black, or whatever—that even though we don't like them, we haven't yet learned how to function without them. And each of these castes, if you will, has people who quarrel with one another over what to put in their place."

The Conservatives Rahim had pointed to were then joined by a group of blacks. They shook hands and seemed to exchange some pleasantries.

"Well," I said, "I'm really surprised to see that a bunch of Afrikaners—you said they were the Conservatives who wanted to keep apartheid. . . . I'm surprised to see them so friendly to that bunch of Africans."

"Welcome to South Africa!" Rahim laughed. "No matter how hard the political system tries to separate people, they find a way to mingle." He could see I was confused. "What you're looking at is probably a meeting not of friends but of political allies of convenience. The blacks you see talking with the Conservatives are Zulu members of the Inkatha Freedom Party—the IFP, as they call themselves—and of black parties from what we call the 'black homelands' created during apartheid. They all belong to COSAG, the Concerned South Africans Group. A better name might be the Concerned South Africans about Losing their Grip."

"What? Blacks teaming up with whites to keep apartheid?"

"Welcome to South Africa!" Rahim said again. "COSAG is a black–white alliance, not a party. Other parties, especially the ANC and the Communist Party, have nonracial political charters. But not the IFP, the Conservatives, or their ilk. Each of them has either black or white members, but they work with each other for a common goal—or *sort of* a common goal, I should say. They have their differences, too."

We walked into the building, and as we did we were immersed suddenly in a crowd of men and women of different shades and colors entering at the same time.

"You've just been swamped in the ANC tidal wave!" Rahim joked.

"They seem very diverse."

"Yes," he replied. "During its long history, the ANC has been led by black men, but its members tend to reflect the population as a whole. Most ANC members are black, but you'll find Asian, Colored, White, and even Afrikaner members, even in high party positions."

"The image of the ANC we often get in America is that it is made up of black communists."

"You'll find communist members in the ANC," Rahim replied, "but they're not Stalinists or Fidelistas who want a totalitarian system with no personal freedom and the elimination of personal property."

"You're kidding, Rahim. Isn't that what communism is?"

"Spoken like a good American!" Rahim laughed hard now, almost bending over. "Seems you've grown up with some strong prejudices of your own. Come on, let's go inside. Then you'll see."

"Okay, sure, but first another question. Why are they in a faction together—I mean the IFP and Conservatives? I guess my real question, and what I don't get, is how this Multi-Party Negotiating Process is going to strive for equality and democracy with all the country's differences—racial, ethnic, language, and so on. Last night you told me that most of the land is in the hands of whites, all under an authoritarian white regime that has probably violated the rights of the people here who aren't white, and even the rights of some of its own race. So how is this conference going to bring all of these people together and reach an agreement?"

"To quote *Hamlet*, 'That is the question!'" Rahim said with a grin. Once again he was starting to talk like the other Rahim, of last night. "How will we be? What will we be? Will we continue to exist? Can we co-exist? Who are we?" His face became serious again. "I don't know. Nobody knows. I have no idea whether this moment is a bright one or a dark one. We are at present blind." He paused, his eyes staring vacantly past me to the wall. Then he added, "Today's the first of April. Let's hope they don't make fools of us all."

I heard a shout from a doorway, and saw Hashim beckoning.

"Hey, look," said Rahim. "My father needs me to lend him a hand. I'm going to leave you here. You can move around, but stay on the edges. With your backpack and scruffy beard, I don't think you'll be mistaken for some CIA agent. Let's meet later—say for afternoon tea?"

"Okay by me, Rahim. Say half-four?"

"*Half-four*. Already sounding like a South African, eh! Let's meet here. Then we can go get some tea. I know a place across the street that's got good-quality rooibos. Just a few words before I go. We can follow up on them later."

"I'm all ears, Rahim, my man."

"Did you notice the many women downstairs and in the elevator?"

"I was going to ask about that. They were all dressed like professionals; not like building staff, but like businesswomen and lawyers, you know. What's that about?"

"One of the things that surprised us all is that the people who planned this meeting, the MPNP, insisted that it be truly representative. That means not only that twenty-six parties are present— actually more than twenty-six; it's a bit hard to keep count. It also means that for the the MPNP to be truly representative, each delegation must have fifty percent women."

"Man, amazing. Nothing like that in U.S. politics."

"Not here either. Not anywhere in the world. This is new: mandated equal gender representation."

"Wow! Guess I stumbled into the right time to come to South Africa!"

"Really amazing," Rahim said, but with a straight face. "The time is dramatic and unprece-dented, but keep your passport close. We are right on the brink . . ." His lips tightened.

"On the brink?" I pressed him. "What do you mean? With multiracial political negotiations, Mandela free, apartheid in the dustbin, women sharing in political leadership, it looks to me like South Africa is on the brink of changing the world!"

"Maybe, but no one here thinks so," Rahim said. "No one. We might be on the brink of change, but I'm afraid to hope. You've just flown into a country where we read in the news every day of killings all over the country. We are falling apart, John. For three years now, these same people have been trying to agree through negotiations, but have failed. Few think this effort has a chance of success, either. There's so much anger and despair. Things could take a turn for the worse very quickly: we could be approaching a bloodbath."

Rahim was taking short breaths. Suddenly I felt afraid. I thought about calling my parents to arrange for an early trip home.

"We are on the brink," he repeated, "the brink of civil war. We cannot go on as it is."

I stared down. I had nothing to say, nothing at all. Suddenly Rahim cheered up.

"But you, Johnny boy, are in for a good time here! Don't worry! Look, people here can be amazing—all of them, even the spotted ones," he declared, with his ironic smile. "The food, the cities, the music, the landscapes, the animals— there is so much to see and do. South Africa has its problems, of course, but this is a wonderful place. I love my country. I love being a South African. I just wish it would get its act together— you know, make happy."

With that, Rahim headed off toward his father.

On my way down the hallway toward the main conference room, I passed a small room where one of the parties—the ANC, I guessed—was huddling in preparation. The door was ajar, and I could hear music. Inside, men and women in suits were singing in four-part harmony.

Nkosi Sikelel' iAfrika . . .

Lord, bless Africa
May her spirit rise up
Hear thou our prayers
Lord bless us
Your family.

WHAT IS A HISTORICAL ROLE-PLAYING GAME?

Immersive historical role-playing games are an innovative classroom pedagogy that teaches history and related subjects by placing students in moments of heightened historical tension. The class becomes a public body, or private gathering;

students, in role, become particular persons from the period and/or members of factional alliances. Their purpose is to advance an agenda and achieve victory objectives through formal speeches, informal debate, negotiations, vote-taking, and conspiracy. After a few preparatory sessions, the game begins, and the students are in charge. The instructor serves as an adviser/arbiter. Outcomes sometimes vary from the history; a debriefing session sets the record straight.

HOW TO PLAY

The following is an outline of what you will encounter in this game and what you will be expected to do.

Game Setup

The instructor will explicate the historical context of the game before the game formally begins. During the setup period, you will read several different kinds of material:

- The game book (from which you are reading now), which includes historical background, rules and features of the game, core texts, and essential documents
- A role sheet, describing the historical person you will model in the game and, where applicable, the faction to which you belong
- Supplementary documents or books that, if assigned, will provide additional information and arguments for use during the game

Read all of this material before the game begins (or as much as possible, catching up once the game is underway). And just as important, go back and reread these materials throughout the game. A second and third reading while *in role* will deepen your understanding and alter your perspective, since ideas take on a different meaning when seen through the eyes of a particular character. Students who have carefully read the materials and who thoroughly know the rules of the game will do better than those who rely on general impressions.

Game Play

Once the game begins, one student (randomly chosen, elected, or identified by role) will usually preside over the class sessions. Your instructor then becomes the Gamemaster (GM) and takes a seat in the back of the room. While not directing the play of the game, the Gamemaster may do any of the following:

- Pass notes to individuals or factions
- Announce important events, some of which may be the result of student actions, others instigated by the GM
- Perform scheduled interventions, sometimes determined by die rolls
- Interrupt proceedings that have gone off track
- Arbitrate play-related controversies

Generally speaking, you are either are in a faction or outside the factions as an Indeterminate. Some factions include roles that are significantly different from one another, while others do not, but all Indeterminates are different from one another: they operate outside the established factions. In games where the factions are tightly knit groups with fixed objectives, Indeterminates provide the most obvious source of extra support. Cultivating them is, therefore, in the interest of faction members, because one faction will not have the voting strength to prevail without allies. Collaboration and coalition-building are at the heart of every game.

The classroom may sometimes be noisy, with multiple points of focus, because of side conversations, note-passing, and players out of their seats. But these practices can also be disruptive and spoil the effect of formal speeches. Nothing is accomplished by trying to talk over the din to persons not listening, so insist upon order and quiet before proceeding.

When spoken to by a fellow student—whether in class or out of class—always assume that the person may be speaking to you in role. If you need to address a classmate out of role, employ a visual sign, like crossed fingers, to indicate your changed status. It is inappropriate to trade on out-of-class relationships when asking for support or favors.

Work to balance your emotional investment in your role with the need to treat your classmates with respect. Some specific roles may require you to advocate beliefs with which you personally disagree. While such assignments may seem difficult at first, careful study of your role sheet and the readings should help you develop a greater understanding of why this person thought and acted as he or she did. In a few cases, you may even need to promote ideas that are viewed as controversial or offensive in today's society. Again, always go back to the sources: analyze why those ideas made sense for that particular person in that particular time and place, and then advocate those beliefs as persuasively and effectively as you can. If you ever feel uncomfortable or uncertain about your role, you should feel free to speak with your instructor. Remember also that you will have an opportunity during the debriefing session to discuss the differences between your game character and your personal beliefs or values.

Game Requirements

The instructor will lay out the specific requirements for the class. In general, though, this game will have students perform three distinct activities:

- **Reading and Writing**. This standard academic work is carried on more purposefully because what you read is put to immediate use, and what you write is meant to persuade others to act in preferred ways. The reading load may vary with roles (reading done as research is in addition to that done as preparation); the writing requirement is typically a set number of pages per game. In both cases the instructor is free to make adjustments. Papers are often policy statements, but also autobiographies, poems, newspaper articles, clandestine messages, or after-game reflections. Papers often provide the bases of speeches.

- **Public Speaking and Debate**. In most games every player is expected to deliver at least one formal speech (the length of the game and the size of the class will affect the number of speeches). Debate occurs after a speech is delivered. Debate is impromptu, raucous, and fast-paced, and often results in decisions determined by voting.
- **Strategizing.** Communication with other players is essential. You may find yourself writing emails, texting, attending out-of-class meetings, or gathering for meals on a fairly regular basis. The purpose of these communications is to lay out a strategy for advancing your agenda and thwarting the agenda of your opponents, or to hatch plots to ensnare individuals who oppose your cause.

Skill Development

This game provides the opportunity to develop a host of academic and life skills:

- Effective writing
- Public speaking
- Problem solving
- Leadership
- Teamwork
- Adaptation to fast-changing circumstances
- Work under pressure with deadlines to meet

COUNTERFACTUALS

There are three counterfactuals in this game. *Counterfactuals* is the reacting term for features of the game that are not completely consistent with the historical scenario, usually because events or characters are compressed into a shorter setting for the sake of clarity and playability. The first counterfactual is that two of the organizations included in the game version of the MPNP, namely the Pan-Africanist Congress (PAC) and the Azanian People's Organisation (AZAPO), were not present at the historic negotiations because they declined to participate. They have been included here because they represent political views (albeit minority positions) that were part of the general contest for support over new directions for the country; although these groups were absent, the fact is that the participants of the MPNP did consider their positions.

The second counterfactual is that twenty-six parties were represented at the historic MPNP, whereas this game limits the parties to fifteen because they represent accurately the range of positions taken at the talks.

The third counterfactual is that by the time of the conference at Kempton Park, the Natal Indian Congress (NIC) had virtually disappeared, most of its members simply merging into the ANC. The NIC is included in this game, however, because it reflects the views of a significant minority of the population who had a long and rich role to play in opposition to apartheid. While the NIC was not formally at the talks, its concerns and point of view were important features of the political landscape in 1993.

2

Historical Background

MAP

In addition to the map below, detailed maps of the South African landscape, agricultural and mineral production, population, and Homelands can be found at the AGIS (Agricultural Geography Information System) website: http://www.agis.agric.za/agisweb/nr_atlas.

TIMELINE

The following chronology describes the major developments leading up to the Multi-Party Negotiating Process.

1990

2 February   President Frederik Willem de Klerk makes a speech at the opening of Parliament, announcing the end of apartheid laws and declaring, among other measures, the lifting of a thirty-year ban on the African National Congress (ANC), the Pan-Africanist Congress (PAC), and other antiapartheid organizations; the suspension of the death sentence until further review; the release of some political prisoners; and the partial lifting of restrictions on the media and on some detainees.

11 February   Nelson Mandela, leader of the ANC, is freed after twenty-seven years in jail.

2 March   The ANC elects Nelson Mandela as deputy president of the organization. It also announces its decision to move its headquarters from Lusaka to Johannesburg as soon as possible.

31 March   The ANC decides not to hold talks with the South African government, scheduled for 11 April, due to the killing of defenseless demonstrators in Sebokeng. A meeting between Nelson Mandela and Chief Buthelezi of the Inkatha Freedom Party is also called off.

18 April   In a parliamentary speech, President de Klerk rules out any possibility of black majority rule.

20 April   Stating that the arms would be used in a white "counter-revolution," members of a far-right group steal a small arsenal from Air Force Headquarters in Pretoria, including machine-guns and R-1 and R-4 rifles.

27 April   Senior ANC leaders, including Joe Slovo and Thabo Mbeki, return to South Africa after a quarter century in exile.

4 May   At the end of their talks, the ANC and the South African government issues a joint statement entitled "The Groote Schuur Minute," from which arise the following: the establishment of a working group to address the issue of the release of political prisoners, and consideration of temporary immunity from prosecution for selected members of the ANC. The government seeks to modify its security legislation to adapt it to the new situation developing in South Africa, and begins to work toward the lifting of the state of emergency. Both parties pledge once again to try and put an end to the "existing climate of violence and intimidation" and reiterate their "commitment to stability and to a peaceful process of negotiations."

2 June   ANC deputy president Mr. Nelson Mandela and state president F. W. de Klerk hold discussions in Pretoria on the progress that has been made in the implementation of the Groote Schuur Minute and on the need to use effective mechanisms to reduce the level of police violence in the country.

22 June   The offices of Stoffel van der Merwe, Minister of National (Black) Education, and Rolf Meyer, Deputy Constitutional Development Minister, are bombed by white far-right-wing members.

2 July   A week-long labor stayaway, organized by the ANC and its allies, begins in protest against factional black violence in Natal.

6 July   The right-wing bomb campaign continues when a powerful bomb explodes in Johannesburg, injuring twenty-seven people.

14 July   Chief Mangosuthu Gatsha Buthelezi, leader of the Zulu Inkatha Movement, announces the transformation of the Movement into a multiracial political party, the Inkatha Freedom Party (IFP).

29 July   The South African Communist Party (SACP) returns to public political life at its largest rally ever, which is held in the township of Soweto. It introduces its twenty-two-person "interim leadership" to a crowd of forty thousand people.

7 August   The ANC and the South African government issue a joint declaration (the "Pretoria Minute"). The ANC announces that it will immediately suspend all armed actions, while the government considers lifting the state of emergency in Natal "as early as possible"; it vows to continue reviewing the security legislation and its application "in order to ensure free political activity." Both sides pledge to redouble efforts to reduce the level of violence in the country.

17 August   The ANC and the Congress of South African Trade Unions (COSATU) issue statements accusing elements of the South African security forces of orchestrating the conflict in the townships. They state that they have evidence of forged pamphlets being dropped in the migrant workers' hostels, conveying the impression that the ANC wanted to attack Zulu workers and drive them out of the townships.

24 August More than five hundred people die in eleven days of fighting between township residents and migrant Zulu workers in the Pretoria-Witwatersrand-Vaal region, and the government declares a state of emergency in this region.

27 August At a mass funeral held at Jabulani Stadium in Soweto and attended by some six thousand people, Archbishop Desmond Tutu says that a delegation of churchmen will meet President de Klerk to convey to him that there is overwhelming evidence that the police have favored Inkatha in the recent conflict.

20 September The ANC and the IFP announce that they have held high-level talks in Durban to discuss ways of ending violence in Natal and in the townships on the Reef. A joint statement issued at the end of the meeting calls it a "historic" meeting, although the "matters discussed were in the main exploratory in nature."

20 October The formerly whites-only National Party (NP) opens its membership to all race groups.

2 November Chief Mangosuthu Buthelezi and Mr. Andries Treurnicht, leader of the Conservative Party, meet in Durban and issue a joint statement declaring that they are united in the rejection of "domination, terrorism and communism."

16 December The ANC concludes its first national consultative conference held inside South Africa in thirty-one years. The conference, attended by 1,600 delegates, mandates the National Executive Committee to "serve notice on the regime that unless all the obstacles are removed on or before 30 April 1991, the ANC shall consider the suspension of the whole negotiation process," and announces that 1991 will be a "year of mass action." It rejects a call to relax international sanctions against South Africa and approves the creation of "defence units" to protect township residents.

1991

29 January A summit meeting is held in Durban between the ANC and the IFP. The meeting is addressed by Zulu chief Mangosuthu Gatsha Buthelezi and ANC deputy president Nelson Mandela. In a joint statement, both parties express their commitment to political tolerance and call on the security forces to play an effective peacekeeping role.

8 May A broad consensus is reached between the government and the ANC to end black violence in townships; this comes only a day before the ANC's 9th May ultimatum to suspend negotiations unless its demands are met.

12 May Inkatha supporters rampage through a squatter camp in the Kagiso Township in the West Rand, killing at least twenty-two people.

14 May Winnie Mandela is sentenced to six years' imprisonment on charges of kidnapping and being accessory to assault of four township youths at her Soweto home in December 1988. On 3 June 1993, the Supreme Court of Appeal overthrew the assault conviction and reduced her sentence to a $5,000 fine and two years' probation.

23 May President de Klerk says that twenty-one colored representatives have joined the ruling NP.

10 June Retired army major Nico Basson tells reporters that the South African military supplied weapons (such as AK-47 assault rifles) and covert assistance to the IFP in order to weaken the ANC. IFP leader Chief Mangosuthu Gatsha Buthelezi denies these allegations.

5 July The ANC holds its first National Conference in Durban after a break of more than thirty years. Cyril Ramaphosa is appointed its secretary general, Nelson Mandela is elected president, and Walter Sisulu is made deputy president of the organization.

23 July M. Z. Khumalo, personal assistant to Chief Buthelezi, resigns from the IFP after admitting that he acted as a middle man who organized covert funds paid by the Security Police for two Inkatha rallies.

1 August The National Executive Committee (NEC) of the ANC issues a statement calling into question the IFP's "legitimacy as an independent force," criticizing the government's response to revelations on the secret funding of political organizations, and calling for the creation of a "transitional authority charged with the task of preparing the country for a democratic constitution."

15 August The South African government, the ANC, and the IFP agree on a draft National Peace Accord, which they describe as "a firm foundation on which peace in South Africa can be achieved." The accord includes a code of conduct for political parties, a code of conduct for the police and the security forces, provisions for socioeconomic development, and a complex set of enforcement mechanisms.

14 September A National Peace Accord is signed by all major political organizations. The Pan-Africanist Congress (PAC) and Azanian People's Organisation (AZAPO) attend the proceedings but refuse to sign the accord, while right-wing organizations refuse to participate in the session.

27 November The PAC accuses the ANC of being "guilty of deceit and duplicity" and of undermining the Patriotic Front Alliance "in cahoots with the regime."

8 December At its first legal congress in four decades, the SACP appoints Mr. Chris Hani as its new general secretary.

20 December The first plenary session of the Convention for a Democratic South Africa (CODESA) meets in Johannesburg. Nineteen organizations, as well the government, are represented. CODESA participants set up five working groups that are to report to a second CODESA plenary session before the end of March.

1992

8 January The ANC's NEC rejects President de Klerk's proposals for a referendum as an "attempt to prolong the transition by 10 years or more," and states that the ANC will "strive for the setting up of an Interim Government in the first half of this year, and elections for a Constituent Assembly to be held by December 1992."

24 February President F. W. de Klerk announces that a referendum will be held on 17 March, requesting a mandate to pursue constitutional reform from the white electorate. The ANC submits its constitutional blueprint to CODESA. It suggests a two-phase transitional period of multi-party rule for fifteen months, to be followed by a coalition government for up to five years.

6 March A report on violence published by the Black Sash Repression Monitoring Group states that an estimated eleven thousand persons have been killed in political violence in South Africa since 1986.

18 March In a referendum for whites only, 68.7 percent vote "Yes" in favor of pursuing constitutional reform, while 31.3 percent vote "No." 86 percent of the white voting population participates in the referendum.

3 April ANC president Nelson Mandela calls for an "independent international monitoring force" to help curb violence in South Africa, saying that the government has "abdicated itself from its duties."

13 April ANC president Nelson Mandela announces that he and his wife Winnie plan to separate because of "differences on a number of issues" and "circumstances beyond (their) control."

21 April Five white Democratic Party MPs defect to the ANC.

15 May The second plenary session of CODESA (CODESA II) convenes in Johannesburg.

16 May CODESA talks end in deadlock. The ANC threatens mass action if the government does not compromise on constitutional issues.

25 May Winnie Mandela and the entire executive of the ANC Women's League are suspended.

27 May A Commission of Inquiry regarding the Prevention of Public Violence and Intimidation, headed by Justice Richard Goldstone, denounces the government's failure to "take sufficiently firm steps to prevent criminal conduct by members of the security forces and the police." It also accuses the ANC and the IFP of "resorting to violence and intimidation in their attempts to gain control over geographic areas."

16 June The ANC begins an open-ended campaign of public protest with a day of rallies, work stoppages, and threats of a crippling general strike until the government agrees to terms for the creation of an interim government and an elected assembly to write a new constitution.

17 June Armed attackers shoot and hack their way through the black township of Boipatong, leaving more than forty people dead and scores injured, including women and children. Witnesses report that the violence was perpetrated by residents of a nearby hostel. The ANC states that on the day of the massacre, information had been conveyed to the police on an impending attack in Boipatong, and that police arrived and forcibly removed residents who were patrolling the township in anticipation of the attack. According to the ANC, police were later seen escorting groups of armed men at various points.

21 June ANC president Nelson Mandela announces that he is suspending all talks with the government in the wake of the killings in Boipatong.

23 July An agreement is reached between the South African Police, ANC, SACP, and COSATU on the principles outlined by a panel of experts on how mass demonstrations should be controlled. The IFP states that it was unable to agree to terms restricting the carrying of cultural weapons.

3 August The ANC and its allies lead millions of workers on a nationwide general strike to demand a multiracial interim government by the end of the year and effective steps to halt violence.

7 September Ciskei security forces fire on ANC demonstrators marching toward the capital of the homeland, killing twenty-nine of them and wounding more than two hundred.

10 September Winnie Mandela resigns from the executives of both the ANC and its Women's League.

26 September A bilateral summit between delegations of the ANC and the South African government, led respectively by Nelson Mandela and President de Klerk, is held in Johannesburg. A joint Record of Understanding is published, laying the basis for the resumption of negotiations. Notably, an agreement is reached on the banning of dangerous weapons throughout the country, the fencing of a number of hostels, the release of all remaining political prisoners before 15 November, and the need for an elected Constituent Assembly with a fixed time frame and adequate deadlock-breaking mechanisms.

27 September At a meeting held in Ulundi, IFP leader Chief Gatsha Buthelezi warns that the deals struck between the ANC and the South African government are "illegitimate" and "unimplementable," and that Zulu will continue carrying cultural weapons. He rejects once again the concept of a Constituent Assembly and announces his decision to break off talks with the government.

12 November President F. W. de Klerk spells out a government timetable for a transition to multiracial democracy and states that all-race elections will take place by April 1994.

16 November Judge Richard Goldstone reveals the existence of files containing plans for covert operations aimed at discrediting the ANC's armed wing, the MK, by a military intelligence task force led by former Civil Co-operation Bureau (CCB) member Ferdi Barnard.

19 December President F. W. de Klerk announces that he is either suspending or forcibly retiring twenty-three officers of the South African Defence Force, including two generals and four brigadiers, for illegal or unauthorized activities and malpractice. He also says that further disciplinary action and possible criminal prosecution will follow pending the completion of the probe.

1993

29 January   At the opening of Parliament, President F. W. de Klerk warns that South Africa will be plunged into a Yugoslav-style civil war if democratic negotiations fail. Multiparty constitutional talks are set to resume in March.

16 February   The ANC expresses deep concern about revelations that the South African Defence Force had a budget of R. 4.38 billion for its secret Special Defence Account during the previous financial year. It also states that massive expenditure on covert projects together with recent revelations that, despite repeated promises, Battalions 31 and 32 have not yet been disbanded, cast doubt on the good faith and sincerity with which the South African government is negotiating.

17 February   The Commonwealth Observer Mission to South Africa (COMSA) concludes that, based on its homicide rate, this country is "one of the world's most violent." COMSA further concludes that South Africa's best hope of containing the violence is to move speedily toward democratic elections and a durable resolution of the country's political crisis.

5–6 March   A multiparty planning and negotiations conference puts constitutional negotiations firmly on track by deciding to establish a new forum before 5 April.

1 April   Representatives from twenty-six South African political parties and organizations resume multi-party negotiations, marking the start of serious deliberations on the transition since the collapse of CODESA.

THE STRUGGLE FOR A DEMOCRATIC SOUTH AFRICA

Toward the Multi-Party Negotiating Process (MPNP)

(Names in **bold** are the most important names to remember.)

In 1990 South Africa's prime minister, F. W. **de Klerk** (pronounced deh-KLAYRK), announced to the all-white Parliament in Cape Town his decision to end apartheid. His speech stunned white South Africans, excited the disenfranchised millions of "non-whites" in that country, and dazzled the world.[1] For more than forty years, de Klerk's **Nationalist Party** had dominated political life in South Africa under the banner of apartheid[2] (an elaborate legal system privileging the white minority at the heavy expense of all others), enforced their will on a resisting majority with military and police violence, and silenced all opposition with imprisonment, detentions, exile, and executions. Since the Nationalists took power in 1948, South Africa had become one of the world's pariahs.

Yet, apartheid South Africa also seemed to be invincible. It found ways to keep the life-lines open. With quiet help from an impressive array of trading partners and collaborators in the West, the Soviet Bloc, Israel, Arab states, and the East, apartheid South Africa had built up a first-world economy and made itself into a leading military force in the southern hemisphere. Though Western governments openly criticized South Africa for its apartheid policies, back-door dealings were common. The West needed South Africa's protection of the vital sea-lane around the Cape of Good Hope, on which massive oil tankers made their way from the Middle East to refineries in Europe and the United States. And the West feared Soviet attempts to expand their influence into Africa, and worried about its support for the leading organization working to upend apartheid—the **ANC** and its guerrilla wing, **Umkhonto we Sizwe** ("Spear of the Nation," also referred to as "MK"—pronounced um-KONT-o way SEEZ-way). The Western fear of a communist takeover of South Africa was nearly as old as the Cold War itself, and for years the Nationalist Party had exploited this for its own benefit, by tarring the ANC and other liberation movements as puppets of the communist "onslaught."

1. De Klerk Address to Parliament, 2 February 1990.
2. Afrikaans for "separateness."

As of 1989, South Africa had withstood internal opposition and political and social isolation from the outside world that had built up steadily over the previous four decades. South African athletes were unwelcome elsewhere, and many of the world's academics, scientists, professional athletes, and tourists placed South Africa "off limits," refusing to go there. The antiapartheid forces in the West had increasing success in calling for sanctions against trade and investment in South Africa. During the 1980s inside the apartheid nation, momentum against the government grew with the rise of the United Democratic Front—uniting hundreds of community organizations protesting against white-controlled local governments in black townships and reserves (the infamous "Homelands").[1] At the same time, U.S. Congress enacted sanctions against U.S.–South Africa trade, and Mikhail Gorbachev's "Glasnost" policy began dismantling the Union of Soviet Socialist Republics (aka the U.S.S.R.) and ultimately allowed the Berlin Wall to come down.

White South Africa, however, still looked strong. True, the Nationalists had lost the use of the "communist threat," but the Reagan and Bush administrations and the Thatcher government in the United Kingdom were reluctant to push South Africa toward democracy. In 1989, the ANC remained on America's list of "terrorist organizations," and Nelson Mandela, symbolic leader of the ANC, was still in jail serving a life sentence.

De Klerk's Thunderbolt

Then, on 2 February, 1990, de Klerk suddenly declared that his government, with immediate effect, was declaring an end to apartheid,

legalizing the ANC and all other opposition parties, releasing political prisoners, abolishing state of emergency regulations, and starting negotiations with all parties to create what he described as

> a *new democratic constitution, universal franchise*, no domination, *equality* before an independent judiciary, protection of minorities as well as individual rights, *freedom of religion*, a sound economy based on proven economic principles and private enterprise, and dynamic programmes directed at better education, health services, housing and social conditions for all (emphasis added).

But it was what de Klerk said next that riveted the attention of the nation and the entire world:

> In this connection Mr. Nelson Mandela could play an important part. The government has noted that he has declared himself to be willing to make a constructive contribution to the peaceful political process in South Africa.
>
> I wish to put it plainly that the government has taken a firm decision to release Mr. Mandela unconditionally.[2]

South Africans and indeed people all around the world were shocked. Why had de Klerk made such a sudden and radical change? In fact, the ruling NP leadership was beginning to realize that apartheid was no longer sustainable economically, not only because of global sanctions but also because institutionalized inequalities were inefficient, expensive, and unpopular. Even before the election of de Klerk, unknown to everyone but a few, the government had launched secret negotiations with the most influential man in South Africa, Nelson **Mandela** (pronounced mahn-DAY-lah).

---

1. "Townships" refer to urban areas restricted to residents of one of the official non-white racial categories (Asian, Black, Colored). "Reserves" refer to rural areas restricted to "Natives" (i.e., black Africans). In 1948, when the white government relabeled Natives as Bantu, they were called "Bantustans," and in the 1970s, when Black replaced Bantu as the official race label, these areas were renamed "Homelands."

2. De Klerk Address to Parliament, 2 February 1990.

Madiba (*mah-DEE-bah*)

Nine days later (11 February 1990), seventy-two-year-old Nelson Rolihlahla Mandela, who had spent the past twenty-seven years behind bars, walked out of Victor Verster Prison into the warm February Cape Town sun a free man, embraced his wife **Winnie**, and strolled down the street smiling, holding her hand, and waving to masses of ecstatic well-wishers, of all colors, who hemmed them in. After being whisked by motorcade into the center of the city, Mandela walked out onto a balcony above a crowd of tens of thousands, and proclaimed,

Amandla! Amandla! i-Afrika mayibuye! (Power! Power! Africa has come back!)[1]

All of this—from Mandela's release into the arms of his wife to his speech of triumph before those for whom, during the long hard years of repression, he had symbolized hope and determination—was televised live around the world.

Mandela had been charged in 1962 with leaving the country without a passport and inciting workers to strike. He was sentenced on 7 November 1962 to five years in prison. In October 1963 he and others were put on trial for sabotage in what became known as the Rivonia Trial. On 12 June, Mandela and seven others were sentenced to life imprisonment. His real crime, though, had been his outspoken role as a critic of the apartheid system. While he had initially embraced Gandhian principles of non-violent resistance, after a tragic massacre in Sharpeville in 1960 he publicly concluded that Africans had a right to defend themselves and to their own liberation by any means, including the use of force. Subsequently, he helped to form the MK (Umkhonto we Sizwe). As a leader of this organization, he was considered a threat to the state.

The exhilaration over Mandela's release lasted for weeks. Spontaneous celebrations broke out in all parts of South Africa. Mandela toured the country, speaking before ever more enormous crowds, and speaking freely, about freedom and peace for all. Jubilation inside the country was matched in the world's capitals, where thousands of South African exiles had been awaiting the liberation of their country, in some cases for decades. Visions of a glorious new South Africa inspired their singing and dancing and gave birth to new plans for the future.

Children in cities far away from South Africa, fluent in their adoptive countries' languages and cultural milieux, heard their parents discussing in agitated tones how they must quickly sell their property, book air tickets, pack, and fly everyone back home. For these youngsters, born in exile, this so-called home was a mysterious place that had always caused their parents pain. Now, suddenly, it had become a source of joy.

Nelson Mandela, affectionately dubbed "Madiba,"[2] was adored by millions, at home and abroad, as a savior of their purpose and protector of their future. Mandela had for twenty-seven years been an unseen symbol of the liberation struggle and the sacrifice Africans were willing to make for freedom. He had continued to provide some general guidance to the ANC from behind bars. His willingness to suffer for his people, therefore, meant that he emerged with an unimpeachable moral authority. But really, who was he? His years in prison had elevated him to near-mythical status. And what power did he have at that moment, other than to draw crowds and ignite dancing in the streets? He had no organization in South Africa behind him—the ANC had been crushed inside the country years ago and driven into exile. Apart from the enthusiasm of those who wanted to see, hear, and touch him, like Christ come again, he had literally only the clothes he wore. Yes, he stood ramrod straight in his spare, six-foot frame, but he was gray and old. Would he try to command the

---

1. Nelson Mandela, "On Release from Prison."

2. *Madiba* is the name of Mandela's royal clan, found among the Xhosa-speaking peoples of the Eastern Cape, South Africa.

masses that seemed almost to worship him? Or had his years in prison and his advanced age sapped him of the strength even to try? Would he convert his name, built on silent resistance, into the voice of a movement bent on reprisal? Or did he have a short memory? He seemed not to be bitter, and he seemed to smile into everyone's heart. He emerged from prison a warm presence, generous in spirit, but many wondered if his stature would be great enough to rein in the forces that were certain to collide.

Perhaps in that glorious moment in Cape Town, Madiba was just what he had always been: a symbol of hope needed by those staring into fear, and nothing more; a man who was powerless save as a mere reflection of their differing dreams. Maybe he was a symbol of hope for all who dared not ask for a promise. As joyously as they reveled in his release, all realized that Mandela's freedom meant that South Africa was everyone's country now—and no one's. Before February 1990, apartheid had separated South Africans in all spheres of life, but after de Klerk's announcement, all South Africans were in it together, without anyone, high or low, knowing what was likely to happen next. For apartheid had not permitted, much less prepared, South Africans to pull in the same direction. It had created a country of people accustomed to pushing, being pushed, or pushing back. And now, without someone taking charge, people began to feel that they were being sucked into a vacuum.

The Multi-Party Talks (Kempton Park, April 1993)

You are among the South Africans who, since Mandela's release, are still struggling to find a solution to building the New South Africa. For three long years, others have tried to reach an agreement, only to fail. Every attempt to resolve differences has faltered because of a lack of compromise, violence in the streets and countryside, and mutual accusations of political groups jostling for power. At first, de Klerk pinned his hopes on dealing with Mandela, and Mandela with de Klerk. But they found it hard, if not impossible, to trust one another. Meanwhile, others clamored to be included in deliberations that would determine the postapartheid future. So, efforts were made to include more voices, to create a representative deliberative body, but such talks also collapsed before any progress could be made.

Your task, then, is to achieve what others could not—a formula that all can accept and with which the country can establish a constitution, conduct free elections, and *create a government* that will not oppress any of its citizens. In short, you must come up with a formula for a democratic South Africa. None before you have succeeded, though many have tried. Thousands have died in this political struggle, and during your talks more deaths are likely. As your talks begin, few South Africans believe that South Africa is capable of guaranteeing its people a safe and prosperous future. And though many believe there is still a chance, the multi-party talks are regarded increasingly as perhaps the country's last hope.

The issues that have to be resolved are thorny and complex. You are tasked with creating a new constitution, just as de Klerk called for. But what does that mean? Even seemingly small matters carry significance, and things you take for granted might be called into question. Assuming the New South Africa is democratic, *what form of government* will it need? Will power be shared among South Africa's groups heretofore divided under apartheid? How soon can elections be called and fairly supervised? Will you and other delegates at the talks draw up the *future constitution*, or should that be left for the first elected government? Who will rule the country until that time? *Who will be in the police, in the army*, and who will command them? (Can those now in uniform, those who enforced apartheid, be trusted to defend the elections and the new government?) What will be the *flag* of the new South Africa, and what will be its national anthem? How many *official languages* will the future South Africa have?

Those of you attending the multi-party talks represent a broad spectrum of political, social, racial, and economic groupings; you include moderates and radicals, leftists and rightists, capitalists and communists, businessmen and unionists, separatists and unionists. The only two principles all of you can agree on, apart from the need to meet, is that the country as a whole cannot revert to apartheid and that the future South Africa must respect persons of all colors, languages, and faiths.

One of the great surprises to come from the preparations for the MPNP has been a fresh attitude toward gender. It has been agreed that each delegation at Kempton Park must consist of an equal number of men and women, reflecting publicly for the first time the importance of women in the social and political life of the nation. South Africa is the first nation in history to require full participation of women in the drafting of a national constitution. This step is surprising, given that all South Africans, whether white, black, Asian, or colored, were part of deeply patriarchal communities. But in 1993, even lip service to gender equality is another sign that fundamental changes are taking place.

Before you can begin discussions with other South Africans about finding common ground, however, it is important to remind yourselves how the long struggle over apartheid has divided you and made it so difficult for you to understand one another, even now, after apartheid has come to an end.

South Africans All
White South Africans

Among the white population, who had dined at the tall table of privilege for generations, and occupied all positions of power in government, business, finance, and industry, de Klerk's announcement rang like a relief to some, a release for others, and like an abdication to many more. Apartheid created diverse economic, educational, and political opportunities for Afrikaners that greatly elevated and secured their position in South African society. By reserving the lion's share

of resources for *die Volk*,[1] apartheid produced world-class achievers in the academic, artistic, literary, scientific, medical, financial, and business professions, who in turn often questioned the principle of white privilege and yearned for an end to South Africa's isolation and its race-based society. Some bolted from the Dutch Reformed Church in protest; a few even joined the ANC. But for many others, apartheid fostered delusions of self-grandeur and blindness as to the aspirations of others, all built on fear. The Afrikaner-dominated Nationalist Party reflected these tendencies as strongly as any other group. De Klerk's followers, the moderates, thought that by ending apartheid and convening all political voices to construct a democratic South Africa, persons of all colors would flock to their reformed ranks and make them the party of the future. Within months of de Klerk's release of Mandela, however, it was becoming clear that they had figured wrong. Few "non-whites" showed any interest in the NP. The party began to lose some of its old members and, instead of growing, it shrank.

The growing nationalist **Conservative** Party (CP) thought de Klerk a foolish upstart and worked to undermine him; its members were determined to keep apartheid. While the nation celebrated Mandela's release, thousands of CP followers—men, women, children—assembled in downtown **Pretoria**, a few miles from de Klerk's offices in the massive Union Building, and demanded de Klerk's head.

"We want to stay a nation of whites!" said some.

"We will not tolerate de Klerk's treason!" said others.

CP leader Dr. Andries Treurnicht accused de Klerk of "sacrificing the Afrikaners" to the blacks and branded Mandela as one who "incited people to kill whites." The CP was strongest among the white-controlled **South African Defence Force (SADF)** and the **South African Police (SAP)**. And

---

1. Literally "the people," an Afrikaans term favored by white nationalists for whom it carried the meaning of "chosen people."

to their right, among the military and police and apartheid's assassination squadrons, were the ultra-white supremacists, bent on fomenting violence to prevent the spread of democracy and keeping Afrikaners firmly on top. According to them, whites would survive either by slamming back into place the lid of absolute control or by retreating en masse to another territory and creating a "white fatherland."

Most English South African whites belonged to the NP; a few were Conservatives, too, and some, like a small minority of Afrikaners, were in the small liberal parties that had opposed the extremes of apartheid policies. Some stood atop South Africa's largest banks and mining companies, and had lobbied the Nationalist government to negotiate with the ANC. They knew apartheid had cost South Africa millions through sanctions and disinvestment and considered a peaceful transition to democracy as necessary for restoring the South African economy. Intellectuals in the English universities and in political movements such as the **SACP** were also working to end apartheid.

But when it came to full democracy, all but a handful of whites—Afrikaners, English—feared the real article. De Klerk had caught everyone off guard. Whether English- or Afrikaans-speaking, whites made up the overwhelming number of government bureaucrats, academics, and civil servants. How would their all-white institutions include others? Must they give up their positions in the New South African government? Just how far was democracy supposed to go? Must they hand over their jobs and paychecks to make way for blacks? And what of the white population at large, especially the majority who lived comfortably in the middle-class sections of city and town enclaves? Would democracy mean that they would lose their servants? Their all-white neighborhoods and schools? Would their children have a chance in a democratic South Africa? They might accept that de Klerk's decision to end apartheid was necessary, but they did not want it to come too quickly or at their own expense.

More than any other group of Afrikaners upset by de Klerk were those living in the hundreds of rural towns and on thousands of farms. In the vast stretches of the Transvaal, Orange Free State, Natal, and the Cape, South Africa's food supply was produced on white-owned land using non-white labor. Unless whites remained in control in South Africa, what would become of their land, their docile labor force, and the large government subsidies that kept them afloat during South Africa's periodic droughts? And most importantly, would others, especially the blacks, who made up the vast majority of the rural population, refuse to work for them, or take their land?

They, and all the other whites scattered about this vast country, amounted to less than 12 percent of the entire population. De Klerk was letting open the floodgates. Was it probable, if not certain, that blacks would turn on the whites who were the source of their misery? Would a "democratic" government in a country that was 75 percent black become just a "black" government bent on redistributing wealth, confiscating property, and wreaking vengeance on a rich white minority? Surely, whites would be overwhelmed. In the cities, in towns, and on farms, four out of five whites feared for their physical safety if black South Africans controlled the government.

Black South Africans

Seventy-five percent of South Africans were what the whites once had labeled "kaffirs," then relabeled "natives," then "Bantus" and recently, "blacks." Other labels were also used by whites—Zulus, Tswanas, Xhosas, Sothos, Ndebeles, and so on—mainly to convince themselves that they could differentiate among them.[1] But for the most part,

1. Such terms (e.g., *Zulu*), are commonly heard in the West in the same breath as "tribe," a nonsensical and often pejorative concept used to promote ethnic identity for pseudocultural or political ends. For example, the architects of apartheid promoted tribal labels to demodernize black South Africans (i.e., to make them seem

whites found blacks indecipherable outside these neat, imposed categories. What all in the country understood, however, was that blacks, these three South Africans out of every four, ranked at the bottom of the apartheid caste system. Blacks were the dispossessed. With a few exceptions, they could not own property, have a business, move freely, choose where they could live or work, remain in school past primary level, gain pay equal to others outside their caste, vote, hold office, speak their minds in public, marry or even flirt across the color line, or live above the poverty line. They made up the overwhelming proportion of the nation's criminals, crime victims, prostitutes, street gangs, street cleaners, slum dwellers, squatters, migrants, unemployed, rail and bus commuters, alcoholics, single parents and orphans. In this "first-world country," blacks made up almost all of its legions of malnourished, diseased, and illiterate.

All South Africans knew, too, that blacks stood for something. They had led the protest against apartheid through their political and community organizations, demonstrations, strikes, boycotts, stay-at-homes, and guerrilla resistance. As political prisoners, they filled South Africa's cells, court dockets, and death rows, as well as its stacks of lists of assassinations and deaths in detention. Tens of thousands lived in exile in Botswana, Swaziland, Lesotho, Zambia, England, Canada, Scandinavia, France, Germany, and the United States. Blacks were the backbone and head of the liberation movement, its guerrilla forces, whether underground in South Africa or training in exile. They were the muscle of a feisty, resilient labor movement in South Africa. Out of sight and sound, thousands of their men were miles underground at any minute day or night blasting and loading the ore headed up the shafts to be extracted for South Africa's exports in gold, nickel, diamonds, plati-

num, uranium, copper, zinc, cadmium, coal, and titanium. In the township slums and mining compounds, black South Africans created a modern African harmonic jazz culture that soared above the mire, captured each moment of life through South Africa's thick and thin, and rhythmized resistance to apartheid. "Our liberation struggle," said jazz pianist Dollar Brand (Abdullah Ibrahim), "was the world's first to be fought in four-part harmony."[1] South Africa was built on their backs and derived from them its sense of the whole. How is it possible to define this three-quarters of the people, the twenty-nine million, for whom democracy had been a dream until Madiba walked out of prison?

The Resistance

Let us begin by separating out those who resisted apartheid, generation by generation. Africans respect, or should respect, their elders. We can attribute a good share of the adulation Madiba enjoyed to this very fact. His generation led the fight against apartheid in its early years, that is, from 1948 to 1964, when organized political protest inside the country was still possible. Before the architects of apartheid could establish a system of tight controls, Mandela and others publicly and legally challenged individual apartheid laws. Though accustomed to segregation laws, and familiar enough with English and Afrikaner methods of keeping South Africa a "white man's country," Mandela's generation had greater access to education, property, and financial resources than apartheid would later permit. Before apartheid got its teeth into the country, Mandela's generation had produced an articulate, skilled, and knowledgeable middle class of teachers, lawyers, nurses, academics, journalists, and writers. For the most part, this striving black middle class became apartheid's principal target, because people like Mandela contradicted—and publicly rejected—the

quaint and primitive), thereby distancing them from "advanced" white South Africans. The terms *Zulu*, *Tswana*, etc. make more sense when understood as first-language groups.

1. From the documentary film *Amandla! A Revolution in Four-Part Harmony* (2002).

principle of white supremacy. Thousands of the educated black elite were imprisoned, detained, driven into exile, or, increasingly, silenced.

The children of this generation grew up under apartheid, and had fewer resources than their parents. Instead of living in lively multiracial, privately owned neighborhoods, which apartheid destroyed, they were packed into government-owned townships far from the cities. They suffered most when it came to education. They attended shabby, ill-equipped, crowded schools, in which African languages, and eventually Afrikaans, were taught at the expense of English, and where science, math, and knowledge of the outside world were de-emphasized. The few who managed to qualify for university had to attend all-black institutions run by Afrikaners, where exploration, questioning, and learning beyond the limits placed by apartheid were grounds for expulsion. The aim of education under apartheid was to reserve higher knowledge for whites, and suit blacks for servile, lowly positions. To use Dr. Nthatho Motlhana's metaphor, "blacks were not supposed to graze in the green pastures over there."[1] Theirs was an angry generation.

With their parents cowed or in jail, these youngsters became the source of resistance to apartheid in the 1970s. Their massive protest against Afrikaans instruction on 16 June 1976 in Soweto, and the ensuing wave of student strikes that spread throughout the country, became—and remains—a day on which black South Africans mark the beginning of the final stage of the liberation struggle. This rebellious generation, inspired by such leaders as Steve **Biko** (BEE-ko) and Mamphela Ramphele (Mahm-PAY-lah ram-PAY-lay) and notions of "Black Consciousness" and "Neo-Marxist Analysis" failed to dislodge apartheid, however, just as their parents had failed through protest. Thousands of these youngsters were killed or, if they had not already fled South Africa into exile, imprisoned. Many of those who escaped

linked up with the organizations-in-exile formed by their parents, principally the ANC and the **PAC,** and signed on as soldiers with MK forces training in Zambia, Tanzania, Angola, Libya, and Algeria.[2]

The next generation of black South Africans emerged after the South African government crushed the 1970s protests. Activists inside South Africa, backed by clandestine ANC operatives infiltrating the country from abroad, formed community-based organizations opposed to apartheid government policies. They were particularly successful in leading resistance to Pretoria's attempts to impose "local self-government." In the 1980s, NP president P. W. Botha (BOW-tah) wanted to create the impression abroad that black South Africans enjoyed a form of democracy, i.e., local governments, in which township councils and the like would be elected by the residents and run their internal affairs. It was clear to antiapartheid forces that, instead of democracy, Botha had in mind the hand-picking of councilors.

Soon ANC-backed local organizations all over South Africa joined in a loose alliance known as the **United Democratic Front** (UDF). The UDF helped to organize protests against these puppet governments and expose them as a sham, in front of the foreign and local journalists and photographers that Botha's reform posture had to allow into the troubled areas. Meanwhile, in black townships near all the urban centers, school-age youngsters formed gangs to attack the schools and close them down. They threw rocks at township police and armed SAP and SADF squads sent into break up protests and demonstrations. This youth-led popular protest often turned ugly. If anyone among them was suspected of spying for the police, a mere allegation could lead to his or her seizure right out in public. After being beaten to a pulp by the mob, the accused would be

1. From the documentary, *Apartheid, Part III* (1987).

2. The ANC's military wing was known as Umkhonto we Sizwe ("Spear of the Nation"); that of the PAC was called Poqo ("We Go It Alone"). The PAC's force was later renamed the Azanian People's Liberation Army (APLA).

executed there and then in a grisly fashion known as "necklacing," in which a tire was hung around the victim's neck, doused with gasoline, and set alight. In short, the combined efforts of the UDF and unruly schoolchildren made the townships "ungovernable" for the NP. The collapse of schools and services also meant that these children constituted black South Africa's first illiterate urban generation.

Homelands: Apartheid's Plan to Separate Blacks from One Another

Not all black South Africans saw or responded to apartheid in the same way. Essentially, under apartheid all blacks were powerless, their life hard-scrabble. Individuals' duties to others could seem, and often were, insurmountable. Parents determined to provide for their children had to work for poor pay, often in demeaning conditions, in white areas miles away from their own miserable dwellings in townships or squatter camps, keeping them separated from their children for long hours. Day care was out of the question. For the very poor, who squatted in reach of the towns and cities where most jobs were available, getting (and keeping) work meant commuting three to four hours *each way*, by bus. That meant arising sometimes as early as 3 A.M. and arriving back home (if one could call it that) at 10 or 11 P.M. And most adults were lucky to have work at all. Unofficially, the unemployment rate among black adults exceeded 40 percent. Squatter slums and impoverished townships bred black-on-black violence, crime, and a whole range of social pathologies. In the rural South African "homelands"—Bophuthatswana, Venda, QwaQwa, Transkei, Ciskei—and KwaZulu-Natal, were stashed the most impoverished of black South Africans, mostly women, children and the elderly.

The only substantive rewards apartheid made available to black South Africans were given in return for cooperation. Apart from black labor, which supported all the major industries— agricultural, mining, manufacturing—black South

Africans were needed in large numbers to run the apparatus of apartheid itself. The SAP was black South Africa's leading full-opportunity employer. Once in uniform, a black police officer received housing for himself and his family, along with medical care, school fees, paid leave, and pension plan. Plainclothesmen did even better. The SADF recruited thousands of black soldiers at junior rank, deploying them to defend South Africa from the "communist onslaught," (a catch-phrase used to brand the ANC and other resistance organizations as agents of Moscow) and help patrol South Africa's townships and rural areas.

Other financially attractive options were created in abundance for those running the homelands. Since the 1960s the NP had propped up these fake states as examples of white South Africa's generosity and willingness to give blacks their "independence." Each had a capital, with fancy offices, parliaments, and a bureaucracy complete with its own security forces (headed by white South Africans or "trusted" black ex-SAP careerists), all paid for by Pretoria. Atop these homeland governments sat well-paid "presidents" or "prime ministers," who were chauffeured about in limousines, lived in luxurious homes, and were assisted by bundles of loyalists expecting their due. In the homeland countryside, appointed "chiefs" were also in Pretoria's pocket. This entire edifice, funded and controlled by white South Africa, was also a conduit channeling information to white authorities in Pretoria about antiapartheid activities.

Homeland leaders were persons of considerable power. In KwaZulu Chief Mangosuthu (Gatsha) **Buthelezi** (boot-eh-LAY-zee) built a base for himself as a champion of a unified South Africa that incorporated traditional African institutions, often denouncing apartheid and even rejecting the "offer" of "independent" Homeland status for KwaZulu pressed for by the government. In taking these stands, Buthelezi helped to complicate the political picture in South Africa, for he was regularly accused by many South Africans of being a collaborator with the government he sometimes vociferously opposed, and he stood firm as a consistent opponent of the ANC-UDF blanket form of democracy for all. In KwaZulu, Buthelezi's paramilitary units attacked communities known to sympathize with the ANC and the UDF. ANC and Umkhonto we Sizwe retaliation was not uncommon. Thousands died.

Apart from controlling black South Africans, the homelands provided white South Africans sources of entertainment and self-indulgence unavailable in white South Africa itself. In places like Sun City, nestled in the hills of **Bophuthatswana** (boh-poo-tah-TSWAH-nah), what was illegal in South Africa—gambling, porno films and interracial sex (i.e., white men hiring black prostitutes)—were to be had scarcely more than hour's drive from Pretoria, the administrative capital of apartheid. The money-spinning culture of the homelands made white businessmen like Sol Kerzner fabulously rich, and gave celebrity whites in the West, like Frank Sinatra and Jack Nicklaus, a stage for their talent and the proceeds to match, all the while claiming to be performing in an independent country where there was no racial discrimination. The president of Bophuthatswana, Lucas **Mangope** (mah-NGO-pay) along with his cabinet and their wives, could expect free accommodation at Sun City for their holiday breaks.

In the urban townships, where the national government owned the land, rented all the dwellings, determined the local laws and regulations, and enforced it with the SAP and SADF, working for apartheid was less obvious, but widespread. Petty criminals, and the not-so-petty, who fell afoul of the law, could be back on the streets in short order if they agreed to cooperate. The police developed extensive networks of spies in the townships by giving common criminals time off, immunity from prosecution, or release from custody, with cash to boot, in return for the names of people in the townships suspected of leading protests, organizing boycotts, or working with one of the banned political organizations. And among the protestors arrested in sweeps and jailed for months without charge the police found individuals they could "turn" (convert into spies). These protestors-become-police-informers were the counterparts to the "askaris," ex-ANC guerrillas captured in the "border wars" in Southwest Africa and Rhodesia. Once "turned," their assured execution as traitors should they cross back into ANC territory, these ex-freedom fighters became effective counterinsurgency troopers fighting alongside whites in uniform in defense of apartheid. Ever creative, apartheid found ways of arming groups of warlords and thugs (*amatsotsi*) operating in the homelands and townships and who, in return for attacking people or groups associated with the liberation struggle, received cash and police protection, if not a blind eye to their illegal actions.

Religious Affiliations

Black South Africans were divided along class and religious lines, as well. The educated elite, which began to emerge in the early 1900s, adopted Christianity as part of their elevated social status. A few were Roman Catholic, but the overwhelming proportion were Protestant—Methodist, Presbyterian, Lutheran, African Methodist Episcopal, Anglican, Congregational, Church of Christ, Baptist, and even Dutch Reformed. Their churches were instrumental in leading black South Africa's challenges to segregation and apartheid. The older, prominent members of the liberation struggle, such as Mandela and Oliver Tambo, came from these churches and were taught in their schools, which prized academic excellence. The Anglican Archbishop of Cape Town, Rev. Desmond **Tutu**, who moved into the international spotlight in the 1980s as a champion of racial justice for all South Africans, was the end-product of a long line of Christian voices coming from black congregations.

However, the overwhelming majority of black South African Christians came from the less educated, generally impoverished parts of rural and urban South Africa. Numbering more than 4.5 million, they belonged to what have been labeled "independent churches," because they rejected any ties to the European or American churches. Their small congregations were scattered all over South Africa, and on Sunday they were easily recognized by their colorful costumes, in contrast to the formal Western dress seen in black Christian Protestant churches. By far the largest of the independents was the Zionist Christian Church ("Zett-C-C"), which blended African with Christian religious teachings and emphasized faith-healing and biblicism. Its members congregated every Easter weekend at Archbishop Lekganyane's headquarters in Morija, outside the northern Transvaal town of Pietersburg (now Polokwane). Customarily, one million ZCC members bussed and taxied themselves to Morija for this occasion. In contrast to the Protestant mainline churches, members of the independent churches stayed away from politics and concentrated their attention on supporting emotionally and materially their fellow members. Their quiet approach to life's difficulties gained the praise of the Nationalist government, and it was common for the South African president himself to visit Morija each Easter and sit next to Bishop Lekganyane.

Black South Africans often found it difficult to know where other black South Africans stood, on which side of the apartheid fence. Fear of being arrested, jailed, or killed by police acting on informer reports that police had little way of verifying, created a sense of suspicion that infected relationships, in the community, in neighbor-hoods, and within families. A visit from a cousin or a sibling's child enquiring about the family could mark the beginning of one's imprisonment, if not virtual disappearance, for years. The release of Mandela did little to calm apprehension, because in 1990, the SAP and SADF remained the sole source of armed authority in South Africa, their connections and networks among black South Africans remained intact, as if Mandela were still behind bars.

The Coloureds

Almost as numerous as the white population in South Africa were the people labeled with one of apartheid's four racial categories as "Coloured." Numbering close to 3.3 million in 1991, they occupied the caste above the Blacks, which meant they were encouraged to think of themselves as a distinct group, albeit beneath the whites. In apartheid's view, the Coloured were racially mixed, the by-product of "sins past" when South Africans, especially in the "Cape," intermingled much more commonly than they were permitted to after 1948. The ancestors of the Coloureds included the Dutch, French, and Portuguese (all of whose descendants were to call themselves Afrikaners), together with their slaves brought in from Indonesia, India, Madagascar, Mozambique, and West Africa, and lastly peoples indigenous to the Cape—the click-speaking Khoikhoi (Hottentots to the Dutch) and San ("Bushmen"). The Coloureds represented the world's only blend of Europe, southern Africa and Asia. All spoke Afrikaans, the first language of the apartheid state, as their mother tongue. Truth be told, this people of mixed origin created this creole language, which white nationalists adopted late in the nineteenth century as their own.

The vast majority of the Coloureds lived in the Cape Province, all the way from **Cape Town** east into the lush hills and valleys, north into stark mountain ranges, then onto the arid Karoo plateau and all the way through the northern Cape to the border of South West Africa, and into Botswana. They were a working class and small farmer element for the most part, with skills that main-tained the fishing industry, sheep and cattle farming, construction, restaurants, workshops, and the extensive Cape vineyards. In Cape Town their families had created a distinct urban culture, with a pronounced Indonesian influence, Muslim clerics and mosques, and radiant "coon" festivals. Cape Coloured cuisine became the standard by which Afrikaners judged how well one ate. Coloreds away from Cape Town identified more closely with the Afrikaners than they did with black Africans, accepting the names given by whites ages ago to their slave ancestors (January, April, and the like), worshiping in the Dutch Reformed Church (Coloured section), and speaking English only as a second language.

This people, who bridged South Africa's racial divide, were in fact caught in the middle. They enjoyed few rights or privileges under apartheid, and suffered as much as black South Africans. They were driven away from the urban areas where they had owned property for generations and stuffed into townships and districts ill-equipped or serviced. The vast majority were poor, their children forced to attend sub-standard schools, their families confined to sub-standard housing, and their men and women prone to alcoholism. In the 1980s, when President Botha created a special Parliament for Coloureds (and Asians) and invited all to vote for their representatives, only a small minority of Coloured voters participated. Like black South Africans, most Coloureds wanted apartheid to end. Some of their leaders, such as Alan **Boesak** (BOW-sack), joined the antiapartheid movement. Yet, apart from some of their radicalized youth in the 80s, few Coloureds joined the liberation struggle or identified wholly with the aims of the ANC, PAC, and other organizations led by black South Africans. They were like the white South Africans in that they had misgivings about a South Africa in which they would continue to remain a minority, separated by their distinctive past and culture, and their Afrikaans language held against them by a democratically elected, black majority government. Mandela's release from prison, therefore, was good news, but for many Coloureds not necessarily a cause for celebration.

The Asians
Apartheid's fourth caste was reserved for "Asians," people who in 1991 amounted to less than one million South Africans, or roughly 2.6 percent. Though the smallest of the four castes, they were a significant component of the South African social and economic landscape. This term *Asian* was in

fact preferred by the people it identified (though many called themselves "Indians" and many would have preferred to be called South African) because "Asian" embraced the diversity of Hindu and Muslim peoples from the Indian subcontinent which included modern Pakistan, where a good portion of South African Asians originated. Asians had been present in South Africa since the nineteenth century (though one maverick historian argues for a pre-historic link), when Hindu laborers were imported to work the sugar plantations in Natal, along the Indian Ocean coast. By the twentieth century, Asians were an important element in the commercial life of Natal's major port city, Durban, and Asian merchants were to be found in all the commercial urban centers of South Africa, particularly in the Witwatersrand (the cities spread atop South Africa's world-famous, massive "gold reef," the popular term for the massive gold seam below). Their earnings from commerce were used to build up their small communities, especially their schools, and a professional class began to emerge. English was their main language, a Western style of dress common among their menfolk, and they were permitted, under apartheid laws, to own property in their residential and commercial sections of town. They constituted also a caste, one that rarely married outside its own, a practice which apartheid reinforced.

Within the Asian community, however, along with a desire and the means to acquire an education was a strong tradition of protest against white racial supremacy and for democratic institutions. The great Mahatma Gandhi began his campaign for India's self-government after he was thrown off a train between Durban and Johannesburg, and Gandhi's India became the United Nations' and British Commonwealth's leading opponent of apartheid. As lawyers, Asians defended black South Africans being tried by under apartheid laws, as activists they helped draft the Freedom Charter, and like Mac **Maharaj** (mah-hah-RAJ) they joined the ANC and worked to liberate South Africa while in exile (Maharaj had been Madiba's cell-mate on Robben Island). Like the Coloured populations, the vast majority of Asians rejected Botha's special Parliament for this racial group. As much, perhaps even more than, black South Africans as a group, the Asians called for full democracy. That did not mean, however, that the prospect of a black-ruled nation necessarily cheered them on. They were mindful of what had happened in other parts of Africa where Asians had made their homes and stayed on after black Africans took charge, such as in Kenya, Uganda, Tanzania, Zambia, Botswana, Zimbabwe, and Mozambique. The impact of independence on Asians in these countries had been mixed, from the Uganda dictatorship of Idi Amin which seized their properties and kicked them out willy-nilly, to the non-racial democracy of Botswana, just across the South Africa border, where the small Asian community flourished.

The Road to the Multi-Party Talks: The Struggle for Power

When the euphoria of Mandela's release faded, the South African mood turned anxious. Mandela's immense stature made the ANC an automatic partner with de Klerk's NP to negotiate South Africa's future. But in early 1990 the ANC was little more than a mirage. Only just unbanned, the party had virtually no offices in South Africa, no staff, and no funds. Its leaders were arriving from overseas, with the daunting task of finding jobs and accommodating their families while having at the same time to turn to urgent political matters and deal with people they hardly knew, if at all. ANC followers inside South Africa, in turn, had no firsthand experience of the exiles just returned. No internal elections were held and all ANC leaders *assumed* their roles, rather than waiting to be chosen. It would take nearly a year for the ANC to organize its first conference. In the meantime, there was lots of jostling. Prominent local figures, like chief labor unionist Cyril Ramaphosa, switched in a snap to the ANC. Ramaphosa, for his part, quickly scaled his way to the top. Neverthe-less, from the get-go, de Klerk put all his chips on the ANC, negotiating only with Mandela's organization, which he knew to be in national disarray. Perhaps he meant it that way, so that he could keep the initiative in his hands and control the negotiating process. By the same token, de Klerk was too new as prime minister to be trusted by the ANC, and many onlookers were upset that de Klerk was talking only with the ANC. Quickly, violently, attempts were made to scuttle the talks. Even before de Klerk and Mandela could sit down together, political acrimony and blood-letting erupted.

February–December 1990

Mandela's speech the day of his release[1] made it clear that he had no illusions about the future and was prepared for the long haul. To the Nationalist Party, he let it be known that he would not call on his ANC organization's MK to put down their arms and suspend the armed struggle, that he would not appeal to the international community to lift the sanctions against South Africa that helped to force de Klerk's hand. The NP would have to make the necessary, concrete steps to end apartheid. Promises were not enough; the proof must be in the pudding. He saw his role as appealing to all others, those excluded by apartheid, to unite. Within days of his Cape Town address, Mandela was in Durban, near to where hundreds had died in the past few years in clashes between ANC/UDF followers and those of Gatsha Buthelezi. He called for peace.[2]

Mandela's appeal carried little force. Within weeks, clashes had broken out once again in Edendale, **KwaZulu-Natal;** the rampaging lasted more than a week, causing eighty deaths and leaving thousands homeless. Uniformed police officers stood by. Those supporting homeland leaders were not about to let the ANC have its way. On the other side of South Africa, in Bophuthatswana, security police rounded up

1. Mandela, "On Release from Prison."
2. Mandela, "Address to Rally in Durban," 25 February 1990.

hundreds of ANC supporters and threw them in jail. And south of **Johannesburg** at **Sebokeng**, the police opened fire on a large ANC gathering, without warning, killing 17 and injuring nearly 450. There was a general feeling that de Klerk was promoting all the violence.

Disturbed by these attacks but interpreting them as the bitter fruit of recent years, Mandela's organization moved toward talks with de Klerk's negotiating team. By March, the ANC had opened its first office, in Johannesburg, and by May, ANC leaders in exile were arriving from overseas to join Mandela. ANC leaders called for an end to violence and asked that negotiations be given a chance to yield results. At first, once the talks were underway, relief seemed to be at hand. De Klerk pledged to release all remaining political prisoners expeditiously, end some emergency regulations, and work with the ANC to end violence.[1] A spell of calm began.

It did not last. In spite of a second round of talks and another agreement,[2] clashes erupted again in KwaZulu-Natal between the ANC and Buthelezi's brand-new political organization, the **Inkatha** (een-KAH-tah) **Freedom Party (IFP)**. Migrant hostel dwellers in the mining towns along the Witwatersrand ("the Reef") were whipped into an attacking force by the IFP and were used to target nearby residents labeled as pro-ANC. More than five hundred people died, again while the police were present. Meanwhile, back in KwaZulu-Natal, violence continued, making these weeks some of "the bloodiest in South African history."[3] The Goldstone Commission investigating the Sebokeng massacre pointed the finger directly at the police.[4]

The ANC had had enough. They threatened to pull out of the talks and began forming armed "self-defence units." De Klerk responded with new emergency laws, "Operation Iron Fist,"

giving power to the SADF and SAP to impose curfews, mount roadblocks, run house-to-house searches, and fence in squatter camps with razor wire, ostensibly as a way of controlling the violence. This angered the ANC further. Mandela accused de Klerk's government of causing all the trouble, and in November, as if to confirm Mandela's view, the independent Harms Commission on death squads implicated the head of the SADF, Gen. Magnus Malan. The ANC suspended the talks. In December, addressing the ANC's first consultative conference inside South Africa in forty-odd years, Mandela accused the Nationalist government of using violence to destabilize the ANC. He demanded that the ANC, and all South Africans, join a mass campaign to oppose opening the tricameral Parliament in January, scrap the existing government (including the homelands), and form an "interim government" and "legislative assembly."[5] He called for the armed struggle to continue and asked the world to keep its sanctions in place. De Klerk offered no response. At the end of 1990, South Africa was back where it had been the previous February, when Mandela stepped out of Victor Verster Prison and spoke to the Cape Town crowd.

1991

Into January and the months ahead, the scale of political violence intensified. Politically related killings totaled 169 that month, 93 in February, and an incredible 277 in March. These bloody attacks were concentrated in KwaZulu-Natal and the cities of the Reef, and were most intense between the IFP and ANC. The ANC were on the receiving end most of the time, as happened in January in Sebokeng, when a group of "vigilantes" killed thirty-five ANC members at a political gathering. Meanwhile

1. "Document 17: The Groote Schuur Minute, 4 May 1990."
2. "Document 18: The Pretoria Minute, 6 August 1990."
3. Allister Sparks, "South African Police Criticized in Natal Violence."
4. Beresford, "Judge Condemns SA Riot Police."

5. "Keynote Address of Comrade Nelson R. Mandela, Deputy President of the ANC, to the ANC National Consultative Conference, 14–16 December 1990," Nelson Mandela Foundation, accessed 26 November 2016, http://db.nelsonmandela.org/speeches/pub_view.asp?pg=item&ItemID=NMS053&txtstr=ANC.

armed gangs, emerging from nowhere, attacked rail commuters from the townships and assaulted funeral vigils and processions. Invariably, the police were either silent onlookers or absent altogether. The IFP were implicated, as were the police, but accusations were made on both sides. The IFP claimed 180 of its leaders had been assassinated by the ANC; the police accused the ANC's MK units of killings; while the ANC claimed that eighty of its leading activists had been done in. Groups of white right-wingers were parading about, brandishing their guns in public, too, though the police seemed ever-present and quick to separate them from those who objected to their presence.

Sensing that South Africa was edging toward the cliff, Mandela met with Buthelezi to reach a truce, and the ANC invited the PAC, **AZAPO** (the Azanian People's Organisation, a small group of black intellectuals calling for a Socialist South Africa run by black Africans), and the IFP for joint talks. In the place of the ANC–NP negotiation approach, which had gone nowhere, Mandela proposed an all-party conference to push negotiations forward. De Klerk seemed open, but then he pulled back, fearing that his position in his own party would be viewed as shaky if the ANC was seen as taking the lead. Finally, in late April, as violence continued unabated, Mandela issued an ultimatum to de Klerk to set up a multi-party commission to address it. Wanting talks to resume, and needing ANC's cooperation, de Klerk agreed to a multi-party "Peace Conference" in June.

Meanwhile, both the NP and ANC were busy consolidating their positions. De Klerk's party was moving to reclaim its control over the negotiating process and get international support for the lifting of sanctions by posing as an antiapartheid champion. Apartheid was declared a "sin against God;" the National majority in Parliament dismantled old apartheid laws such as the Group Areas Act and opened its membership to all persons. But for its part, the ANC was gaining more ground. In his frequent trips overseas, Mandela raised millions in funding for the ANC. In June, before the Peace Conference, the ANC held its forty-eighth national conference, its first since 1959, where Nelson Mandela was duly elected president and a constitution was adopted.[1] To the worry of many onlookers, half of the ANC's NEC also belonged to the SACP.

As the talks got underway, the minority all-white, liberal Democratic Party dropped a bombshell claim in Parliament: that the National government was actively funding the IFP and its armed units. The press jumped on the story and released more details, linking this support to the SAP and SADF, and to the violence launched against ANC followers in IFP areas. It embarrassed de Klerk, who claimed that others in his government were responsible, but the admissions weakened his hand. He removed Gen. Malan of the SADF and General Adriaan Vlok of the SAP and in September signed the Peace Accord, which conceded to the ANC's call for multi-party talks.[2] In October, the ANC formed the Patriotic Front with the PAC and convened a conference attended by ninety-two organizations. ANC seemed much strengthened for the bargaining that lay ahead.

In December 1991, the CODESA met in Johannesburg, attended by fifteen political parties (including all parties in the tricameral Parliament, except the white right-wing CP) and representatives from **Ciskei** (sih-SKY), Bophuthatswana, Transkei, and Venda. Their agreed purpose was "to set in motion the process of drawing up and establishing a constitution" that would guarantee a multi-party, non-racial, non-sexist democracy.[3]

1. African National Congress. "ANC Constitution." The National Conference was attended by elected representatives from ANC chapters around the country, whereas the ANC's Consultative Conference, held the previous December, was attended by ANC members prior to any local elections.

2. The National Peace Accord, 14 September 1991, http://www.incore.ulst.ac.uk/services/cds/agreements /pdf/sa4.pdf.

3. "Document 22: CODESA I Declaration of Intent, December 1991."

1992

Over the next six months it became clear that CODESA was not a multi-party conference but another NP–ANC affair. The positions of other parties did not matter. Starting from a strong position, it thought, the ANC pushed its agenda for an interim government and a temporary constitution until a future Constituent Assembly could be democratically elected. When de Klerk dragged his feet, the ANC made compromises to pull him along, at which point the Patriotic Front crumbled. The PAC pulled out, AZAPO rejected the multi-party approach, and the SACP moved into closer association with COSATU, the leading trade union organization. All were critical of the ANC for moderating its positions and dealing with the NP on its own, rather than operating out in the open. The IFP remained deeply suspicious of Mandela and his followers, as outbreaks of IFP–ANC violence continued in KwaZulu-Natal and the Reef.

Meanwhile, de Klerk gambled his future by holding a referendum in May among white voters as to whether the NP should continue negotiations. A resounding 68 percent voted yes, but rather than move closer to Mandela, de Klerk hardened his position. He wanted a CODESA constitution that was permanent, and one that protected regional autonomy and required substantial super-majorities (more than the ANC could hope to achieve) to alter it. In brief, it was a prescription for giving the white minority and the homelands a veto over South Africa's future and denying the ANC majority control. When talks resumed on 15 May ("CODESA II"), Mandela began trading accusations with de Klerk and threatened to pull the ANC out of negotiations and "plug into the power of the masses." On 16 June, the ANC launched a "mass action campaign" calling for commuter and rent boycotts, strikes, and anti-homeland demonstrations.

The anti-ANC reaction was immediate. On 17 June, hundreds of IFP "warriors" from a nearby hostel, armed with guns, spears, and machetes, rampaged through the squatter shack town of

Boipatong (BOY-pah-TONG), massacring thirty-nine men, women, and children and wounding seriously at least thirty others. Minister of Law and Order Captain Craig Kotze blamed the ANC, but survivors told reporters that they saw police assisting the marauders and even firing on the Boipatong squatters. No arrests were made. In early September, after the ANC had stepped up its campaign against the homelands, a major clash occurred at Bisho, the homeland capital of Ciskei. At CODESA II in June, Brigadier Oupa Gqozo had declared Ciskei a "sovereign independent state" rather than continue participating in the talks. The ANC supported protests in the Ciskei from that point and in early August assembled thirty thousand people to march on Bisho. They were turned back, but in early September another more determined march, led by SACP member Ronnie Kasrils, reached the Bisho stadium. The Ciskein army opened fire, killing twenty-nine people and wounding hundreds.

The surge of events placed Mandela in a quandary. Though feeling betrayed by de Klerk's hard line, he was doubtful that the prime minister was able to control the violence. In other words, the threat of the "**Third Force**" (white police and soldiers fomenting violence through city gangs and homeland security forces)[1] was real. The ANC's inability to deliver results in CODESA and the Mass Action Campaign, at the same time, was unleashing the more radical elements, who were much less inhibited than the moderates about confrontations and using violence against their opponents. The SACP Secretary General was Chris **Hani** (HAH-nee), an ANC member and ex-MK commander and at that point an outspoken proponent of confrontation. After Mandela, he was the best known and most popular liberation figure. De Klerk used the SACP connection to hurt the ANC. Trying to drive a wedge between this old alliance, which Mandela was dedicated to preserving, de Klerk argued that

1. Jacques Pauw, "Violence: The Role of the Security Forces."

he could not convince enough whites to back him as long as the SACP was involved. Targeting the SACP stirred up white anticommunist anxieties and gained de Klerk international support in the West as the leader of the more reasonable party. Even white moderates held the ANC responsible for the Bisho tragedy, because the SACP was involved.

De Klerk needed Mandela and a moderate ANC. The May referendum demonstrated that his base strongly favored negotiations, and the outbreaks of violence, which seemed beyond his control (or so he said), pressured him to compromise, just as they did Mandela. Within two weeks after Bisho, the adversaries-cum-partners were back together trying to find common ground. The result was the Record of Understanding.[1] They agreed to pursue bilateral discussions rather than try at once to resume the CODESA "multi-party" talks, seemingly unable to determine how to get anyone else around the table, much less keep them there. De Klerk agreed to a constitutional non-racial interim government, and Mandela agreed to quiet the mass action campaign.

The initial response from other key, interested parties was first outrage, then a scramble for partners. Buthelezi accused the NP and ANC of conniving for their own ends and threatened KwaZulu-Natal's secession from South Africa. On the white right, opposition to de Klerk remained solid, but without any plan to cope with the changes being propelled by the Record of Understanding. Key CP members bolted to form a new coalition, the Afrikaner Volksunie (Union of the Afrikaner People—AVU), to campaign for an Afrikaner "Homeland." AVU leaders and other right-wing groups in turn also began meeting actively with Gatsha Buthelezi and other homeland leaders, forming a conservative black and white coalition, the Concerned South Africans Group (COSAG), to oppose the moderate de Klerk/ Mandela position and press for regional states. De

Klerk tried to siphon off some of that conservative support and hold his moderate base by calling for strong regional governments in the new South Africa and "special majorities" to prevent any single party—read the ANC—from controlling the national government. On the left, ANC militants objected to Mandela's September compromise with de Klerk, and AZAPO declared itself forever out of the negotiating process, preferring instead to start a militant program of action to ensure, in the words of its president, Itumeleng Jerry Mosala, "the liberation of our people."[2] ANC leaders were embarrassed further by revelations in the press, backed by Amnesty International investigations, that torture and summary executions had taken place in MK camps in Angola, Zambia, and Tanzania. Though he claimed no responsibility for these atrocities, Mandela soon apologized on behalf of his organization. His moral high ground, nevertheless, was being eroded. Nor did it help the ANC that Winnie Mandela, who had separated from her husband and had been put on trial for participating in murders in Soweto in the 1980s, was posing as the radical voice of the urban poor in the townships and squatter camps. She attacked her own husband and his leadership group as participating in a "disastrous" negotiation process the aim of which, she declared, was to satisfy the personal ambitions of a "black elite."[3] Once again, the ANC felt alone, isolated. De Klerk, always quick to pounce on ANC weaknesses to boost his image among his wavering supporters, blamed the ANC and the IFP for all the political violence that continued in spite of the Accord. But, as always portraying himself as the best hope, de Klerk declared that negotiations were the only way to avoid civil war.

In spite of its weakened position, or perhaps because of it, the ANC pressed ahead with de Klerk in restarting multi-party talks. In late 1992, the

1. "Record of Understanding between ANC and NP, 26 September 1992."

2. SA Report, 4 Dec. 1992, as reproduced in *Facts and Reports*, 22 (18 Dec. 1992), YZ8.

3. David Beresford, *The Guardian (UK)*.

ANC had thrown a juicy bone to the tens of thousands of white civil servants, who constituted one of de Klerk's shakier constituencies, with Joe Slovo's idea of a "sunset government," which would guarantee white bureaucrats their jobs years after a new government was formed. Slovo's proposal was significant, not only because of its content but because Slovo was the senior SACP member (above Chris Hani) in the ANC. His move demonstrated that both sides of the ANC–SACP coalition desired a democratic South Africa above their ideological preferences.[1] In early 1993, the secretive but influential *Broederbond,*" made up of the most influential Afrikaners in all sectors of South Africa, came out in favor of negotiations, strengthening both de Klerk's and the ANC's appeal to the extremes on the right and left to join in the talks. Although Buthelezi publicly rejected resuming a multi-party conference, he knew he had no choice but to join once it convened.

Thus, in April 1993, after three years of conflict, failed negotiations, deaths due to political violence, and the emergence of scores of armed militant groups, all opposed to a democratic South Africa on de Klerk and Mandela's terms, hundreds of representatives of all but the most extreme wings of political views convened at Kempton Park, Johannesburg, to see what the future held.

The prospects for agreement, as always, seemed remote. Pessimism about the future, too, was increasing. Many thought South Africa was coming apart at the seams. Although an enormous majority (87 percent) of South Africans supported negotiations, almost as high a proportion (85 percent) felt unsafe in their own communities because of the violence, and the barely 50 percent who had hope for the future in 1992 had not increased by mid-1993, while those who had less hope had increased from 24 to 35 percent. Fewer than half believed that Africans and whites shared enough values to create a democratic South Africa.[2] The downward trend in attitudes was reflected in other disturbing developments. Since Mandela's release, the South African economy had suffered negative growth, and unemployment was rising. The ANC estimated that more than 5 billion South African rand had been illegally exported out of the country, as whites prepared to emigrate. Domestic and foreign investments were at all-time lows. At an all-time high was the accelerating crime rate, with a murder committed every 30 minutes, rape every 21, robbery every 6.6, and housebreaking every 3.5. An estimated 20,135 persons were murdered in 1992. Since February 1990, more than eight thousand people had died in political violence, mostly in clashes between the IFP and ANC. But in late 1992 and early 1993, the rate of black-on-white and white-on-black violence, though small in comparison to black-on-black violence, was increasing as armed extremist groups and deranged individuals targeted innocents simply because of their race. By 1993, 3,488,951 firearm licenses had been issued in South Africa, an average increase of 537 per day over the previous year. The country seemed headed for the civil war that for years many South Africans feared might be the ultimate outcome of the collapse of apartheid. All those attending the MPNP at Kempton Park understood the need to pull South Africa back from the abyss, but they arrived knowing that previous conferences, whether bilateral or the multi-lateral CODESA I and II, had failed to agree on fundamental steps to take the country forward. In the months leading up to the MPNP, including the March planning conference, it was agreed that the MPNP must create a government of national unity, in the following way. First, a constitution would be drawn up to determine the shape of the interim government that would replace the existing Parliament and rule South Africa until such time as a final constitution was adopted.

1. For Slovo's thoughts on the transition to democracy, refer to his article "Has Socialism Failed?" in the Supplemental Readings.

2. Johnson and Schlemmer, *Launching Democracy in South Africa*, tables 3.35, 3.37, 3.40.

For the talks, now in your hands, to succeed, therefore, the following issues will have to be addressed and resolved:

1. Federal vs. centralized form of government: Will South Africa be governed by a central government, or would the laws governing its people reside mostly in the provinces? In either case, what role would the provinces have in the larger South Africa, and how would their boundaries be determined?
2. Will power be shared in the new South Africa in Parliament and at the executive level (including the cabinet), or will it be winner-take-all?
3. When will elections be called to choose representatives to the interim government?
4. What will become of the Homeland territories, their governments, and their institutions? Will any be entitled to form independent states, such as an Afrikaner homeland?
5. Will the constitution contain a bill of rights? If so, what will it contain?
6. What will become of the existing SADF and the SAP? Will they continue as before, or will their members be suspended and required to reapply for admission along with all other South Africans? Who will command these army and police forces? In this respect, what should become of members of the armed resistance forces, such as Umkhonto we Sizwe and the Azanian People's Liberation Army (APLA)? Will they be integrated into the SADF? If so, to what level of authority?
7. What will be the flag of the new South Africa and its national anthem? Must the existing flag and anthem go?
8. How many official languages will the future South Africa have?

3
The Game

"The Collapse of Apartheid" is, like all reacting games, a role-playing experience. That means that you will assume a persona quite different from your own. You must adopt your role's goals and learn to think like the person you are portraying, allowing the character's perceptions to influence your reasoning. This of course requires both information (you will need to read more than just the role description) and imagination (written materials won't tell you what to think about everything you encounter; you will have to learn to think from another perspective).

Students in this reacting game will be members of the Multi-Party Negotiating Process (MPNP) Talks held at Kempton Park in 1993. Your principal job is to construct a new constitution for a post-apartheid South Africa, though you will have some preliminary issues to attend to as well. All players will have a role or identity that was present at or relevant to the actual negotiations in 1993. Some of you will be members of factions and some will not; but all of you have goals that are reflective of the primary concerns of you and your constituents. The gender balance in the game is even, reflecting the actual MPNP, during which organizers strove to ensure a plurality of voices and perspectives in constitution formation; do not forget your gender identity—it is important to keep in mind that matters of equality, justice, rights, and protection relate as much to a person's sex as they do to ethnicity, economic standing, language, or religion. In addition to your individual and faction goals, however, you also hold in common a profound sense of urgency: this is your last chance to settle on a constitution before civil war erupts and leads South Africa to unmitigated disaster and tragedy.

The game will occur in three stages. The game will begin with All-Party Talks in which all participants will be present together to discuss important preliminary issues that the Gamemaster (your course instructor) will explain. In the second part of the game, you will be broken up into three Constitutional Working Groups (CWGs), each of which will have specific duties related to creating a section of the constitution. The duties of each CWG are outlined below. Each CWG will be made up of a mixture of representatives from different parties and factions. This means that it is quite possible that you will not have another representative of your faction in your CWG. In the third and final stage, each CWG will present its constitutional provisions to the MPNP as a whole to be discussed and approved or disapproved.

Each session throughout the game will have a chairperson who will be responsible for organizing and moderating discussion and decision making by the assembly, establishing decision-making procedure, setting the agenda for the day, and pressing the body to respond to any urgent news issues that might (or, rather, will) arise. The historic MPNP rotated this chairpersonship so that each party involved had a chance to preside and none could do so more than once. Similarly, in the game the chair position will change daily. The rotation for this will be established the day before the All-Party Talks begin. Your instructor will explain the process for deciding the chairperson for each session. The chairpersonship is important and can be a powerful influence on the Talks, both in the first two All-Party sessions and in the last two All-Party sessions. In the first two sessions, the most pressing issues will be deciding whether the constitution provided by the MPNP will be permanent or temporary, and whether the MPNP will be shaping a constitution, a framework for a constitution, or principles upon which a constitution will be founded (these issues overlap with the question of permanence); determining how collective decisions will be made in the conference (for example, voting per head or as parties); and deciding who will lead the conference in response to news items. In the last two sessions, the chairperson will set the agenda for constitutional deliberations, manage time, oversee debates, and decide which issues require detailed discussion and which can be treated as secondary (i.e., dealt with if there is time). The chairperson has less to do during the CWGs, unless a collective response to a news item is needed.

It is important to read the documents in the Supplementary Readings that are relevant and useful to your role, as well as do further research. Your role description and goals are designed to give you a firm footing, but you will certainly run into questions, issues, or problems that are not explicitly or implicitly discussed in the description. You must learn as best you can to think like a member of your party and gender. This means you must also *imagine* like a member of your party and gender—try to reason out how someone of your party and gender would have thought through an issue; for indeed, historically the women and men at the MPNP themselves did not always know immediately how to answer some questions or what they should think about certain proposals. In addition, you should *insist* that your colleagues in the MPNP persuade you with reasonable and well-informed ideas that are, as often as possible, substantiated with supporting testimony from respected sources and with factual evidence.

MAJOR ISSUES FOR DEBATE

While institutional segregation based on ethnicity and blatantly racist policies inform its context, this is not a game about race. Some of the characters are themselves racist or at least pursuing what others deem racist agendas, but even they will not engage in debate about race per se and they will not be in a position to make racist statements about others. Rather, this game is about how a nation seeks to revise its self-understanding after decades of systematic injustice.

There are many issues that will be addressed in this process. The most important of these deal with shaping a democracy out of conditions of privilege while maintaining respect for individual rights. This is essentially a question of justice: How does a society transition from being defined by injustice to shaping itself according to just principles? Out of this central problem, a number of major issues emerge.

- Does a truly "representative" government require formal inclusion of minority positions (in the form of quotas, for example), or does it demand strict per capita equality ("one person one vote," for example)?

- How can policy and law help citizens develop trust in each other and in the government after years of injustice and betrayal? Similarly, how can society learn to trust security forces and police?
- Who bears responsibility for injustices committed against the politically marginalized, and what is the relationship of crime to resistance against those injustices?

RULES AND PROCEDURES

Roles

The standard roles in "The Collapse of Apartheid" are fictionalized for two reasons: first, this reflects the important historical feature of the MPNP, namely that for the most part the negotiations sought to bypass the challenges that leading public personalities faced in negotiating peace accords; and second, it allowed the creators of the game to compress the life stories of people in parties into a unified point of view. Many roles have the option for you to choose a historical character who was actually present at the MPNP. It is up to your instructor to determine whether to allow this option or not. If you do choose a historical character, you need to do some additional research on that person and write a 500- to 800-word supplemental biography as well as suggest any additional Objectives (you may not eliminate any objectives already marked out for the role). If you adopt a historical character, you will automatically receive additional Prestige Points.

Prestige Points

The deliberations at the MPNP were complicated not only because of the long history of apartheid and resistance but also because there was a great deal of uncertainty about what the political future would look like. Parties and individuals were not only concerned with creating a smooth constitutional transition from apartheid to democracy, they were also mindful of their own roles in the new South Africa. All characters, therefore, in addition to striving to bring about a peaceful transition from apartheid to democracy, are seeking to enhance the status and influence of their party as well as to ensure their own professional future. To reflect that uncertainty, *The Collapse of Apartheid* uses "Prestige Points" to determine whether parties and/or individuals win or not. Prestige Points are earned both by parties and individuals, not always in the same ways. It is important to know that your instructor may or may not choose to use the point system and playing cards in the game, which can be played equally well without them.

Every party and many individuals start with different numbers of Prestige Points, and their targets to achieve a win are also different. This reflects the historic realities of South Africa, where some parties like the ANC started with immense prestige but also high public expectations, and other parties, such as the Conservative Party, could only hope to build prestige within a small, specific constituency. In some cases, an individual's prestige may grow or diminish at different rates than that of his or her party or faction, and a particular decision's impact on a character's prestige may differ from its impact on his or her party. Public opinion is fluid, unpredictable, and often inconsistent, so that at times what is detrimental to a faction may in fact be beneficial for a faction member.

There will be daily modifications to Prestige Points, based on external events and how you, your party, or the MPNP respond to events that occur in South Africa at large; these will be introduced through Event Cards and Daily News cards. There will also be final adjustments made to personal and party prestige at the end of the game, according to the itemized list of modifiers included in each role sheet.

The MPNP itself can also gain or lose prestige. If its prestige is at zero at the end of the game, everyone loses. Above zero, the lower the prestige of the MPNP the less enthusiasm the South African public has for the constitution it begets.

You and the GM will *both* keep a record of the modulations in your prestige over the course of the game. This may be done through a shared spreadsheet (such as on Google Drive), a daily email from the GM to the class, or in some other fashion. You should also keep a record yourself. Prestige Points are always public and visible to everyone in the game, but your peers will not know your target number to win. *Do not share your PP values with any other player.*

MPNP (Begins with 4 PP)

Score	Result
0 score at end of game	CIVIL WAR—Everyone loses
<3 at end of game	All players and parties −6
>7 at end of game	All players and parties +5

MPNP PP Table

Outcome	Prestige Points
No Constitutional Agreement	−10
Party refuses to sign constitution	−1 for each party; −3 if ANC or NP do not sign
Party leaves MPNP	−1 for each occasion

Cards

There are three types of cards in the game: Event Cards, News Cards, and Gamemaster Cards. All the cards present actual news reports from the time of the MPNP. Because of game compression, some of the cards may be slightly out of sequence chronologically. The cards affect you in four ways: 1) they give you a way to gauge the mood of the country outside of the negotiations at Kempton Park; 2) they may require a response; 3) they award or take away Prestige Points for roles, factions, or even the MPNP as a whole; 4) they may be used as cited references in your written work.

If a response is required (either as indicated on the card or by your GM), the quality of the response will affect your prestige. Types of responses will vary—some may be to demand accountability on the part of another party at the MPNP; some may be to try to quiet the turmoil in your own party; some may be to try to distance yourself or your party from an event; some may be the chairperson of the MPNP relaying a consensus decision of the Talks to try to quiet social disruption. In all cases, a response to a news item given from the podium should be understood to be public and given to the national press, whereas responses from your seat are internal to the MPNP. Even if a news item does not require a response, you may respond to it formally or informally, as you see fit.

You have the option to "spend" Prestige Points in response to the news. To do so, you can announce publicly that you are giving up X number of points in order to help with the crisis. By doing this, you are in essence putting the reputation of your character and/or your party on the line and using your personal or party authority to help relieve troubling situations. It is not an alternative to a well-reasoned public statement, but it can enhance such a statement, give you an influence even if your party is not directly connected to the crisis, or be used to take a personal stand in opposition to your own faction. (For example, if you disagree with others in your faction, you can declare that you are offering X points to appease a constituency or counter the claims of your faction.)

Following are descriptions of the three types of cards:

- **Event Cards** give news on major events which *require* response from certain parties or from the entire MPNP. These are triggered at the start of each new session, when the new chairperson for the session will draw the card, read aloud the news, and pass the card around the room.

- **News Cards** give news of happenings around the country. They are triggered in two ways: 1) one News Card should be drawn after an Event Card at the start of a session, and if any are left for the given day, one should be drawn about 10 minutes before the end of a session; or 2) they are drawn when another card indicates "Draw a News Card."
- **Gamemaster Cards** are other news items that may or may not arise at the discretion of the GM.

Objectives and Victory Conditions

Your grade success in "The Collapse of Apartheid" is based more on performance than on scoring points, so the quality of your critical thinking, your argumentation and questioning, your active participation in discussion, your analysis of texts in light of the issues that arise, and your individual research beyond the simple role description are the true keys to success in the game. However, if your instructor chooses to use points, these can provide added benefits. Your instructor will inform you about the significance of winning and losing to your grade.

Each role has game features associated with it that can help you sort through your priorities and establish a clearer sense of the character. Prestige Points, discussed above, can help you get a sense of how issues relate to each other. Goals are also given for each character. These are the things you seek to accomplish. Some goals are fairly absolute—they are definitive for your character's and his or her party's perspective; these are the "Essential" goals, which should not be compromised except in the last resort. If you compromise "Essential" goals, you have essentially "given up the farm," and your constituency will consider you a sell-out and the proceedings a failure unless you can make a convincing case that such a compromise was unavoidable *and* that it is reasonable from your character's perspective. "Negotiable" goals are also important objectives that you do not want to give up on easily, but which can be modified and shaped more easily than "Essential" goals.

With "Negotiable" goals, it is important to be creative—try to find ways to not abandon them altogether; instead, find ways that they can be made to fit with goals that other parties have. There is also a list of "Catastrophic Outcomes." If these occur, bad things will happen—avoid them. These are sometimes almost opposite to the "Essential" goals, but more often they are other things that can arise in the game, either through outside events or, more likely, because of the goals of other players.

CONSTITUTIONAL WORKING GROUPS (CWGS)

Assignment

- Each group must draft provisions for their part of the constitution that will govern a future South Africa (see guidelines on next page).
- The following week, Group A will present its draft, explain the reasoning behind it, and take questions.
- Group B will then present its draft, etc.
- Group C will then present its draft, etc.

Constitutional Working Groups Outline

Group A: Governmental Structure
- Legislative structure
- Role of central government
- Parliaments
- Provincial governments

Group B: Executive Power
- Executive positions (president, vice presidents, cabinet)
- Role of the Executive
- Armed forces

Group C: Justice
- Human rights
- Crimes under apartheid
- Compensation for historic losses
- Structure of judiciary
- Juries
- Penal system

Guidelines
Duties of Constitutional Working Groups
(Note: The most important issues are in **bold**. Topics do not need to be taken in the order presented here.)

GROUP A: GOVERNMENTAL STRUCTURE
Shape of the Legislature
Structure of the Legislature
- Should the legislature be unicameral or bicameral?

Powers of the Legislature
- What should be the duties of the legislature?
- Should the legislature be able to counter the powers of the executive?
- Limitations on the legislature
- Representation

National Governing System
Relationship between National Government and Regions
Responsibilities of the National Government

National Economy
Industries
Taxation
Land Ownership
- Can the State claim the resources of the soil or under the soil?
- Can private citizens claim the resources that are a part of South Africa?
- Is the land of the State alienable from the State?
- Is the right to private property alienable?
- Is there a difference between the soil and resources under the soil?

Regional Identities
Future of the Homelands
- Should homelands be maintained?
- Should independent or semi-autonomous states be created to represent cultural or national identities?
- Should there be a federal system?
- Should all regional identities be erased?

Principles for Designation of Regions
Regional governments
Regional autonomy
Education
- Do regions control educational curriculum and the distribution of educational resources?
Representation

GROUP B: EXECUTIVE POWERS
Structure of the Executive
Leadership and Titles (President, Prime Minister, Head of State, etc.)
Roles
Cabinet positions

Appointment of the Executive
Selection of Head of State
Selection of Cabinet
Quotas or Minimum Representation (ethnicity, race, gender)

National Security
Leadership of Armed Forces
Membership in Armed Forces
Exclusions from Armed Forces

Internal Security
Internal Security Organizations (e.g., police, national guard, crime investigation)
Leadership of Internal Security Forces
Membership in Internal Security Forces
Exclusions from Internal Security Forces

GROUP C: JUSTICE
Statement on Human Rights
Crimes under Apartheid
Determine Whether Past Crimes Should Be Investigated or Ignored
- Should violent actions done during apartheid be investigated and prosecuted or should they be ignored?
- Should there be a general amnesty for violent actors during apartheid?

- Is there a way to use the investigation of past crimes to encourage a process of reconciliation between people or would such investigations lead to further divisions?
- What are the important elements in the process of reconciliation?

Investigation procedure
- Who will be involved in such investigations?

Conditions for Punishment/Pardon

Compensation for Past Losses or Harm
Criminal Activity by the Apartheid Government
- Should the government compensate proven victims of illegal actions by the government during apartheid?

Land ownership
- How should the State deal with claims of the theft of lands over the past 30, 50, 100, or 400 years?
- Should land be returned to people claiming to have had their land taken from them?
- How will the legitimacy of claims be determined?

Structure of Judiciary
Judicial hierarchy
Appointments/elections
Requirements for eligibility
Instilling trust

Juries
Quotas or minimum representation (ethnicity, race, gender)
Restrictions
Selection

Penal System
Humanitarian code
- Do prisoners have rights?
- Are there guidelines protecting the rights of prisoners and protecting prisoners from certain types of treatment?

Oversight
Qualifications for Prison Directors
Qualifications/Restrictions for Guards

ASSIGNMENTS

The South Africa game has two paper assignments, though your instructor may change this at his or her discretion. Below are the recommended options for paper assignments, but check with your instructor about which option is preferred for your class. All the papers have a persuasive dimension and it is important that you draw support from the core documents (UN Declaration on Human Rights, Freedom Charter, Mandela Speeches) and secondary documents of high significance (the Kairos Document, Verwoerd), as well as documents relating specifically to your roles (listed on the role sheets). In addition, you can draw from the timeline in this Gamebook and from News Reports on the cards for further evidence (cite the information on the header of the card). As in class argumentation, you may not use sources written after 1993, except for gleaning factual information that would have been known at the time. The first paper should be due either the first day of game sessions or sometime in the first week, before CWGs start. The second paper should be turned in after the game is finished.

- Paper #1: In Character (instructor or student chooses one of these options):
  ○ Write a 500- to 700-word newspaper editorial discussing in depth one key constitutional concern (you will develop something of a specialty on this topic). The editorial should be written for a broad audience, and it should be persuasive. Writing should be very concise and efficient, as the 700-word limit is strict and you will be penalized for anything beyond that.
  ○ Write a 1000- to 1300-word White Paper that outlines a problem and proposes a

specific policy solution. The White Paper will make an argument that is aimed at an audience outside your political party—this could be general (all South Africans) or specific (an opposition party).

- Write an 800- to 1200-word speech to your main constituents addressing a specific constitutional problem for South Africa. The speech must persuade the audience (your party) to adopt this issue as a priority in the constitutional deliberations. In addition to developing the problem in depth, it should recommend a strategy or way forward for the party to adopt.

- Paper #2: In Character (instructor or student chooses one of these options):
  - Write a 1000- to 1300-word letter or speech to the role's constituency recommending appropriate reaction to the constitution (or constitutional process, if the constitution was not approved), with particular attention to one issue (or two issues, if they are related). You can recommend that your constituency reject or support the constitution, but you must explain why.
  - Write a 700-word newspaper editorial that focuses on the constitutional process, explaining why it did or did not succeed, in your view. Discuss how that process and its outcomes reflect something of the national character (old or new), how it connects to certain aspects of the history of governance or the culture of struggle, and what it implies about the future.

  - Write a 1000- to 1300-word White Paper that addresses either an issue unresolved by the new constitution (if there is one) or a new issue raised by it, and proposes policy solutions to address that problem. The paper should seek to persuade people outside of your party.
  - Write an 800- to 1200-word letter to your constituents explaining why your position on a specific issue changed and making a case for why the party should also adopt that change.

- Speeches: These have a less structured place in this game than in most reacting games because there is not time to dedicate full class sessions to formal presentations. However, participants are still expected to use clear argumentation, good reasoning, and supporting references in their efforts to persuade. Inevitably, use of the podium comes with advantages not only in game play but also in assessment by your instructor. The podium rule is in effect.

4

Roles and Factions

Delegates to the Multi-Party Negotiating Process

As agreed at the March planning conference, all delegations will consist of, insofar as possible, 50 percent male and 50 percent female representation.

The National Party (NP)
- Three Whites—one woman, two men
- One Coloured—woman

African National Congress (ANC)
- Two from the National Executive Council (NEC)—1 woman
- One from Umkhonto we Sizwe (MK)—man
- One from the African National Congress Women's Wing (ANCWW)—woman
- One from the African National Congress Youth League (ANCYL)—man

Concerned South African Group (COSAG), later Freedom Alliance
- Inkatha Freedom Party (IFP)—woman
- Ciskei—man
- Bophuthatswana—woman
- Afrikaner Volksunie (AVU), later Freedom Front—man
- Conservative Party (CP)—man

Others
- South African Communist Party (SACP)—woman
- Pan-Africanist Congress (PAC)—woman
- Democratic Party (DP)—woman
- Congress of South African Trade Unions (COSATU)—man
- Natal Indian Congress (NIC)—man
- Azanian People's Organisation (AZAPO)—man

THE AFRICAN NATIONAL CONGRESS (ANC)

Roles: Delegates will be representing the ANC National Executive Council (NEC), Umkhonto we Sizwe (MK), the Women's League (ANCWL), and the Youth League (ANCYL). ANC is multiracial, but most heavily populated by blacks.

In 1992, the African National Congress (ANC; originally the South African Native National Congress) was South Africa's oldest political organization, and had campaigned for nonracialism since its formation in 1911. The ANC was the leading party in the fight against segregation and since 1948, against apartheid. In 1959, the ANC split between those who remained committed to nonracialism as understood in the *1955 Freedom Charter* and those who wished to transform South Africa into a country (which they called "Azania") in which only black Africans would be in charge. This offshoot was known as the Pan-Africanist Congress (PAC). One of their representatives is present at the Multi-Party Talks.

Over the years the ANC has developed two major strategies in support of its mission. The first, and oldest, is the continued protest and demonstration against the laws and manifestations of segregation and apartheid. The second began in 1960, after the South African government had imprisoned many of the ANC's leaders involved in protests or had driven them into exile. The ANC created Umkhonto we Sizwe (MK) as its wing for armed resistance and set up camps outside South Africa to equip and train guerrilla forces to sneak back into the country and organize attacks, bombings, sabotage, and other forms of violence directed at the apartheid regime. Some MK leaders, such as Joe Slovo and Chris Hani, became well known and so highly respected that they had reputations second only to the imprisoned Mandela himself.

Over the years, members of the party have worked closely with the one other party that supported nonracialism, the South African Communist Party (SACP). Leading members of the ANC, including its National Executive and high-ranking officers such as Slovo and Hani, were also top SACP officials. A representative of the SACP is present at the Multi-Party Talks, and is expected to work closely with the ANC on a number of issues, though there are things upon which they likely will not agree.

Bear in mind throughout the MPNP that the ANC's virtual leader, Nelson Mandela, now freed, is not present. There are several reasons for this. Mandela has found that by traveling overseas, particularly in the United States where the ANC was until recently a banned "terrorist" organization, he can raise funds in support of ANC activities. The ANC organization, even though it is old, with many followers, is still finding it hard to establish itself. When ANC representatives returned from abroad, they had very little money to set up offices, buy equipment and vehicles, pay themselves and other activists reasonable salaries, and very little time to meet and organize among the South African public. By staying visible both inside South Africa and overseas, ANC members feel that the international community is more likely to put pressure on South Africa to come up with a democratic institution than to return to apartheid. Mandela is also *safer* moving here and there, rather than establishing a routine. There are people in the security forces who want to see the Madiba dead.

Since the release of Mandela, the ANC has discovered it has many enemies, some of whom are prepared to resort to violence. The ANC's major concern is the National Party (NP) government of F. W. de Klerk. Although he is the man who released Mandela, called on the all-white parliament to dismantle apartheid laws, proposed constitutional talks, apologized for apartheid, opened his party's doors to persons of all races, and rejected the right-wing forces in his own party, de Klerk and his delegation to the MPNP are not trusted by the ANC for several reasons. First, the NP's desire for "power-sharing" appears to be a kind of veto power that would keep the NP in control of the future government. Second, de Klerk has been interested in dealing mainly with Mandela on a one-to-one basis, rather than having a broader discussion about South Africa's future. And third, de Klerk seems unable—or unwilling—to prevent his security forces or vigilante groups from directing violence against the ANC and its followers. His claims that "rogue forces," not the government, are responsible for these acts may be either a confession of his weakness or a device to screen himself from underhanded dealings. The ANC believes that de Klerk would feel more comfortable about the future if blacks who had worked with the apartheid regime (such as the homeland leaders) were accommodated into the new structure, as a check on the ANC.

The other major rival for the ANC on the national scene is the Inkatha Freedom Party (IFP), led by Mangosuthu Buthelezi, the shrewd "prime minister" of KwaZulu-Natal, who is, in the universal opinion of the ANC membership, an adroit and calculating politician with a taste for power. While Buthelezi and the IFP will present themselves in very different terms, the ANC sees that IFP leadership is closely linked to the government forces it claims to oppose. After all, it was the government, not "cultural tradition," that created the leadership; the security forces of KwaZulu-Natal are filled with links to the South African Police; and the Zulu identity on which Inkatha rests its stake is a creation of the white government as a means of controlling the African population. No one knows for sure how many of the people of KwaZulu-Natal favor the ANC and how many are committed to the IFP—the violence between the groups and the overt oppression of ANC sympathizers by the regional security forces prevents the acquisition of reliable information—but the leadership of the ANC is confident that a large number in the region are on its side. Of course, Buthelezi would say the same for the IFP. Whatever the truth is, it is clear that there are enough followers of both parties to create a bitter, bloody rivalry.

Within the ANC, there are several semiformal organizations. The Executives are the officials of the organization, most of whom have only recently returned to South African society after years of either self-imposed exile in other countries or imprisonment. These (mostly) men have long histories with the ANC struggle against apartheid and are mostly closely connected to its ideological principles, though not all agree on the use of violence. The armed wing of the ANC, Umkhonto we Sizwe (MK), has sought to protect ANC sympathizers, and uses sabotage and reprisals in resistance to the government. This has included, since the mid-1970s, a deliberate effort to make South Africa ungovernable in order to bring down the apartheid system. More loosely organized but still a formidable force within the ANC and in the townships is the ANC Women's Wing, led by the strong but controversial personality of Winnie Mandela, Madiba's recently estranged wife. The Women's Wing focuses especially on the shameful conditions in the townships, especially the poor educational resources there, and insists that the ANC's push for justice needs to go beyond racial equality to include gender, an issue that some of the leadership, while agreeing in principle, believes will only slow the process of change. Finally, there is the ANC Youth League, a highly activist branch with little organization, centered on the immediate experience of life in the townships. Empowered by the impact of the youth uprising in Soweto in 1976, men and women between the ages of 13 and 25 often gather more or less spontaneously to protest new measures by the government or by anti-ANC parties. It is not uncommon for the youth to be moved to violence, and the very loosely organized Youth League is seen by many in South Africa, including much of the ANC leadership, as a "loose cannon," an unpredictable conglomerate of poorly educated young men and women who have grown up amid perpetual violence, with few opportunities for employment of any sort, and with little hope for any systemic improvement to their lives.

THE NATIONAL PARTY (NP)

Roles: Delegates consist of ministers of the present National Party government, most of whom are Afrikaners. They are led by F. W. de Klerk (who is not present at the MPNP) and a representative from the Coloured population of the Cape.

The National Party represents the moderate, left-of-center majority of whites now governing

South Africa and, under F. W. de Klerk, has taken the crucial steps to end apartheid. Their strongest support comes from the educated members of the state bureaucracy, universities, and the mining, business, and banking sectors of the economy. The moderate wing of the NP realized in the late 1980s that apartheid was obsolete in the modern world and was too costly to uphold. Apartheid also ran counter to the free market liberal economics to which they were ideologically committed. It discouraged investment in the South African economy from overseas, limited South Africa's contact with the western industrialized world, and had caused increasing levels of violence inside the country. Most southern African countries, where plenty of economic opportunities had previously existed for South Africa, had now become South Africa's enemies. Trade in the region had been badly affected, and South Africa had been prevented from opening up markets in the rest of Africa. South Africa's progress in technology and science was also falling behind because of international sanctions, isolation from the world's leading scientific and business circles, and the flight of talent and capital from South Africa's insecurity and violence.

The NP moderates want to modernize South Africa by democratizing it, but they also have economic interests and standards of living to protect, as well as their cultural identity. The NP accepts that all South Africans must be included into a unified, central government, but up to now, they have been cautious. Since Mandela's release, the NP has watched the ANC gain broad support among South Africans while the National Party has steadily lost members, even though de Klerk opened the party to all citizens, regardless of color or other identity. The NP realized that it took a big chance when it released Mandela, dismantled apartheid laws, and rejected those who wanted to keep the NP a whites-only party. Up to 1993, a number of Coloured South Africans, particularly in the Cape Province, have joined the NP ranks, but few Blacks or Asians have entered the party, which,

in spite of its reformed leadership, is still identified with past policies of apartheid.

The NP moderates are seeking to convince those outside its party that the NP is truly committed to democracy and is not acting out of a desire to hold on to power. But at the same time, some NP members fear that the ANC will simply invert power relations in South Africa, force its political will on others, and deprive whites of their property and security.

Another challenge for the NP is how to understand the long-term intentions of its political opponents. For instance, though the Cold War has only recently ended, the language of compromise coming from the Communist Party raises suspicions: Is the offer of the SACP's cooperation simply a façade to mask their radical longer-term intentions to create a new communist system in South Africa? And even if Mandela is honest about what he claims to seek in a nonracial South Africa, will his successors seek to create an authoritarian single-party state?

CONCERNED SOUTH AFRICAN GROUP (COSAG)

This faction has delegates from the Inkatha Freedom Party (IFP), Ciskei, Bophuthatswana, the Afrikaner Volksunie (AVU, later Freedom Front), and the Conservative Party (CP).

COSAG (later known as the Freedom Alliance) is a loose alliance of conservative black and white delegates who are opposed to de Klerk's National Party and the ANC having the determining say in developing a new constitution. Until April 1993, the NP and ANC had tried to negotiate South Africa's future pretty much alone, but opposition from those who later formed COSAG was largely responsible for the collapse of earlier talks. The NP and ANC have accepted COSAG at the talks, and COSAG in turn hopes to get concessions from de Klerk and Mandela's followers.

COSAG consists of both black and white South Africans, some of whom supported apartheid and others who worked within the system, particularly in setting up black homelands. In reality, these groups did not have a lot in common outside of their hostility to the ANC and their somewhat compatible goals for establishing racially or culturally identified "homelands." However, they often drew on a common typology and language to muster support from constituents and the international community—branding the ANC and any other opponents to the status quo as communists and terrorists, and claiming dedication to a free market economic system (even though apartheid depended upon a system that was heavily reliant on state intrusion into the marketplace). This use of language was closely linked with the jargon of international Cold War anxieties, and, in the minds of most of the players (except possibly Buthelezi), was not in reality grounded in ideology.

COSAG has highly placed followers in the South African and homeland security forces, and is popular among the police and military—the persons who not only wear the uniform but who carry arms and who have been locked in combat with the ANC and PAC during the struggles over apartheid. COSAG has resented the domination to date of the negotiations by the NP and the ANC, and what it regards as the designs of those two parties to gain power in a new political system. In addition, COSAG fears that the outcome of any negotiations that involve only the NP and the ANC will be to abolish racial and ethnic identities in South Africa, eliminate the homelands, and persecute whites and blacks who were part of the apartheid system.

Inkatha Freedom Party (IFP)

The IFP is almost entirely a Zulu party, headed by Gatsha Buthelezi (GAH-tsah, boo-tay-LAY-zy), the "traditional prime minister to the Zulu Nation." Buthelezi is highly educated in the western tradition and publicly represents himself as a modernist opposed to apartheid and the creation of homelands. He refused to take Pretoria's offer of "full independence" and preside over the establishment of an independent KwaZulu-Natal.

He also supports democracy in South Africa, as long as it respects "traditional" African cultures and institutions.

Though posing as an opponent to apartheid, the IFP has benefited greatly from Pretoria's recognition of Buthelezi as the "traditional prime minister" and King Goodwill Zwelithini as the Zulu monarch. One of the symbols of Zulu culture has become the *impi*, a traditional Zulu warrior armed with a spear or a gnarled walking stick and a shield. Occasionally, intimidating bands of *impi* will roam through townships chanting and whistling in a show of Zulu solidarity, striking fear into other members of the community. Most people in South Africa are unhappy with the naming of tribal groups by the apartheid government because they believe such designations to be a racist sham that does not correspond to the way Africans historically understood identity; for some in KwaZulu-Natal, however, the tribal designation has relevance as a political identity linked to linguistic and cultural heritage. Many Zulu consider the ANC, despite its antitribalist constitution, to be a political expression of tribes that are rivals to the Zulu, especially the Xhosa. On the other hand, many Zulu in the region are affiliated with the ANC.

The IFP has become a powerful force linking KwaZulu-Natal with the hundreds of thousands of Zulu laborers found in South Africa's urban hostels and mining compounds; it has become a major opponent of the ANC in both these areas. In the 1980s, King Zwelithini called on all Zulu to stay away from all organizations led by non-Zulu, claiming that organizations like the ANC, UDF, and the Congress of South African Trade Unions did not represent "Zulu values." The IFP also gained support from whites in Natal.

Clashes between the IFP and ANC in KwaZulu-Natal have been severe and frequent, with over five thousand deaths in the region and its neighboring townships since 1986. Buthelezi places the blame for this on the ANC's support of violence and its policy of making South Africa ungovernable.

Supporters of the ANC, on the other hand, accuse Buthelezi of masterminding the quelling of any dissent in the region and say that such violence between Africans only serves the defenders of apartheid, a system both sides claim to oppose. Complicating this is the plight of Zulu migrant workers in the townships: they are given the most menial jobs and treated with suspicion by permanent residents, and this has led to frequent conflict with ANC organizations over strikes and stay-aways, things impoverished Zulu cannot afford. The South African army and police have channeled support to the IFP and KwaZulu-Natal officials loyal to Buthelezi. These police also stand aside when armed IFP followers attack pro-ANC civilian settlements. Thousands of ANC supporters have died as a result.

Bophuthatswana, Ciskei

The homelands are very poor and overpopulated. Critics point to the uneven distribution of wealth in these officially "independent" areas—where the general population lives in straitened conditions while the leadership lives in comfort, even luxury—as evidence that the homeland leaders are in collusion with the apartheid government. Indeed, outside the homelands, and to an unknown extent within the homelands, this is generally assumed to be the case, and it is clear that the homeland security forces are tightly linked to the South African Police. But the homeland leaders, who are Africans themselves, maintain that while things are far from perfect in their territories, at least here Africans can rule themselves—though again, this runs counter to the general recognition that the homelands are completely propped up by Pretoria and that their leaders could not last long without formidable government support.

Representatives of Bophuthatswana (Boh-POOH-tah-TSWA-nah) and Ciskei (Sih-SKY) wish these homelands to remain "independent" or, at the least, become part of South Africa only as semi-autonomous states. Lucas Mangope (Mah-NGOH-pay) of Bophuthatswana (president since Bophuthatswana's "independence" in 1976), and

Brigadier Oupa Gqozo (G with a click-OZ-oh) of Ciskei (ruler since the overthrow of President Lenox Sebe in 1990) are fiercely opposed by the ANC. The ANC regards these and other homelands as "intolerable holdovers" from apartheid. It also maintains that such leaders have no legitimate claim to political authority but were simply put in place by Pretoria in the give and take of political patronage. Nonetheless, Mangope and Gqozo (and the South African government) presented the homelands as examples of African self-rule, even sometimes drawing upon images of "traditional leadership" and cultural heritage in order to reinforce such a notion. In reality, though, leadership in the homelands was not assigned through traditional means such as lineage, but instead by a willingness to cooperate with the government of South Africa. Mangope and Gqozo's police and military have tried their best to stamp out the ANC (which they, like Pretoria, call "communist") influence in their respective territories. As recently as September 1992, when seventy thousand ANC supporters tried to march on Ciskei's capital of Bisho, Gqozo's troops fired on them, killing twenty-nine. Mangope's security forces have arrested scores of ANC supporters and imprisoned them.

Bophuthatswana and Ciskei have depended heavily on financial and military support from Pretoria, and now that de Klerk has called for an end to apartheid, delegates from these homelands want the new South African government to continue to support strong provincial administrations or semi-independent states. They certainly do not want to see the creation of a powerful central authority likely to be dominated by the ANC. Key to their claims are the rights of cultural groups to maintain a distinct heritage and identity.

Afrikaner Volksunie (AVU)

Under the leadership of ex-General Constand Viljoen (fill-YOON), the AVU brought together some twenty or more right-wing political groups under the banner of Afrikaner self-determination. At times, some of these right-wing organizations (such as the Afrikaner Resistance Movement—AWB) resort to violence and call for "white secession" from South Africa rather than participating in negotiations. The AVU are the moderates in this coalition, and Viljoen is highly respected among the ranking officers of the existing South African military. The AVU wants to avoid bloodshed while getting constitutional protections for Afrikaners, such as a white homeland.

For the AVU delegates to the MPNP, such protections are not simply an extension of the worn-out racism of the apartheid past. Not only is apartheid untenable, indeed, it is clear that some white people would be perfectly happy working side by side with blacks, and they should have the option to do just that. However, there is much to fear in an abrupt transition to a fully nonracial democracy after such a long time. Families have established themselves over generations and worked hard to reach a certain standard of living—it would be profoundly unjust to forfeit the welfare of future generations to make up for the mistakes of the past. Also, Afrikaners have a unique heritage and culture of which they are very proud, and it is essential that they be provided with the means to protect that identity in the face of what they perceive to be true about the opposition: that it is fueled by an aggressive communist ideology that rejects both patriotic nationalism and even religion (in favor of internationalism and atheism), as well as the principle of free enterprise. Finally, while Mandela may be as peaceable in his old age as he presents himself, that does not guarantee that his subordinates in the ANC will not seek unmitigated power and rob Afrikaners of property and dignity out of greed or revenge for injustices of the past.

Conservative Party (CP)

An offshoot of the National Party, the CP in the 1990s is the principal voice of the diehard, pro-apartheid right-wing, and is made up entirely of Afrikaners. In the eyes of the CP, de Klerk is a traitor to his country and to his people. The prosperity of South Africa in the decades before the 1980s and the introduction of excellent educational institutions, sophisticated medicine, democratic institutions, a modern judiciary, diversified business and industry, and, of course, Christianity are all evidence of the unparalleled contribution of white civilization to southern African life. The sophisticated thought of Nelson Mandela, Stephen Biko, Desmond Tutu, and even the dangerous and despised Chris Hani are all evidence of that very fact, and the role of whites in making South Africa into an international powerhouse should not be taken for granted. Apartheid, Conservative Party members believe, was not a flawed ideology. Rather, its downfall was due to the failure of the government to effectively control communist ANC revolutionary plots and the moral failure of the international community to support the cause of capitalist democracy in the southern hemisphere.

For a time, the CP was convinced that it had a majority following among Afrikaners, but the 1992 referendum revealed that only about 1 in 3 Afrikaners was with the hardliners. Since then the CP has joined the AVU, but has kept its identity as being to the right of the AVU. Although in favor of a white-only state in South Africa, it is willing to work with black members of COSAG in order to weaken the ANC and NP's grip on negotiations. Known for making verbal threats, the CP is also thought by many to be part of a "Third Force" of police and military officers operating as a rogue element in South Africa and opposed to the negotiation process.

SOUTH AFRICAN COMMUNIST PARTY (SACP)

The delegate representing the SACP is a member of a party that has been closely identified with the struggle against segregation and apartheid for decades. The SACP is also an ally of the ANC and, like the ANC, is multiracial. Some SACP members are also ANC members, including its top-ranked leaders, such Umkhonto we Sizwe (MK) Commander Chris Hani.

The SACP is closely identified with socialism. It has argued that apartheid and segregation are the byproducts of capitalism, which is the true enemy of the people. Because of capitalism, black labor has been exploited and their protests have been squashed. Whether the English or the Afrikaners have been in charge in South Africa, the rule has always been the same: the state belongs to those who own the mines, the banks, and the means of production. And those who work in South Africa are controlled by the state for the benefit of big capital, including the big farms owned by whites and run by their poor black laborers, male and female.

In 1990, white SACP leader Joe Slovo wrote in his pamphlet "Has Socialism Failed?" that his party should call for a "multi-party post-apartheid democracy, both in the national democratic and socialist phases. . . ." What Slovo meant is that the SACP would work with the ANC, which the SACP regards as willing to compromise with capitalists, so that democratic government and political stability can come to South Africa as a prelude to moving toward socialism.

PAN-AFRICANIST CONGRESS (PAC)

The PAC delegate to the MPNP belongs to a group that formed in 1959 as an offshoot of the ANC. The PAC took part in the armed struggle against apartheid and created its own guerrilla wing (APLA—Azanian People's Liberation Army).

The PAC, which rejected key elements of the Freedom Charter, came into being as a black nationalist party, believing that Azania (the ancient Greek word for Africa and the PAC's preferred name for South Africa) belongs to the black people, and that the future South Africa should be governed by blacks only because blacks represent the true indigenous inhabitants. With whites completely out of power (not only from government but in all other respects as well), the economic well-being of blacks would be assured. Whites who oppose this idea deserve to be driven out, or worse. The PAC cry of "One Boer, One Bullet" has incited its supporters to kill whites who want to remain in control of South Africa or any part of it.

Over the years, the PAC has changed its tactics, politics, and organization many times and has often suffered from poor leadership. With the release of Mandela, and the return of many refugees to South Africa, the PAC is hoping to rally support among the millions of future black voters who have suffered at the hands of whites and their black allies and hold itself up as their true representative (as opposed to the ANC, which is open to white membership and is ready to accommodate whites in the future South Africa).

The PAC had a rocky relationship with other parties in the earlier negotiations. In November of 1991, it disassociated itself from the final statement read by the two judges chairing the preparatory meeting, saying that it "did not reflect the PAC's position." Several PAC proposals, such as neutral international conveners, the holding of CODESA outside of South Africa, and the opening of CODESA's sessions to the media, were rejected by other parties.

DEMOCRATIC PARTY (DP)

The DP is a small group of liberal whites, both English and Afrikaner, who for years have been opposed to apartheid. However, rather than opt out of the political process and side with blacks, Indians, and coloreds who were excluded, white liberals remained active in white politics and campaigned for seats in parliament. Over the years, these white liberals have organized various political parties, beginning with the United Party, then the Progressive Party, the Reform Party, the Progressive Reform Party, the New Republic Party, and the Progressive Federal Party (PFP).

In the 1987 general election, Denis Worrall, Wynand Malan, and Esther Lategan formed the Independent Movement, but only Wynand Malan won his seat when the partnership disintegrated. Denis Worrall and others then formed the Independent Party (IP), while Esther Lategan and others formed the National Democratic Movement.

In 1988, Zach de Beer became leader of the PFP and continued the negotiations with the Independent Party and the National Democratic Movement. On 8 April 1989, they merged to form the

Democratic Party, which won 36 seats in parliament in the general election. The NP also lost seats to the right wing (Conservative Party), and the loss of support prepared the NP leader, F. W. de Klerk, to announce a radical change in government policy on 2 February 1990.

Zach de Beer, leading what was now the DP, was chosen as the first Management Committee Chairman of CODESA. In CODESA, the DP played a vital role in the negotiation of a proposed Interim Constitution. The principles and ideals of the DP, like many of its earlier political predecessors, included the universal franchise and a democratic, nonracial constitution.

The DP clearly holds some of its major principles in common with the ANC. But its distrust of socialist policies and ideas such as the nationalization of the mining industry may put its delegates closer to the new vision of the National Party on some issues.

CONGRESS OF SOUTH AFRICAN TRADE UNIONS (COSATU)

COSATU, which was formed in 1985, is not a political party and therefore not entitled as such to attend the MPNP. But since Mandela's release, COSATU had become part of a "Tripartite Alliance" with the ANC and SACP, which therefore allowed some of their seats at the MPNP to be used by COSATU.

COSATU is a massive union representing mineworkers and blue collar workers, men and women, almost all black. It was a major force in pressuring the NP to abandon apartheid. Its president, Cyril Ramaphosa, is a brilliant negotiator and tactician. After de Klerk's decision to release Mandela and open South Africa to democracy, COSATU made known its vision of the future: the redistribution of resources and power, requiring state intervention in nationalizing resources and imposing anti-trust legislation, and state control of basic services such as water, transportation, housing, education, and food (these had been at times under private control).

COSATU's vision is socialist. Workplaces would be strictly controlled by government, if not nationalized, and all basic services were to be owned by government and made available to the entire public. As one of its spokesmen declared in 1993, "political freedom will be meaningless unless it is underpinned by economic democracy. As workers, we want houses, free education, affordable and accessible health care, electricity, [and] lower food prices."

NATAL INDIAN CONGRESS (NIC)

This political and social organization is based in Durban, where 80 percent of South African Indians (or more properly "Asians") are found. Its members are part of an old and vast network of Asian activists in Africa and India. Since 1893, when Mahatma Gandhi worked in South Africa, Asians in the NIC and other organizations have opposed racial segregation and apartheid. Until the ANC and SACP were banned in South Africa, the NIC worked with these organizations to protect apartheid policies, and their members were among the signatories of the Freedom Charter (1955).

It has been common among apartheid's opponents to join various organizations challenging NP policy, and thus some members of the NIC have joined the ANC, the SACP, and, during the 1980s, the United Democratic Front. They resisted attempts by the NP to incorporate Indian and Coloured voters into a segregated parliamentary system, and four out of five Indians refused to vote for the pro-parliament South African Indian Congress (SAIC).

Although they are firm opponents of the NP's apartheid policies, members of the NIC are conscious of the peculiar position of Asians in South Africa. Unlike the other three racial (or "population") groups in South Africa, Asians are almost entirely city dwellers, with no ties to any particular territory or province (though they are a large minority in Natal). Moreover, they speak no indigenous languages, using English overwhelmingly, though most speak one of several Indian languages (Hindi, Gujarati, etc.) at home. Asians are successful traders, commercial entrepreneurs, and shopkeepers, and their schools graduate highly literate and educated boys and girls. They are Hindu (57 percent), Muslim (25 percent), and Christian (18 percent), representing the religious diversity in the Indian subcontinent, and retain in their cultural institutions a strong connection with India. Though many have lived in South Africa for three or four generations, they are often looked at by Blacks, Coloureds, and Whites alike as newcomers to South Africa. Will NIC delegates continue to maintain the party's long agreement with the ANC? Will they find affinities with the new goals of the NP (as many Coloureds have), now that apartheid is finished? Or will they identify with the notions of cultural preservation and the diversification of political influence so important to COSAG?

5

Core Texts and Supplemental Readings

The Core Documents for "The Collapse of Apartheid" are the *United Nations Declaration on Human Rights* and *The Freedom Charter*. Other highly important texts such as Verwoerd's explanation of apartheid, Mandela's criticism of apartheid and his testimony at the Rivonia Trial, Steve Biko's articulation of Black Consciousness, and the Kairos Document are included with others in the "Documents" section. There are also Supplemental Readings following. These are of two types: (1) documents relevant for all of the roles; and (2) others of general interest, such as the Negotiation Agreements. You will want to read the Supplemental Documents related to your role. You may also find it advantageous to explore some of the documents related to other parties and factions.

In addition to the documents in "The Collapse of Apartheid," the authors recommend the short narrative history of South Africa by Nancy Clark and William Worger, *South Africa: The Rise and Fall of Apartheid*, published by Routledge.

CORE TEXTS

Universal Declaration of Human Rights (1948)

Editor's Comment: The United Nations was formed in 1947 as an attempt to establish an international body for deliberation and cooperation. In 1948 it published its Declaration of Human Rights (UDHR), which was essentially a universal Bill of Rights for the planet. Most nations—including South Africa, whose delegation was led by Prime Minister Jan Smuts (of the majority United Party, which went on to lose the 1948 election to the National Party, creators of apartheid)—signed the document, a symbol of agreement with its principles and policies. How does this document reflect ideas about the nature of justice? What does it suggest or imply (or what does it not say) about resistance to offenses to human rights and the tools of oppression that people have at their disposal? How does it understand the expressions of the essential elements of freedom and equality, and why does it choose to identify those things it does? Are there passages that might be especially problematic for some governments, such as the apartheid government of

South Africa? Are there passages that could be inter-
preted in ways that might not be "western"? Does it
present the notion of "nationality" in ways that could
be problematic for some groups or in conflict with
ideas of cultural identity? How does it deal with the
inherent tensions between individual liberty and social
welfare?

Preamble: Whereas recognition of the inherent dignity and of the equal and inalienable rights of all members of the human family is the foundation of freedom, justice and peace in the world,

Whereas disregard and contempt for human rights have resulted in barbarous acts which have outraged the conscience of mankind, and the advent of a world in which human beings shall enjoy freedom of speech and belief and freedom from fear and want has been proclaimed as the highest aspiration of the common people,

Whereas it is essential, if man is not to be compelled to have recourse, as a last resort, to rebellion against tyranny and oppression, that human rights should be protected by the rule of law,

Whereas it is essential to promote the development of friendly relations between nations,

Whereas the peoples of the United Nations have in the Charter reaffirmed their faith in fundamental human rights, in the dignity and worth of the human person and in the equal rights of men and women and have determined to promote social progress and better standards of life in larger freedom,

Whereas Member States have pledged themselves to achieve, in cooperation with the United Nations, the promotion of universal respect for and observance of human rights and fundamental freedoms,

Whereas a common understanding of these rights and freedoms is of the greatest importance for the full realization of this pledge,

Now, therefore, The General Assembly proclaims this Universal Declaration of Human Rights as a common standard of achievement for all peoples and all nations, to the end that every individual and every organ of society, keeping this Declaration constantly in mind, shall strive by teaching and education to promote respect for these rights and freedoms and by progressive measures, national and international, to secure their universal and effective recognition and observance, both among the peoples of Member States themselves and among the peoples of territories under their jurisdiction.

Article I: All human beings are born free and equal in dignity and rights. They are endowed with reason and conscience and should act towards one another in a spirit of brotherhood.

Article 2: Everyone is entitled to all the rights and freedoms set forth in this Declaration, without distinction of any kind, such as race, colour, sex, language, religion, political or other opinion, national or social origin, property, birth or other status. Furthermore, no distinction shall be made on the basis of the political, jurisdictional or international status of the country or territory to which a person belongs, whether it be independent, trust, non-self-governing or under any other limitation of sovereignty.

Article 3: Everyone has the right to life, liberty and security of person.

Article 4: No one shall be held in slavery or servitude; slavery and the slave trade shall be prohibited in all their forms.

Article 5: No one shall be subjected to torture or to cruel, inhuman or degrading treatment or punishment.

Article 6: Everyone has the right to recognition everywhere as a person before the law.

Article 7: All are equal before the law and are entitled without any discrimination to equal protection of the law. All are entitled to equal protection against any discrimination in violation of this Declaration and against any incitement to such discrimination.

Article 8: Everyone has the right to an effective remedy by the competent national tribunals for acts violating the fundamental rights granted him by the constitution or by law.

Article 9: No one shall be subjected to arbitrary arrest, detention or exile.

Article 10: Everyone is entitled in full equality to a fair and public hearing by an independent and impartial tribunal, in the determination of his rights and obligations and of any criminal charge against him.

Article 11: 1. Everyone charged with a penal offence has the right to be presumed innocent until proved guilty according to law in a public trial at which he has had all the guarantees necessary for his defence. 2. No one shall be held guilty of any penal offence on account of any act or omission which did not constitute a penal offence, under national or international law, at the time when it was committed. Nor shall a heavier penalty be imposed than the one that was applicable at the time the penal offence was committed.

Article 12: No one shall be subjected to arbitrary interference with his privacy, family, home or correspondence, nor to attacks upon his honour and reputation. Everyone has the right to the protection of the law against such interference or attacks.

Article 13: 1. Everyone has the right to freedom of movement and residence within the borders of each State. 2. Everyone has the right to leave any country, including his own, and to return to his country.

Article 14: 1. Everyone has the right to seek and to enjoy in other countries asylum from persecution. 2. This right may not be invoked in the case of prosecutions genuinely arising from non-political crimes or from acts contrary to the purposes and principles of the United Nations.

Article 15: 1. Everyone has the right to a nationality. 2. No one shall be arbitrarily deprived of his nationality nor denied the right to change his nationality.

Article 16: 1. Men and women of full age, without any limitation due to race, nationality or religion, have the right to marry and to found a family. They are entitled to equal rights as to marriage, during marriage and at its dissolution. 2. Marriage shall be entered into only with the free and full consent of the intending spouses. 3. The family is the natural and fundamental group unit of society and is entitled to protection by society and the State.

Article 17: 1. Everyone has the right to own property alone as well as in association with others. 2. No one shall be arbitrarily deprived of his property.

Article 18: Everyone has the right to freedom of thought, conscience and religion; this right includes freedom to change his religion or belief, and freedom, either alone or in community with others and in public or private, to manifest his religion or belief in teaching, practice, worship and observance.

Article 19: Everyone has the right to freedom of opinion and expression; this right includes freedom to hold opinions without interference and to seek, receive and impart information and ideas through any media and regardless of frontiers.

Article 20: 1. Everyone has the right to freedom of peaceful assembly and association. 2. No one may be compelled to belong to an association.

Article 21: 1. Everyone has the right to take part in the government of his country, directly or through freely chosen representatives. 2. Everyone has the right to equal access to public service in his country. 3. The will of the people shall be the basis of the authority of government; this shall be expressed in periodic and genuine elections which shall be by universal and equal suffrage and shall be held by secret vote or by equivalent free voting procedures.

Article 22: Everyone, as a member of society, has the right to social security and is entitled to realization, through national effort and international co-operation and in accordance with the organization and resources of each State, of the economic, social and cultural rights indispensable for his dignity and the free development of his personality.

Article 23: 1. Everyone has the right to work, to free choice of employment, to just and favourable conditions of work and to protection against unemployment. 2. Everyone, without any discrimination, has the right to equal pay for equal work. 3. Everyone who works has the right to just and favourable remuneration ensuring for himself and his family an existence worthy of human dignity, and supplemented, if necessary, by other means of social protection. 4. Everyone has the right to form and to join trade unions for the protection of his interests.

Article 24: Everyone has the right to rest and leisure, including reasonable limitation of working hours and periodic holidays with pay.

Article 25: 1. Everyone has the right to a standard of living adequate for the health and well-being of himself and of his family, including food, clothing, housing and medical care and necessary social services, and the right to security in the event of unemployment, sickness, disability, widowhood, old age or other lack of livelihood in circumstances beyond his control. 2. Motherhood and childhood are entitled to special care and assistance. All children, whether born in or out of wedlock, shall enjoy the same social protection.

Article 26: 1. Everyone has the right to education. Education shall be free, at least in the elementary and fundamental stages. Elementary education shall be compulsory. Technical and professional education shall be made generally available and higher education shall be equally accessible to all on the basis of merit. 2. Education shall be directed to the full development of the human personality and to the strengthening of respect for human rights and fundamental freedoms. It shall promote understanding, tolerance and friendship among all nations, racial or religious groups, and shall further the activities of the United Nations for the maintenance of peace. 3. Parents have a prior right to choose the kind of education that shall be given to their children.

Article 27: 1. Everyone has the right freely to participate in the cultural life of the community, to enjoy the arts and to share in scientific advancement and its benefits. 2. Everyone has the right to the protection of the moral and material interests resulting from any scientific, literary or artistic production of which he is the author.

Article 28: Everyone is entitled to a social and international order in which the rights and freedoms set forth in this Declaration can be fully realized.

Article 29: 1. Everyone has duties to the community in which alone the free and full development of his personality is possible. 2. In the exercise of his rights and freedoms, everyone shall be subject only to such limitations as are determined by law solely for the purpose of securing due recognition and respect for the rights and freedoms of others and of meeting the just requirements of morality, public order and the general welfare in a democratic society. 3. These rights and freedoms may in no case be exercised contrary to the purposes and principles of the United Nations.

Article 30: Nothing in this Declaration may be interpreted as implying for any State, group or person any right to engage in any activity or to perform any act aimed at the destruction of any of the rights and freedoms set forth herein.

Hendrik F. Verwoerd: Explaining Apartheid (1950)

(from a Parliamentary speech)
Editor's Comment: Hendrik Verwoerd, the Minister of Native Affairs in the first National Party government in 1948 and later Prime Minister, is widely credited as the "architect of apartheid." Does he explain apartheid in terms of advantaging Europeans over Africans? If not, then how did he legitimize a system of social and political segregation? Does Verwoerd have a notion of justice? Upon what assumptions about race, cultural identity, and economics does his explanation rest?

I wish to accede to the wish which, I understand, has long been felt by members of this council, namely that a member of the Government should explain the main features of what is implied by the policy of Apartheid.

Within the compass of an address I have, naturally, to confine myself to the fundamentals of the Apartheid policy and to the main steps following logically from the policy. Further details and a fuller description of the reasons and value of what is being planned will have to remain in abeyance today. Properly understood, however, these main features will elucidate what will be done and how this will be as much in the interests of the Bantu as in those of the European.

As a premise, the question may be put: Must Bantu and European in future develop as inter-mixed communities, or as communities separated from one another in so far as this is practically possible? If the reply is "intermingled communities" then the following must be understood. There will be competition and conflict everywhere. So long as the points of contact are still comparatively few, as is the case now, friction and conflict will be few and less evident. The more this intermixing develops, however, the stronger the conflict will become. In such conflict, the Europeans will, at least for a long time, hold the stronger position, and the Bantu be the defeated party in every phase of the struggle. This must cause to rise in him an increasing sense of resentment and revenge. Neither for the European, nor for the Bantu, can this, namely increasing tension and conflict, be an ideal future, because the inter-mixed development involves disadvantage to both.

Perhaps, in such an eventuality, it is best frankly to face the situation which must arise in the political sphere. In the event of an intermixed development, the Bantu will undoubtedly desire a share in the government of the intermixed country. He will, in due course, not be satisfied with a limited share in the form of communal representation, but will desire full participation in the country's government on the basis of an equal franchise. For the sake of development of this demand, he will desire the same in the social, economic and other spheres of life, involving in due course, intermixed residence, intermixed labour, intermixed living, and, eventually, a miscegenated population—in spite of the well-known pride of both the Bantu must, in the political sphere, have as their object equal franchise with the European.

Now examine the same question from the European's point of view. A section of the Europeans, consisting of both Afrikaans- and English-speaking peoples, says equally clearly that, in regard to the above standpoint, the European must continue to dominate what will be the European part of South Africa. It should be noted that, not-withstanding false representations, these Europeans do not demand domination over the whole of South Africa, that is to say, over the Native territories according as the Bantu outgrow the need for their trusteeship. Because that section of the European population states its case very clearly, it must not be accepted, however, that the other section of the European population will support the above possible future demand of the Bantu. That section of the European population (English as well as Afrikaans) which is prepared to grant representation to the Bantu in the country's government does not wish to grant anything beyond communal representation, and that on a strictly limited basis. They do not yet realize that a balance of power may thereby be given to the non-European with which an attempt may later be made to secure full and equal franchise on the same voter's roll. The moment they realize that, or the moment when the attempt is made, this later section of the European population will also throw in its weight with the first section in the interests of European supremacy in the European portion of the country. This appears clearly from its proposition that, in its belief on the basis of an inherent superiority, or greater knowledge, or whatever it may be, the European must remain master and leader. The section is, therefore, also a protagonist of separate residential areas, and of what it calls separation.

My point is this that, if mixed development is to be the policy of the future in South Africa, it will lead to the most terrific clash of interests imaginable. The endeavours and desires of the Bantu and the endeavours and objectives of *all* Europeans will be antagonistic. Such a clash can only bring unhappiness and misery to both. Both Bantu and European must, therefore, consider in good time how this misery can be averted from themselves and from their descendants. They must find a plan to provide the two population groups with opportunities for the full development of their respective powers and ambitions without coming into conflict.

The only possible way out is the second alternative, namely, that both adopt a development divorced from each other. That is all that the word apartheid means. Any word can be poisoned by attaching a false meaning to it. That has happened to this word. The Bantu have been made to believe that it means oppression, or even that the Native territories are to be taken away from them. In reality, however, exactly the opposite is intended with the policy of apartheid. To avoid the above-mentioned unpleasant and dangerous future for both sections of the population, the present Government adopts the attitude that it concedes and wishes to give to others precisely what it demands for itself. It believes in the supremacy (*baasskap*) of the European in his sphere but, the, it also believes equally in the supremacy (*baasskap*) of the Bantu in his own sphere. For the European child, it wishes to create all the possible opportunities for its own development, prosperity and national service in its own sphere; but for the Bantu is also wishes to create all the opportunities for the realization of ambitions and the rendering of service to *their* own people. There is thus no policy of oppression here, but one of creating a situation which has never existed for the Bantu; namely, that, taking into consideration their languages, traditional, history and different national communities, they may pass through a development of their own. That opportunity arises for them as soon as such a division is brought into being between them and the Europeans that they need not be the imitators and henchmen of the latter.

The next question, then, is how the division is to be brought about so as to allow the European and the Bantu to pass through a development of their own, in accordance with their own traditions, under their own leaders in every sphere of life.

It is perfectly clear that it would have been the easiest—an ideal condition for each of the two groups—if the course of history had been different. Suppose there had arisen in Southern Africa a state in which only Bantu lived and worked, and another in which only Europeans lived and worked. Each could then have worked out is own destiny in its own way. This is not the situation today, however, and planning must in practice take present day actualities of life in the Union into account. We cannot escape from that which history has brought in its train. However, this easiest situation for peaceful association, self-government and development, each according to its own nature and completely apart from one another, may, in fact, be taken as a yardstick whereby to test plans for getting out of the present confusion and difficulties. One may, so far as is practicable, try to approach this objective in the future.

The realities of today are that a little over one-third of the Bantu resides, or still has its roots, in what are unambiguously termed Native territories. A little over a third lives in the countryside and on the farms of Europeans. A little less than a third lives and works in the cities, of whom a section have been detribalized and urbanized. The apartheid policy takes this reality into account.

Obviously, in order to grant equal opportunities to the Bantu, both in their interests as well as those of the Europeans, its starting-point is the native territories. For the present, these territories cannot provide the desired opportunities for living and development of their inhabitants and their children, let alone to more people. Due to neglect of their soil and over-population by man and cattle, large numbers are even now being continuously forced to go and seek a living under the protection of the European and his industries. In these circumstances it cannot be expected that the Bantu community will so provide for itself and so progress as to allow ambitious and developed young people to be taken up by their own people in their national service out of their own funds. Accordingly, as a flourishing community arises in such territories, however, the need will develop for teachers, dealers, clerks, artisans, agricultural experts, leaders of local and general governing bodies of their own. In other words, the whole superstructure of administrative and professional people arising in every prosperous community will then become necessary. Out first aim as a Government is, therefore, to lay the foundation of a prosperous producing community through soil reclamation and conservation methods and through the systematic establishment in the Native territories of Bantu farming on an economic basis.

The limited territories are, however, as little able to carry the whole of the Bantu population of the reserves of the present and the future—if all were to be farmers—as the European area would be able to carry all the Europeans if they were all to be farmers, or as England would be able to carry its whole population if all of them had to be landowners, farmers, and cattle breeders. Consequently, the systematic building up of the Native territories aims at a development precisely as in all prosperous countries. Side by side with agricultural development must also come an urban development founded on industrial growth. The future Bantu towns and cities in the reserves may arise partly in conjunction with Bantu industries of their own in those reserves. In their establishment Europeans must be prepared to help with money and knowledge, in the consciousness that such industries must, as soon as is possible, wholly pass over into the hands of the Bantu.

On account of the backlog, it is conceivable, however, that such industries may not develop sufficiently rapidly to meet adequately the needs of the Bantu requiring work. The European industrialist will, therefore, have to be encouraged to establish industries within the European areas near such towns and cities. Bantu working in those industries will then be able to live within their own territories, where they have their own schools, their own traders, and where they govern themselves. Indeed, the kernel of the apartheid policy is that, as the Bantu no longer need the European, the latter must wholly withdraw from the Native territories.

What length of time it will take the Bantu in the reserves to advance to that stage of self-sufficiency and self-government will depend on his own industry and preparedness to grasp this opportunity offered by the apartheid policy for self-development and service to his own nation.

This development of the reserves will not, however, mean that all Natives from the cities or European countryside will be able, or wish, to trek to them. In the countryside there has, up to the present, not been a clash of social interests. The endeavour, at any rate for the time being, must be to grant the Bantu in town locations as much self-government as is practicable under the guardianship of the town councils, and to let tribal control of farm Natives function effectively. There the residential and working conditions will also have to enjoy special attention so that the Bantu community finding a livelihood as farm labourers may also be prosperous and happy. Here the problem is rather how to create better relationships, greater stability, correct training and good working conditions. Apart from the removal of black spots (like the removal of white spots in the Native areas), the policy of apartheid is for the time being, not so much an issue at this juncture, except if mechanization of farming should later cause a decrease in non-European labourers.

Finally, there are the implications of the apartheid policy in respect of European cities. The primary requirement of this policy is well known, namely, that not only must there be separation between European and non-European groups, such as the Bantu, the coloured, and the Indian, shall live in their own residential areas. Although considerable numbers of Bantu who are still rooted in the reserves may conceivably return thither, particularly according as urban and industrial development take place, or even many urbanized Bantu may proceed thence because of the opportunities to exercise their talents as artisans, traders, clerks or professionals, or to realize their political ambitions—large numbers will undoubtedly still remain behind in the big cities. For a long time to come, this will probably continue to be the case.

For these Bantu also, the Apartheid policy and separate residential areas have great significance.

The objective is, namely, to give them the greatest possible measure of self-government in such areas according to the degree in which local authorities, who construct these towns, can fall into line. In due course, too, depending on the ability of the Bantu community, all the work there will have to be done by their own people, as was described in connection with the reserves. Even within a European area, therefore, the Bantu communities would not be separated for the former to oppress them, but to form their own communities within which they may pursue a full life of work and service.

In view of all this, it will be appreciated why the Apartheid policy also takes an interest in suitable education for the Bantu. This, in fact, brings in its train the need for sufficiently competent Bantu in many spheres. The only and obvious reservation is that the Bantu will have to place his development and his knowledge exclusively at the service of his own people.

Co-operation in implementing the apartheid policy as described here is one of the greatest services the present leader of the Bantu population can render his people. Instead of striving after vague chimeras and trying to equal the European in an intermingled community with confused ideals and inevitable conflict, he can be a national figure helping to lead his own people along the road of peace and prosperity. He can help to give the children and educated men and women of his people an opportunity to find employment or fully to realize their ambitions within their own sphere or, where this is not possible, as within the Europeans' sphere, employment and service within segregated areas of their own.

I trust that every Bantu will forget the misunderstandings of the past and choose not the road leading to conflict, but that which leads to peace and happiness for both the separate communities. Are the present leaders of the Bantu, under the influence of communist agitators, going to seek a form of equality which they will not get? For in the long run they will come up against the whole of the European community, as well as the large section of their own compatriots who prefer the many advantages of self-government within a community of their own. I cannot believe that they will. Nobody can reject a form of independence, obtainable with everybody's co-operation, in favour of a futile striving after that which promises to be not freedom but downfall.

The Freedom Charter (1955)

Adopted at the Congress of the People, Kliptown, on 26 June 1955[1]

Editor's Comment: The Freedom Charter was the outcome of a non-racial meeting of antiapartheid organizations from all over South Africa, though the majority in attendance at the Kliptown meeting were Black, Coloured, and Asian members of the African National Congress and whites of the Congress of Democrats. The Charter stood as the major statement of principles opposed to racially based government until the end of apartheid itself. Many who signed it were arrested and put on trial for treason. In what ways does the Freedom Charter draw from the UN Declaration on Human Rights? How does it particularize the demand for justice and liberty to the South African context? Are there aspects of the Freedom Charter that seem to point to inadequacies in the UDHR or suggest a different way of thinking about "justice"?

We, the People of South Africa, declare for all our country and the world to know:

that South Africa belongs to all who live in it, black and white, and that no government can justly claim authority unless it is based on the will of all the people;

that our people have been robbed of their birthright to land, liberty and peace by a form of government founded on injustice and inequality;

that our country will never be prosperous or free until all our people live in brotherhood, enjoying equal rights and opportunities;

1. Used by permission of the ANC Archives.

that only a democratic state, based on the will of all the people, can secure to all their birthright without distinction of colour, race, sex or belief;

And therefore, we, the people of South Africa, black and white together equals, countrymen and brothers adopt this Freedom Charter;

And we pledge ourselves to strive together, sparing neither strength nor courage, until the democratic changes here set out have been won.

The People Shall Govern! Every man and woman shall have the right to vote for and to stand as a candidate for all bodies which make laws;

All people shall be entitled to take part in the administration of the country;

The rights of the people shall be the same, regardless of race, colour or sex;

All bodies of minority rule, advisory boards, councils and authorities shall be replaced by democratic organs of self-government.

All National Groups Shall Have Equal Rights!

There shall be equal status in the bodies of state, in the courts and in the schools for all national groups and races;

All people shall have equal right to use their own languages, and to develop their own folk culture and customs;

All national groups shall be protected by law against insults to their race and national pride;

The preaching and practice of national, race or colour discrimination and contempt shall be a punishable crime;

All apartheid laws and practices shall be set aside.

The People Shall Share in the Country's Wealth!

The national wealth of our country, the heritage of South Africans, shall be restored to the people;

The mineral wealth beneath the soil, the Banks and monopoly industry shall be transferred to the ownership of the people as a whole;

All other industry and trade shall be controlled to assist the wellbeing of the people;

All people shall have equal rights to trade where they choose, to manufacture and to enter all trades, crafts and professions.

The Land Shall Be Shared Among Those Who Work It!

Restrictions of land ownership on a racial basis shall be ended, and all the land re-divided amongst those who work it to banish famine and land hunger;

The state shall help the peasants with implements, seed, tractors and dams to save the soil and assist the tillers;

Freedom of movement shall be guaranteed to all who work on the land;

All shall have the right to occupy land wherever they choose;

People shall not be robbed of their cattle, and forced labour and farm prisons shall be abolished.

All Shall Be Equal Before the Law!

No-one shall be imprisoned, deported or restricted without a fair trial; No-one shall be condemned by the order of any Government official;

The courts shall be representative of all the people;

Imprisonment shall be only for serious crimes against the people, and shall aim at re-education, not vengeance;

The police force and army shall be open to all on an equal basis and shall be the helpers and protectors of the people;

All laws which discriminate on grounds of race, colour or belief shall be repealed.

All Shall Enjoy Equal Human Rights!

The law shall guarantee to all their right to speak, to organise, to meet together, to publish, to preach, to worship and to educate their children;

The privacy of the house from police raids shall be protected by law;

All shall be free to travel without restriction from countryside to town, from province to province, and from South Africa abroad;

Pass Laws, permits and all other laws restricting these freedoms shall be abolished.

There Shall Be Work and Security!

All who work shall be free to form trade unions, to elect their officers and to make wage agreements with their employers;

The state shall recognise the right and duty of all to work, and to draw full unemployment benefits;

Men and women of all races shall receive equal pay for equal work;

There shall be a forty-hour working week, a national minimum wage, paid annual leave, and sick leave for all workers, and maternity leave on full pay for all working mothers;

Miners, domestic workers, farm workers and civil servants shall have the same rights as all others who work;

Child labour, compound labour, the tot system and contract labour shall be abolished.

The Doors of Learning and Culture Shall Be Opened!

The government shall discover, develop and encourage national talent for the enhancement of our cultural life;

All the cultural treasures of mankind shall be open to all, by free exchange of books, ideas and contact with other lands;

The aim of education shall be to teach the youth to love their people and their culture, to honour human brotherhood, liberty and peace;

Education shall be free, compulsory, universal and equal for all children; Higher education and technical training shall be opened to all by means of state allowances and scholarships awarded on the basis of merit;

Adult illiteracy shall be ended by a mass state education plan;

Teachers shall have all the rights of other citizens;

The colour bar in cultural life, in sport and in education shall be abolished.

There Shall Be Houses, Security, and Comfort!

All people shall have the right to live where they choose, be decently housed, and to bring up their families in comfort and security;

Unused housing space to be made available to the people;

Rent and prices shall be lowered, food plentiful and no-one shall go hungry;

A preventive health scheme shall be run by the state;

Free medical care and hospitalisation shall be provided for all, with special care for mothers and young children;

Slums shall be demolished, and new suburbs built where all have transport, roads, lighting, playing fields, creches and social centres;

The aged, the orphans, the disabled and the sick shall be cared for by the state;

Rest, leisure and recreation shall be the right of all:

Fenced locations and ghettoes shall be abolished, and laws which break up families shall be repealed.

There Shall Be Peace and Friendship!

South Africa shall be a fully independent state which respects the rights and sovereignty of all nations;

South Africa shall strive to maintain world peace and the settlement of all international disputes by negotiation—not war;

Peace and friendship amongst all our people shall be secured by upholding the equal rights, opportunities and status of all;

The people of the protectorates Basutoland, Bechuanaland and Swaziland shall be free to decide for themselves their own future;

The right of all peoples of Africa to independence and self-government shall be recognised, and shall be the basis of close co-operation.

Let all people who love their people and their country to say, as we say here:

These freedoms we will fight for, side by side, throughout our lives, until we have won our liberty!

Nelson Mandela: "Verwoerd's Grim Plot" (1959)

Editor's Comment: Mandela's article appeared in Liberation: A Journal of Democratic Discussion, *published in Johannesburg from 1953 to 1959. Mandela, then president of the ANC, offers a detailed refutation of the argument that the apartheid government's form of "Bantu Self-government" was in any way intended to give black South Africans independence, freedom, or democracy. How does Mandela challenge Hendrik Verwoerd's apology for apartheid? What does Mandela have to say about the use of language? What are the fundamental assumptions about humanity, society, and justice that influence Mandela's position?*

No. 36, May 1959[1]

> "South Africa belongs to all who live in it, black and white."
>
> —*The Freedom Charter.*

> "All the Bantu have their permanent homes in the reserves and their entry into other areas and into the urban areas is merely of a temporary nature and for economic reasons. In other words, they are admitted as work-seekers, not as settlers."
>
> —*Dr. W. W. M. Eiselen, Secretary of the Department of Bantu Administration and Development.*
> (Article in *Optima,* March 1959)

The two statements quoted above contain diametrically opposite conceptions of this country, its future and its destiny. Obviously they cannot be reconciled. They have nothing in common, except that both of them look forward to a future state of affairs rather than that which prevails at present.

At present South Africa does not "belong"—except in a moral sense—to all. 97 per cent of the country is legally owned by members (a handful of them at that) of the dominant white minority. And at present by no means "all" Africans have their "permanent homes" in the Reserves. Millions of Africans were born and have their permanent homes in the towns and cities and elsewhere outside the reserves, have never seen the reserves and have no desire to go there.[2]

It is necessary for the people of this country to choose between these two alternative paths. It is assumed that readers of "Liberation" are familiar with the detailed proposals contained in the Charter. Let us therefore, as calmly and objectively as we can, study the alternatives submitted by the Nationalist Party.

Partition

The newspapers have christened the Nationalists' plan as one for "Bantustans." The hybrid word is, in many ways, extremely misleading. It relates to the partitioning of India, after the reluctant departure of the British, and as a condition thereof, into two separate States, Hindustan and Pakistan. There is no real parallel with the Nationalists' proposals, for

a. India and Pakistan constitute two completely separate and politically independent States,
b. Muslims enjoy equal rights in India; Hindus enjoy equal rights in Pakistan,
c. Partition was submitted to and approved by both parties, or at any rate fairly widespread and Influential sections of each.

---

1. Used by permission of the Nelson Mandela Foundation.

2. According to the 1951 census, trust land locations and reserves accounted for only two and a half million out of a total African population of, at that time, eight and a half million. A further two and a half million, nearly, were on European-owned farms. The rest were mainly in urban areas, with the Witwatersrand alone accounting for over a million Africans. (*Official Year Book 1956–57,* p. 718)

The Government's plans do not envisage the partitioning of this country into separate, self-governing States. They do not envisage equal rights, or any rights at all, for Africans outside the reserves. Partition has never been approved of by Africans and never will be. For that matter it has never been really submitted to or approved of by the Whites. The term "Bantustan" is therefore a complete misnomer, and merely tends to help the Nationalists perpetrate a fraud.

Let us examine each of these aspects in detail.

"Bantu Self-Government"

It is typical of the Nationalists' propaganda techniques that they describe their measures in misleading titles, which convey the opposite of what the measures contain. Verwoerd called his law greatly extending and intensifying the pass laws the "Abolition of Passes" Act. Similarly, he has introduced into the current Parliamentary session a measure called the "Promotion of Bantu Self-Government Bill." It starts off by decreeing the abolition of the tiny token representation of Africans (by Whites) in Parliament and the Cape Provincial Council.

It goes on to provide for the division of the African population into eight "ethnic units" (the so-called Bantustans).[1] These units, it is declared, are to undergo a "gradual development to self-government."

This measure was described by the Prime Minister, Dr. Verwoerd, as a "supremely positive step" towards placing Africans "on the road to self-government" (in his policy statement of January 27). Mr. De Wet Nel, B.A.D. Minister, said the people in the reserves "would gradually be given more powers to rule themselves."

The White Paper

The scheme is elaborated in a White Paper, tabled in the House of Assembly, to "explain" the

1. They are as follows: North and South Sotho, Swazi, Tsonga, Tswana, Venda, Xosa, and Zulu.

Bill. According to this document, immediate objects of the Bill are:

a. The recognition of the so-called Bantu National Units and the appointment of Commissioners-General whose task will be to give guidance and advice to the units in order to promote their general development, with special reference to the administrative field;

b. The linking of Africans working in urban areas with territorial authorities established under the Bantu Authorities Act, by conferring powers on the Bantu Authorities to nominate persons as their representatives in urban areas;

c. The transfer to the Bantu Territorial Authorities, at the appropriate time, of land in their areas at present held by the Native Trust;

d. The vesting in territorial Bantu Authorities of legislative authority and the right to impose taxes, and to undertake works and give guidance to subordinate authorities;

e. The establishment of territorial boards for the purpose of temporary liaison through commissioners-general if during the transition period the administrative structure in any area has not yet reached the stage where a territorial authority has been established;

f. The abolition of representation in the highest European governing bodies.

"Further Objects"

According to the same White Paper the Bill has the following further objects:

a. The creation of homogeneous administrative areas for Africans by uniting the members of each so-called national group in the national unit, concentrated in one coherent homeland where possible;

b. The education of Africans to a sound understanding of the problems of soil conservation and agriculture so that all rights over and responsibilities in respect of soil in African areas may be assigned to them. This includes the gradual replacement of European agricultural officers of all grades by qualified and competent Africans;

c. The systematic promotion of diverse economy in the African areas, acceptable to Africans and to be developed by them;

d. The education of the African to a sound understanding of the problems and aims of Bantu Education so that by decentralisation of powers, responsibility for the different grades of education may be vested in them;

e. The training of Africans with a view to effectively extending their own judicial system and their education to a sound understanding of the common law with a view to transferring to them responsibility for the administration of justice in their areas;

f. The gradual replacement of European administrative officers by qualified and competent Africans;

g. The exercise of legislative powers by Africans in respect of their areas, at first on a limited scale, but with every intention of gradually extending this power.

A Heavy Price

It will be seen that the African people are asked to pay a very heavy price for this so-called "self-government" in the Reserves. Urban Africans—the workers, business men and professional men and women, who are the pride of our people in their stubborn and victorious march towards modernisation and progress—are to be treated as outcasts: not even "settlers" like Dr. Verwoerd. Every vestige of rights and opportunities will be ruthlessly destroyed. Everywhere outside the reserves an African will be tolerated only on condition that it is for the convenience of the Whites.

There will be forcible uprooting and mass removals of millions of people ("homogeneous administrative areas"—see (a) under "Further Objects" above). The reserves, already intolerably overcrowded, will be crammed with hundreds of thousands more people evicted by the Government.

In return for all these hardships, in return for Africans abandoning their birthright as citizens, pioneers and inhabitants of South Africa, the Government promises them "self-government" in the tiny 13 per cent that their greed and miserliness "allocates" to us. But what sort of self-government is this that is promised?

What Sort of Self-Government?

There are two essential elements to self-government, as the term is used and understood all over the modern world. They are:

1. **Democracy**. The organs of Government must be representative. That is to say they must be the freely-chosen leaders and representatives of the people, whose mandate must be renewed at periodic democratic elections.

2. **Sovereignty**. The Government thus chosen must be free to legislate and act as it deems fit on behalf of the people, not subject to any limitations upon its powers by any alien or internal authority.

Now neither of these two essentials is present in the Nationalist plan. . . . No provision is made for elections. The Nationalists say that Chiefs, not elected legislatures, are "the Bantu tradition."

There was a time when, like all peoples on earth, Africans conducted their simple communities through Chiefs, advised by tribal councils and mass meetings of the people. In those times the Chiefs were indeed representative governors. Nowhere, however, have such institutions survived the complexities of modern industrial civilisation. Moreover, in South Africa, we all know full well that no Chief can retain his post unless he submits to Verwoerd, and many Chiefs who sought the interest of their people before position and self-advancement have, like President Luthuli, been deposed.

Thus, the proposed Bantu Authorities will not be, in any sense of the term, representative or democratic.

No Sovereignty

In spite of all their precautions to see that their "Territorial Authorities"—appointed by themselves, subject to dismissal by themselves, under constant control by their Commissioners-General and their B.A.D.—never become authentic voices of the people, the Nationalists are determined to see that even these puppet bodies never enjoy any real power of sovereignty.

. . . What are we to think, then, in the same article, when Dr. Eiselen comes right out into the open, and declares:

> The utmost degree of autonomy in administrative matters which the Union Parliament is likely to be prepared to concede to these areas will stop short of actual surrender of sovereignty by the European trustee, and there is therefore no prospect of a federal system with eventual equality among members taking the place of the South African Commonwealth.

There is no sovereignty, then. No autonomy. No democracy. No self-government. Nothing but a crude, empty fraud, to bluff the people at home and abroad, and to serve as a pretext for heaping yet more hardships and injustices upon the African people.

The Economic Aspect

Politically, the talk about self-government for the reserves is a swindle. Economically, it is an absurdity.

The few scattered African reserves in various parts of the Union, comprising about 13 per cent of the least desirable land area, represent the last shreds of land ownership left to the African people of their original ancestral home. After the encroachments and depredations of generations of European land-sharks, achieved by force and by cunning, and culminating the outrageous Land Acts from 1913 onwards, had turned the once free and independent Tswana, Sotho, Xhosa, Zulu and other peasant farmers of this country into a nation of landless outcasts and roving beggars, humble "work-seekers" on the mines and the farms where yesterday they had been masters of the land, the new White masters of the country generously "presented" the few miserable areas that were left to remain as reservoirs and breeding-grounds for black labour. These are the reserves.

It was never claimed or remotely considered by the previous Governments of the Union that these reserves could become economically self-sufficient "national homes" for 9,600,000 African people of this country. That final lunacy was left to Dr. Verwoerd, Dr. Eiselen and the Nationalist Party.

The facts are—as every reader who remembers M. Mbeki's brilliant series of articles on the Transkei in *Liberation* will be aware—that the reserves are congested distressed areas, completely unable to sustain their present populations. The majority of the adult males are always away from home working in the towns, mines or European-owned farms. The people are on the verge of starvation.

"Rural Locations"

The Government has already established a number of "rural locations" townships in the reserves. The Eiselen article says a number more are planned: he mentions a total of no less than 96. Since the residents will not farm, how will they manage to keep alive, still less pay rent and taxes, and support the traders, professional classes and civil servants whom the optimistic Eiselen envisages as making a living there?

. . . Even if many industries moved, or were forced to move, to the border areas around the reserves it would not make one iota of difference to the economic viability of the reserves themselves. The fundamental picture of the Union's economy would remain fundamentally the same as at present: a single integrated system based upon the exploitation of African labour by White capitalists.

Economically, the "Bantustan" concept is just as big a swindle as it is politically.

Self-Determination

Thus we find, if we really look into it that this grandiose "partition" scheme, this "Supremely positive step" of Dr. Verwoerd, is—like all apartheid schemes—merely a lot of high-sounding double-talk to conceal a policy of ruthless oppression of the non-Whites and of buttressing the unwarranted privileges of the White minority, especially the farming, mining and financial circles.

Even if it were not so, however; even if the schemes envisaged a genuine sharing-out of the country on the basis of population figures, and a genuine transfer of power to elected representatives of the people, it would remain fundamentally unjust and dangerously unstable unless it were submitted to, accepted and endorsed by all parties to the agreement. To think otherwise is to fly in the face of the principle of self-determination, which is upheld by all countries and confirmed in the United Nations Charter, to which this country is pledged.

Now even Dr. Eiselen recognises, to some extent, this difficulty. He pays lip-service to the Atlantic Charter and appeals to "Western democracy." He mentions the argument that apartheid would only be acceptable "provided that the parties concerned agreed to this of their own free will." And then he most dishonestly evades the whole issue. "There is no reason for ruling out apartheid on the grounds that the vast majority of the population opposes it," he writes. "The Bantu as a whole do not demand integration, a single society. This is the ideal merely of a small minority."

Even Dr. Eiselen, however, has not got the audacity to claim that the African people actually favour apartheid or partition. Let us state clearly the facts of the matter, with the greatest possible clarity and emphasis.

No Serious or Responsible Leader, Gathering, or Organisation of the African People Has Ever Accepted Segregation, Separation or the Partition of This Country in Any Shape or Form.

At Bloemfontein in 1956, under the auspices of the United African clergy, perhaps the most widely-attended and representative gathering of African representatives, of every shade of political opinion ever held, unanimously and uncompromisingly rejected the Tomlinson Report, on which the Verwoerd plan is based, and voted in favour of a single society.

Even in the rural areas, where dwell the "good" (i.e., simple and ignorant) "Bantu" of the Imagination of Dr. Verwoerd and Dr. Eiselen, attempts to impose apartheid have met, time after time, with furious, often violent resistance. Chief after Chief has been deposed or deported for resisting "Bantu Authorities" plans. Those who, out of shortsightedness, cowardice or corruption, have accepted these plans have earned nothing but the contempt of their own people.

Serious Misstatements

It is a pity that, on such a serious subject, and at such a crucial period, serious misstatements should have been made by some people who purport to speak on behalf of the Africans.

. . . The leading organisation of the African people is the African National Congress. Congress has repeatedly denounced apartheid. It has repeatedly endorsed the Freedom Charter, which claims South Africa "for all its people." It is true that, occasionally individual Africans become so depressed and desperate at Nationalist misrule that they tend to clutch at any straw, that they tend to say: give us any little corner where we may be free to run our own affairs; but Congress has always firmly rejected such momentary tendencies and refused to barter our birthright, which is South Africa, for such illusory "Bantu-stans."

Let the People Speak!

Here, indeed, Mr. Nokwe has put his finger on the spot. There is no need for Dr. Eiselen, Mrs. Ballinger or The World to argue about "what the Africans think" about the future of this country. Let the people speak for themselves! Let us have a free vote and a free election of delegates to a national convention, irrespective of colour or nationality. Let the Nationalists submit their plan, and the Congress its Charter. If Verwoerd and Eiselen think the Africans support their scheme they need not fear such a procedure. If they are not prepared to submit to public opinion then let them stop parading and pretending to the outside world that they are democrats, and talking revolting nonsense about "Bantu self-government."

Dr. Verwoerd may deceive the simple-minded Nationalist voters with his talk of Bantustans, but he will not deceive anyone else, neither the African people, nor the great world beyond the borders of this country. We have heard such talk before, and we know what it really means.

Like everything else that has come from the Nationalist Government, it spells nothing but fresh hardships and sufferings to the masses of the people.

Sinister Design

Behind the fine talk of "self-government" is a sinister design.

The abolition of African representation in Parliament and the Cape Provincial Council shows that the real purpose of the scheme is not to concede autonomy to Africans but to deprive them of all say in the government of the country in exchange for a system of local Government controlled by a Minister who is not responsible to them but to a Parliament in which they have no voice. This is not autonomy but autocracy.

Contact between the Minister and the Bantu Authorities will be maintained by five Commissioners-General. These officials will act as the watchdogs of the Minister to ensure that the "Authorities" strictly toe the line. Their duty will be to ensure that these authorities should not become "the voice of the African people but that of the Nationalist Government."

. . . Nowhere in the Bill or in the various Proclamations dealing with the creation of Bantu Authorities is there provision for democratic elections by Africans falling within the jurisdiction of the Authorities.

In the light of these facts it is sheer nonsense to talk of South Africa as being about to take a "supremely positive step" towards placing Africans on the road to self-government—or of having given them more powers to rule themselves. As Dr. Eiselen clearly pointed out in his article in *Optima*, the establishment of the Bantustans will not in any way affect white supremacy since even in such areas whites will stay supreme. The Bantustans are not intended to voice aspirations of the African people; they are instruments for their subjection. Under the pretext of giving them self-government the African people are being split up into tribal units in order to retard their growth and development into full nationhood.

The Chief Target

The new Bantu Bill and the new policy behind it will bear heavily on the peasants in the reserves. But it is not they who are the chief target of Verwoerd's new policy.

His new measures are aimed, in the first place, at the millions of Africans in the great cities of this country, the factory workers and intellectuals who have raised the banner of freedom and democracy and human dignity, who have spoken forth boldly the message that is shaking Imperialism to its foundations throughout this great Continent of Africa.

The Nationalists hate and fear that banner and that message. They will try to destroy them, by striking with all their might at the standard bearers and vanguard of the people, the working class.

Behind the "self-government" talk lies a grim programme of mass evictions, political persecution and police terror. It is the last desperate gamble of a hated and doomed fascist autocracy—which, fortunately, is soon due to make its exit from the stage of history.

Nelson Mandela: "I Am Prepared to Die" (1964)

Nelson Mandela's statement from the dock at the opening of the defence case in the Rivonia Trial Pretoria Supreme Court, 20 April 1964[1]

Editor's comment: Nelson Mandela delivered this address to the court, when he was on trial for his life, and prior to his sentencing. He was found guilty of sabotage and sentenced to life in prison. Apart from revealing his personal reasons and motivations in opposing apartheid, Mandela's statement provides a concise and detailed history of the efforts of the African National Congress and others over the previous decades to achieve a non-racial democracy. On 11 June 1964, at the conclusion of the trial, Mandela and seven others—Walter Sisulu, Govan Mbeki, Raymond Mhlaba, Elias Motsoaledi, Andrew Mlangeni, Ahmed Kathrada, and Denis Goldberg—were convicted. Mandela was found guilty on four charges of sabotage and like the others was sentenced to life imprisonment. What is Mandela's position on the use of violence? As someone who was seeking to establish a just system in South Africa, should Mandela be seen as a peacemaker? How does Mandela describe his relationship to communism and why is that significant?

I am the First Accused.

I hold a Bachelor's Degree in Arts and practised as an attorney in Johannesburg for a number of years in partnership with Oliver Tambo. I am a convicted prisoner serving five years for leaving the country without a permit and for inciting people to go on strike at the end of May 1961.

At the outset, I want to say that the suggestion made by the State in its opening that the struggle in South Africa is under the influence of foreigners or communists is wholly incorrect. I have done whatever I did, both as an individual and as a leader of my people, because of my experience in South Africa and my own proudly felt African background, and not because of what any outsider might have said.

In my youth in the Transkei I listened to the elders of my tribe telling stories of the old days. Amongst the tales they related to me were those of wars fought by our ancestors in defence of the fatherland. The names of Dingane and Bambata, Hintsa and Makana, Squngthi and Dalasile, Moshoeshoe and Sekhukhuni, were praised as the glory of the entire African nation. I hoped then that life might offer me the opportunity to serve my people and make my own humble contribution to their freedom struggle. This is what has motivated me in all that I have done in relation to the charges made against me in this case.

Having said this, I must deal immediately and at some length with the question of violence. Some of the things so far told to the Court are true and some are untrue. I do not, however, deny that I planned sabotage. I did not plan it in a spirit of recklessness, nor because I have any love of violence. I planned it as a result of a calm and sober assessment of the political situation that had arisen after many years of tyranny, exploitation, and oppression of my people by the Whites.

I admit immediately that I was one of the persons who helped to form Umkhonto we Sizwe, and that I played a prominent role in its affairs until I was arrested in August 1962.

In the statement which I am about to make I shall correct certain false impressions which have been created by State witnesses.[2] Amongst other things, I will demonstrate that certain of the acts referred to in the evidence were not and could not have been committed by Umkhonto. I will also deal with the relationship between the African National Congress and Umkhonto, and with the part which I personally have played in the affairs of both organizations. I shall deal also with the part played by the Communist Party. In order to explain these matters properly, I will have to explain what

---

1. Used by permission of the Nelson Mandela Foundation.

2. State witnesses in the trial whose names were withheld for their protection.

Umkhonto set out to achieve; what methods it prescribed for the achievement of these objects, and why these methods were chosen. I will also have to explain how I became involved in the activities of these organizations.

I deny that Umkhonto was responsible for a number of acts which clearly fell outside the policy of the organisation, and which have been charged in the indictment against us. I do not know what justification there was for these acts, but to demonstrate that they could not have been authorized by Umkhonto, I want to refer briefly to the roots and policy of the organization.

I have already mentioned that I was one of the persons who helped to form Umkhonto. I, and the others who started the organization, did so for two reasons. Firstly, we believed that as a result of Government policy, violence by the African people had become inevitable, and that unless responsible leadership was given to canalize and control the feelings of our people, there would be outbreaks of terrorism which would produce an intensity of bitterness and hostility between the various races of this country which is not produced even by war. Secondly, we felt that without violence there would be no way open to the African people to succeed in their struggle against the principle of white supremacy. All lawful modes of expressing opposition to this principle had been closed by legislation, and we were placed in a position in which we had either to accept a permanent state of inferiority, or to defy the Government. We chose to defy the law. We first broke the law in a way which avoided any recourse to violence; when this form was legislated against, and then the Government resorted to a show of force to crush opposition to its policies, only then did we decide to answer violence with violence.

But the violence which we chose to adopt was not terrorism. We who formed Umkhonto were all members of the African National Congress, and had behind us the ANC tradition of non-violence and negotiation as a means of solving political disputes. We believe that South Africa belongs to all the people who live in it, and not to one group, be it black or white. We did not want an interracial war, and tried to avoid it to the last minute. If the Court is in doubt about this, it will be seen that the whole history of our organization bears out what I have said, and what I will subsequently say, when I describe the tactics which Umkhonto decided to adopt. I want, therefore, to say something about the African National Congress.

The African National Congress was formed in 1912 to defend the rights of the African people which had been seriously curtailed by the South Africa Act, and which were then being threatened by the Native Land Act. For thirty-seven years— that is until 1949—it adhered strictly to a constitutional struggle. It put forward demands and resolutions; it sent delegations to the Government in the belief that African grievances could be settled through peaceful discussion and that Africans could advance gradually to full political rights. But White Governments remained unmoved, and the rights of Africans became less instead of becoming greater. In the words of my leader, Chief Luthuli, who became President of the ANC in 1952, and who was later awarded the Nobel Peace Prize:

> "Who will deny that thirty years of my life have been spent knocking in vain, patiently, moderately, and modestly at a closed and barred door? What have been the fruits of moderation? The past thirty years have seen the greatest number of laws restricting our rights and progress, until today we have reached a stage where we have almost no rights at all."

Even after 1949, the ANC remained determined to avoid violence. At this time, however, there was a change from the strictly constitutional means of protest which had been employed in the past. The change was embodied in a decision which was taken to protest against apartheid legislation by peaceful, but unlawful, demonstrations against certain laws. Pursuant to this policy the ANC launched the Defiance Campaign, in which I was placed in charge of volunteers. This campaign was based on the principles of passive resistance. More than 8,500 people defied apartheid laws and went to jail. Yet there was not a single instance of violence in the course of this campaign on the part of any defier. I and nineteen colleagues were convicted for the role which we played in organizing the campaign, but our sentences were suspended mainly because the Judge found that discipline and non-violence had been stressed throughout. . . . The volunteers were not, and are not, the soldiers of a black army pledged to fight a civil war against the whites. They were, and are, dedicated workers who are prepared to lead campaigns initiated by the ANC to distribute leaflets, to organize strikes, or do whatever the particular campaign required. They are called volunteers because they volunteer to face the penalties of imprisonment and whipping which are now prescribed by the legislature for such acts.

During the Defiance Campaign, the Public Safety Act and the Criminal Law Amendment Act were passed. . . . The Government has always sought to label all its opponents as communists. This allegation has been repeated in the present case, but as I will show, the ANC is not, and never has been, a communist organization.

In 1960 there was the shooting at Sharpeville, which resulted in the proclamation of a state of emergency and the declaration of the ANC as an unlawful organization. My colleagues and I, after careful consideration, decided that we would not obey this decree. The African people were not part of the Government and did not make the laws by which they were governed. We believed in the words of the Universal Declaration of Human Rights, that "the will of the people shall be the basis of authority of the Government," and for us to accept the banning was equivalent to accepting the silencing of the Africans for all time. The ANC refused to dissolve, but instead went underground. We believed it was our duty to preserve this organization which had been built up with almost fifty years of unremitting toil. I have no doubt that no self-respecting White political organization would disband itself if declared illegal by a government in which it had no say.

In 1960 the Government held a referendum which led to the establishment of the Republic. Africans, who constituted approximately 70 per cent of the population of South Africa, were not entitled to vote, and were not even consulted about the proposed constitutional change. All of us were apprehensive of our future under the proposed White Republic, and a resolution was taken to hold an All-In African Conference to call for a National Convention, and to organize mass demonstrations on the eve of the unwanted Republic. . . . As all strikes by Africans are illegal, the person organizing such a strike must avoid arrest. I was chosen to be this person, and consequently I had to leave my home and family and my practice and go into hiding to avoid arrest.

The stay-at-home, in accordance with ANC policy, was to be a peaceful demonstration. Careful instructions were given to organizers and members to avoid any recourse to violence. The Government's answer was to introduce new and harsher laws, to mobilize its armed forces, and to send Saracens,[1] armed vehicles, and soldiers into the townships in a massive show of force designed to intimidate the people. This was an indication that the Government had decided to rule by force alone, and this decision was a milestone on the road to Umkhonto.

Some of this may appear irrelevant to this trial. In fact, I believe none of it is irrelevant because it will, I hope, enable the Court to appreciate the attitude eventually adopted by the various persons and bodies concerned in the National Liberation Movement. When I went to jail in 1962, the dominant idea was that loss of life should be avoided. I now know that this was still so in 1963.

I must return to June 1961. What were we, the leaders of our people, to do? Were we to give in to

1. Saracens are British-made armored military troop carriers.

the show of force and the implied threat against future action, or were we to fight it and, if so, how?

We had no doubt that we had to continue the fight. Anything else would have been abject surrender. Our problem was not whether to fight, but was how to continue the fight. We of the ANC had always stood for a non-racial democracy, and we shrank from any action which might drive the races further apart than they already were. But the hard facts were that fifty years of non-violence had brought the African people nothing but more and more repressive legislation, and fewer and fewer rights. It may not be easy for this Court to understand, but it is a fact that for a long time the people had been talking of violence—of the day when they would fight the White man and win back their country—and we, the leaders of the ANC, had nevertheless always prevailed upon them to avoid violence and to pursue peaceful methods. When some of us discussed this in May and June of 1961, it could not be denied that our policy to achieve a non-racial State by non-violence had achieved nothing, and that our followers were beginning to lose confidence in this policy and were developing disturbing ideas of terrorism.

It must not be forgotten that by this time violence had, in fact, become a feature of the South African political scene. . . . Already small groups had arisen in the urban areas and were spontaneously making plans for violent forms of political struggle. . . . It was increasingly taking the form, not of struggle against the Government though this is what prompted it—but of civil strife amongst themselves, conducted in such a way that it could not hope to achieve anything other than a loss of life and bitterness.

At the beginning of June 1961, after a long and anxious assessment of the South African situation, I, and some colleagues, came to the conclusion that as violence in this country was inevitable, it would be unrealistic and wrong for African leaders to continue preaching peace and non-violence at a time when the Government met our peaceful demands with force.

This conclusion was not easily arrived at. It was only when all else had failed, when all channels of peaceful protest had been barred to us, that the decision was made to embark on violent forms of political struggle, and to form Umkhonto we Sizwe. We did so not because we desired such a course, but solely because the Government had left us with no other choice. In the *Manifesto of Umkhonto* published on 16 December 1961, which is Exhibit AD, we said:

"The time comes in the life of any nation when there remain only two choices—submit or fight. That time has now come to South Africa. We shall not submit and we have no choice but to hit back by all means in our power in defence of our people, our future, and our freedom."

This was our feeling in June of 1961 when we decided to press for a change in the policy of the National Liberation Movement. I can only say that I felt morally obliged to do what I did. . . . As far as the ANC was concerned, it formed a clear view which can be summarized as follows:

a. It was a mass political organization with a political function to fulfil. Its members had joined on the express policy of non-violence.
b. Because of all this, it could not and would not undertake violence. This must be stressed. One cannot turn such a body into the small, closely knit organization required for sabotage. Nor would this be politically correct, because it would result in members ceasing to carry out this essential activity: political propaganda and organization. Nor was it permissible to change the whole nature of the organization.
c. On the other hand, in view of this situation I have described, the ANC was prepared to depart from its fifty-year-old policy of non-violence to this extent that it would no longer disapprove of properly controlled violence.

Hence members who undertook such activity would not be subject to disciplinary action by the ANC.

I say "properly controlled violence" because I made it clear that if I formed the organization I would at all times subject it to the political guidance of the ANC and would not undertake any different form of activity from that contemplated without the consent of the ANC. And I shall now tell the Court how that form of violence came to be determined.

As a result of this decision, Umkhonto was formed in November 1961. When we took this decision, and subsequently formulated our plans, the ANC heritage of non-violence and racial harmony was very much with us. We felt that the country was drifting towards a civil war in which Blacks and Whites would fight each other. We viewed the situation with alarm. Civil war could mean the destruction of what the ANC stood for; with civil war, racial peace would be more difficult than ever to achieve. . . . The avoidance of civil war had dominated our thinking for many years, but when we decided to adopt violence as part of our policy, we realized that we might one day have to face the prospect of such a war. . . . We did not want to be committed to civil war, but we wanted to be ready if it became inevitable.

Four forms of violence were possible. There is sabotage, there is guerrilla warfare, there is terrorism, and there is open revolution. We chose to adopt the first method and to exhaust it before taking any other decision.

In the light of our political background the choice was a logical one. Sabotage did not involve loss of life, and it offered the best hope for future race relations. Bitterness would be kept to a minimum and, if the policy bore fruit, democratic government could become a reality.

The initial plan was based on a careful analysis of the political and economic situation of our country. We believed that South Africa depended to a large extent on foreign capital and foreign trade. We felt that planned destruction of power plants, and interference with rail and telephone communications, would tend to scare away capital from the country, make it more difficult for goods from the industrial areas to reach the seaports on schedule, and would in the long run be a heavy drain on the economic life of the country, thus compelling the voters of the country to reconsider their position.

Attacks on the economic life lines of the country were to be linked with sabotage on Government buildings and other symbols of apartheid. These attacks would serve as a source of inspiration to our people. . . . This then was the plan. Umkhonto was to perform sabotage, and strict instructions were given to its members right from the start, that on no account were they to injure or kill people in planning or carrying out operations. . . . For instance, Umkhonto members were forbidden ever to go armed into operation. Incidentally, the terms High Command and Regional Command were an importation from the Jewish national underground organization Irgun Zvai Leumi, which operated in Israel between 1944 and 1948

. . . The Manifesto of Umkhonto was issued on the day that operations commenced. The response to our actions and Manifesto among the white population was characteristically violent. The Government threatened to take strong action, and called upon its supporters to stand firm and to ignore the demands of the Africans. The Whites failed to respond by suggesting change; they responded to our call by suggesting the laager.[1]

In contrast, the response of the Africans was one of encouragement. Suddenly there was hope again. Things were happening. People in the townships became eager for political news. A great deal of enthusiasm was generated by the initial successes, and people began to speculate on how soon freedom would be obtained.

But we in Umkhonto weighed up the white response with anxiety. The lines were being drawn.

---

1. A protective camp. The term is used figuratively to refer to a reactively defensive mentality rather than as a recognition of the grievances of Africans.

The whites and blacks were moving into separate camps, and the prospects of avoiding a civil war were made less. The white newspapers carried reports that sabotage would be punished by death. If this was so, how could we continue to keep Africans away from terrorism?

Already scores of Africans had died as a result of racial friction. . . . On 21 March 1960, sixty-nine unarmed Africans died at Sharpeville.

How many more Sharpevilles would there be in the history of our country? And how many more Sharpevilles could the country stand without violence and terror becoming the order of the day?

. . . Experience convinced us that rebellion would offer the Government limitless opportunities for the indiscriminate slaughter of our people. But it was precisely because the soil of South Africa is already drenched with the blood of innocent Africans that we felt it our duty to make preparations as a long-term undertaking to use force in order to defend ourselves against force. If war were inevitable, we wanted the fight to be conducted on terms most favourable to our people. The fight which held out prospects best for us and the least risk of life to both sides was guerrilla warfare. We decided, therefore, in our preparations for the future, to make provision for the possibility of guerrilla warfare.

All whites undergo compulsory military training, but no such training was given to Africans. It was in our view essential to build up a nucleus of trained men who would be able to provide the leadership which would be required if guerrilla warfare started. We had to prepare for such a situation before it became too late to make proper preparations. It was also necessary to build up a nucleus of men trained in civil administration and other professions, so that Africans would be equipped to participate in the government of this country as soon as they were allowed to do so.

At this stage it was decided that I should attend the Conference of the Pan-African Freedom Movement for Central, East, and Southern Africa, which was to be held early in 1962 in Addis Ababa, and, because of our need for preparation, it was also decided that, after the conference, I would undertake a tour of the African States with a view to obtaining facilities for the training of soldiers, and that I would also solicit scholarships for the higher education of matriculated Africans. Training in both fields would be necessary, even if changes came about by peaceful means. . . . I started to make a study of the art of war and revolution and, whilst abroad, underwent a course in military training. If there was to be guerrilla warfare, I wanted to be able to stand and fight with my people and to share the hazards of war with them.

I also made arrangements for our recruits to undergo military training. But here it was impossible to organize any scheme without the co-operation of the ANC offices in Africa. I consequently obtained the permission of the ANC in South Africa to do this. To this extent then there was a departure from the original decision of the ANC, but it applied outside South Africa only. The first batch of recruits actually arrived in Tanganyika when I was passing through that country on my way back to South Africa.

. . . I wish to turn now to certain general allegations made in this case by the State. But before doing so, I wish to revert to certain occurrences said by witnesses to have happened in Port Elizabeth and East London. I am referring to the bombing of private houses of pro-Government persons during September, October and November 1962. I do not know what justification there was for these acts, nor what provocation had been given. But if what I have said already is accepted, then it is clear that these acts had nothing to do with the carrying out of the policy of Umkhonto.

One of the chief allegations in the indictment is that the ANC was a party to a general conspiracy to commit sabotage. I have already explained why this is incorrect but how, externally, there was a departure from the original principle laid down by the ANC. There has, of course, been overlapping of functions internally as well, because there is a difference between a resolution adopted in the atmosphere of a committee room and the concrete difficulties that arise in the field of practical activity. At a later stage the position was further affected by bannings and house arrests, and by persons leaving the country to take up political work abroad. This led to individuals having to do work in different capacities. But though this may have blurred the distinction between Umkhonto and the ANC, it by no means abolished that distinction. Great care was taken to keep the activities of the two organizations in South Africa distinct. The ANC remained a mass political body of Africans only carrying on the type of political work they had conducted prior to 1961. Umkhonto remained a small organization recruiting its members from different races and organizations and trying to achieve its own particular object. . . . Another of the allegations in the indictment is that Rivonia was the headquarters of Umkhonto. This is not true of the time when I was there. I was told, of course, and knew that certain of the activities of the Communist Party were carried on there. But this is no reason (as I shall presently explain) why I should not use the place.

I came there in the following manner:

1. As already indicated, early in April 1961 I went underground to organize the May general strike. My work entailed travelling throughout the country, living now in African townships, then in country villages and again in cities . . .
2. In October, Arthur Goldreich informed me that he was moving out of town and offered me a hiding place there. A few days thereafter, he arranged for Michael Harmel to take me to Rivonia. I naturally found Rivonia an ideal place for the man who lived the life of an outlaw. Up to that time I had been compelled to live indoors during the daytime and could only venture out under cover of darkness. But

at Liliesleaf[1] [Farm, Rivonia]. I could live differently and work far more efficiently.

3. For obvious reasons, I had to disguise myself and I assumed the fictitious name of David. In December, Arthur Goldreich and his family moved in. I stayed there until I went abroad on 11 January 1962. As already indicated, I returned in July 1962 and was arrested in Natal on 5 August.
4. Up to the time of my arrest, Liliesleaf Farm was the headquarters of neither the African National Congress nor Umkhonto. With the exception of myself, none of the officials or members of these bodies lived there, no meetings of the governing bodies were ever held there, and no activities connected with them were either organized or directed from there. On numerous occasions during my stay at Liliesleaf Farm I met both the Executive Committee of the ANC, as well as the NHC, but such meetings were held elsewhere and not on the farm.
5. Whilst staying at Liliesleaf Farm, I frequently visited Arthur Goldreich in the main house and he also paid me visits in my room. We had numerous political discussions covering a variety of subjects. We discussed ideological and practical questions, the Congress Alliance, Umkhonto and its activities generally, and his experiences as a soldier in the Palmach, the military wing of the Haganah. Haganah was the political authority of the Jewish National Movement in Palestine.
6. Because of what I had got to know of Goldreich, I recommended on my return to South Africa that he should be recruited to Umkhonto. I do not know of my personal knowledge whether this was done.

1. Liliesleaf was the name of the farm in the district of Rivonia on the northern outskirts of Johannesburg where the arrests took place. At the time, it was leased to Arthur Goldreich.

Another of the allegations made by the State is that the aims and objects of the ANC and the Communist Party are the same. I wish to deal with this and with my own political position, because I must assume that the State may try to argue from certain Exhibits that I tried to introduce Marxism into the ANC. The allegation as to the ANC is false . . .

The ideological creed of the ANC is, and always has been, the creed of African Nationalism. It is not the concept of African Nationalism expressed in the cry, "Drive the White man into the sea." The African Nationalism for which the ANC stands is the concept of freedom and fulfillment for the African people in their own land. The most important political document ever adopted by the ANC is the "Freedom Charter." It is by no means a blueprint for a socialist state. It calls for redistribution, but not nationalization, of land; it provides for nationalization of mines, banks, and monopoly industry, because big monopolies are owned by one race only, and without such nationalization racial domination would be perpetuated despite the spread of political power. It would be a hollow gesture to repeal the Gold Law prohibitions against Africans when all gold mines are owned by European companies. In this respect the ANC's policy corresponds with the old policy of the present Nationalist Party which, for many years, had as part of its programme the nationalization of the gold mines which, at that time, were controlled by foreign capital. Under the Freedom Charter, nationalization would take place in an economy based on private enterprise. The realization of the Freedom Charter would open up fresh fields for a prosperous African population of all classes, including the middle class. The ANC has never at any period of its history advocated a revolutionary change in the economic structure of the country, nor has it, to the best of my recollection, ever condemned capitalist society.

As far as the Communist Party is concerned, and if I understand its policy correctly, it stands for the establishment of a State based on the principles of Marxism. Although it is prepared to work for the Freedom Charter, as a short-term solution to the problems created by white supremacy, it regards the Freedom Charter as the beginning, and not the end, of its programme.

The ANC, unlike the Communist Party, admitted Africans only as members. Its chief goal was, and is, for the African people to win unity and full political rights. The Communist Party's main aim, on the other hand, was to remove the capitalists and to replace them with a working-class government. The Communist Party sought to emphasize class distinctions whilst the ANC seeks to harmonize them. This is a vital distinction.

It is true that there has often been close co-operation between the ANC and the Communist Party. But co-operation is merely proof of a common goal—in this case the removal of white supremacy—and is not proof of a complete community of interests.

The history of the world is full of similar examples. Perhaps the most striking illustration is to be found in the co-operation between Great Britain, the United States of America, and the Soviet Union in the fight against Hitler. Nobody but Hitler would have dared to suggest that such co-operation turned Churchill or Roosevelt into communists or communist tools, or that Britain and America were working to bring about a communist world

. . . I joined the ANC in 1944, and in my younger days I held the view that the policy of admitting communists to the ANC, and the close co-operation which existed at times on specific issues between the ANC and the Communist Party, would lead to a watering down of the concept of African Nationalism. At that stage I was a member of the African National Congress Youth League, and was one of a group which moved for the expulsion of communists from the ANC. This proposal was heavily defeated. Amongst those who voted against the proposal were some of the most conservative sections of African political opinion. They defended the policy on the ground that from its inception the ANC was formed and built up, not as a political party with one school of political thought, but as a Parliament of the African people, accommodating people of various political convictions, all united by the common goal of national liberation. I was eventually won over to this point of view and I have upheld it ever since.

It is perhaps difficult for white South Africans, with an ingrained prejudice against communism, to understand why experienced African politicians so readily accept communists as their friends. But to us the reason is obvious. Theoretical differences amongst those fighting against oppression is a luxury we cannot afford at this stage. What is more, for many decades, communists were the only political group in South Africa who were prepared to treat Africans as human beings and their equals; who were prepared to eat with us, talk with us, live with us, and work with us. They were the only political group which was prepared to work with the Africans for the attainment of political rights and a stake in society. Because of this, there are many Africans who, today, tend to equate freedom with communism.

. . . It is not only in internal politics that we count communists as amongst those who support our cause. In the international field, communist countries have always come to our aid. In the United Nations and other Councils of the world the communist bloc has supported the Afro-Asian struggle against colonialism and often seems to be more sympathetic to our plight than some of the Western powers. Although there is a universal condemnation of apartheid, the communist bloc speaks out against it with a louder voice than most of the white world. In these circumstances, it would take a brash young politician, such as I was in 1949, to proclaim that the Communists are our enemies.

I turn now to my own position. I have denied that I am a communist, and I think that in the circumstances I am obliged to state exactly what my political beliefs are.

I have always regarded myself, in the first place, as an African patriot. . . . Today I am attracted by the idea of a classless society, an attraction which springs in part from Marxist reading and, in part,

from my admiration of the structure and organization of early African societies in this country. The land, then the main means of production, belonged to the tribe. There were no rich or poor and there was no exploitation.

It is true, as I have already stated, that I have been influenced by Marxist thought. But this is also true of many of the leaders of the new independent States. Such widely different persons as Gandhi, Nehru, Nkrumah, and Nasser all acknowledge this fact. We all accept the need for some form of socialism to enable our people to catch up with the advanced countries of this world and to overcome their legacy of extreme poverty. But this does not mean we are Marxists.

Indeed, for my own part, I believe that it is open to debate whether the Communist Party has any specific role to play at this particular stage of our political struggle. The basic task at the present moment is the removal of race discrimination and the attainment of democratic rights on the basis of the Freedom Charter. In so far as that Party furthers this task, I welcome its assistance. I realize that it is one of the means by which people of all races can be drawn into our struggle.

From my reading of Marxist literature and from conversations with Marxists, I have gained the impression that communists regard the parliamentary system of the West as undemocratic and reactionary. But, on the contrary, I am an admirer of such a system.

The Magna Carta, the Petition of Rights, and the Bill of Rights are documents which are held in veneration by democrats throughout the world.

I have great respect for British political institutions, and for the country's system of justice. I regard the British Parliament as the most democratic institution in the world, and the independence and impartiality of its judiciary never fail to arouse my admiration.

The American Congress, that country's doctrine of separation of powers, as well as the independence of its judiciary, arouses in me similar sentiments.

I have been influenced in my thinking by both West and East. All this has led me to feel that in my search for a political formula, I should be absolutely impartial and objective. I should tie myself to no particular system of society other than of socialism. I must leave myself free to borrow the best from the West and from the East . . .

There are certain Exhibits which suggest that we received financial support from abroad, and I wish to deal with this question

. . . As I understand the State case, and in particular the evidence of "Mr. X," the suggestion is that Umkhonto was the inspiration of the Communist Party which sought by playing upon imaginary grievances to enroll the African people into an army which ostensibly was to fight for African freedom, but in reality was fighting for a communist state. Nothing could be further from the truth. In fact the suggestion is preposterous. Umkhonto was formed by Africans to further their struggle for freedom in their own land. Communists and others supported the movement, and we only wish that more sections of the community would join us.

Our fight is against real, and not imaginary, hardships or, to use the language of the State Prosecutor, "so-called hardships." Basically, we fight against two features which are the hallmarks of African life in South Africa and which are entrenched by legislation which we seek to have repealed. These features are poverty and lack of human dignity, and we do not need communists or so-called "agitators" to teach us about these things.

South Africa is the richest country in Africa, and could be one of the richest countries in the world. But it is a land of extremes and remarkable contrasts. The whites enjoy what may well be the highest standard of living in the world, whilst Africans live in poverty and misery. Forty per cent of the Africans live in hopelessly overcrowded and, in some cases, drought-stricken Reserves, where soil erosion and the overworking of the soil makes it impossible for them to live properly off the land. Thirty per cent are labourers, labour tenants, and squatters on white farms and work and live under conditions similar to those of the serfs of the Middle Ages. The other 30 per cent live in towns where they have developed economic and social habits which bring them closer in many respects to white standards. Yet most Africans, even in this group, are impoverished by low incomes and high cost of living.

The highest-paid and the most prosperous section of urban African life is in Johannesburg. Yet their actual position is desperate. The latest figures were given on 25 March 1964 by Mr. Carr, Manager of the Johannesburg Non-European Affairs Department. The poverty datum line for the average African family in Johannesburg (according to Mr. Carr's department) is R42.84 per month. He showed that the average monthly wage is R32.24 and that 46 per cent of all African families in Johannesburg do not earn enough to keep them going.

Poverty goes hand in hand with malnutrition and disease. The incidence of malnutrition and deficiency diseases is very high amongst Africans. Tuberculosis, pellagra, kwashiorkor, gastro-enteritis, and scurvy bring death and destruction of health. The incidence of infant mortality is one of the highest in the world . . .

The complaint of Africans, however, is not only that they are poor and the whites are rich, but that the laws which are made by the whites are designed to preserve this situation. There are two ways to break out of poverty. The first is by formal education, and the second is by the worker acquiring a greater skill at his work and thus higher wages. As far as Africans are concerned, both these avenues of advancement are deliberately curtailed by legislation.

The present Government has always sought to hamper Africans in their search for education. One of their early acts, after coming into power, was to stop subsidies for African school feeding. Many African children who attended schools depended on this supplement to their diet. This was a cruel act.

There is compulsory education for all white children at virtually no cost to their parents, be they rich or poor. Similar facilities are not provided for the African children, though there are some who receive such assistance. African children, however, generally have to pay more for their schooling than whites. According to figures quoted by the South African Institute of Race Relations in its 1963 journal, approximately 40 per cent of African children in the age group between seven to fourteen do not attend school. For those who do attend school, the standards are vastly different from those afforded to white children. In 1960–61 the per capita Government spending on African students at State-aided schools was estimated at R12.46. In the same years, the per capita spending on white children in the Cape Province (which are the only figures available to me) was R144.57. Although there are no figures available to me, it can be stated, without doubt, that the white children on whom R144.57 per head was being spent all came from wealthier homes than African children on whom R12.46 per head was being spent.

The quality of education is also different. According to the Bantu Educational Journal, only 5,660 African children in the whole of South Africa passed their Junior Certificate in 1962, and in that year only 362 passed matriculation.[1] This is presumably consistent with the policy of Bantu education about which the present Prime Minister said, during the debate on the Bantu Education Bill in 1953:

"When I have control of Native education I will reform it so that Natives will be taught from childhood to realize that equality with Europeans is not for them. . . . People who believe in

equality are not desirable teachers for Natives. When my Department controls Native education it will know for what class of higher education a Native is fitted, and whether he will have a chance in life to use his knowledge."

The other main obstacle to the economic advancement of the African is the industrial colour-bar under which all the better jobs of industry are reserved for Whites only. Moreover, Africans who do obtain employment in the unskilled and semi-skilled occupations which are open to them are not allowed to form trade unions which have recognition under the Industrial Conciliation Act. This means that strikes of African workers are illegal, and that they are denied the right of collective bargaining which is permitted to the better-paid White workers . . .

The Government often answers its critics by saying that Africans in South Africa are economically better off than the inhabitants of the other countries in Africa. I do not know whether this statement is true and doubt whether any comparison can be made without having regard to the cost-of-living index in such countries. But even if it is true, as far as the African people are concerned it is irrelevant. Our complaint is not that we are poor by comparison with people in other countries, but that we are poor by comparison with the white people in our own country, and that we are prevented by legislation from altering this imbalance.

The lack of human dignity experienced by Africans is the direct result of the policy of white supremacy. White supremacy implies black inferiority. Legislation designed to preserve white supremacy entrenches this notion. Menial tasks in South Africa are invariably performed by Africans. When anything has to be carried or cleaned the white man will look around for an African to do it for him, whether the African is employed by him or not. Because of this sort of attitude, whites tend to regard Africans as a separate breed. They do not look upon them as people with families of their own; they do not realize that they have emotions—that

---

1. The Junior Certificate examination was generally taken by white children at the age of 15 and they could not normally leave school before this. Matriculation was taken two years later and qualified students for higher education. The educational system, however, ensured that very few Africans reached Junior Certificate level, so that what represented a basic standard for whites was one of achievement for Africans. Even fewer attained matriculation level.

they fall in love like white people do; that they want to be with their wives and children like white people want to be with theirs; that they want to earn enough money to support their families properly, to feed and clothe them and send them to school. And what "house-boy" or "garden-boy" or labourer can ever hope to do this?

Pass laws, which to the Africans are among the most hated bits of legislation in South Africa, render any African liable to police surveillance at any time. I doubt whether there is a single African male in South Africa who has not at some stage had a brush with the police over his pass. Hundreds and thousands of Africans are thrown into jail each year under pass laws. Even worse than this is the fact that pass laws keep husband and wife apart and lead to the breakdown of family life.

Poverty and the breakdown of family life have secondary effects. Children wander about the streets of the townships because they have no schools to go to, or no money to enable them to go to school, or no parents at home to see that they go to school, because both parents (if there be two) have to work to keep the family alive. This leads to a breakdown in moral standards, to an alarming rise in illegitimacy, and to growing violence which erupts not only politically, but everywhere. Life in the townships is dangerous. There is not a day that goes by without somebody being stabbed or assaulted. And violence is carried out of the townships in the white living areas. People are afraid to walk alone in the streets after dark. Housebreakings and robberies are increasing, despite the fact that the death sentence can now be imposed for such offences. Death sentences cannot cure the festering sore.

Africans want to be paid a living wage. Africans want to perform work which they are capable of doing, and not work which the Government declares them to be capable of. Africans want to be allowed to live where they obtain work, and not be endorsed out of an area because they were not born there. Africans want to be allowed to own land in places where they work, and not to be obliged to live in rented houses which they can never call their own. Africans want to be part of the general population, and not confined to living in their own ghettoes. African men want to have their wives and children to live with them where they work, and not be forced into an unnatural existence in men's hostels. African women want to be with their menfolk and not be left permanently widowed in the Reserves. Africans want to be allowed out after eleven o'clock at night and not to be confined to their rooms like little children. Africans want to be allowed to travel in their own country and to seek work where they want to and not where the Labour Bureau tells them to. Africans want a just share in the whole of South Africa; they want security and a stake in society.

Above all, we want equal political rights, because without them our disabilities will be permanent. I know this sounds revolutionary to the whites in this country, because the majority of voters will be Africans. This makes the white man fear democracy.

But this fear cannot be allowed to stand in the way of the only solution which will guarantee racial harmony and freedom for all. It is not true that the enfranchisement of all will result in racial domination. Political division, based on colour, is entirely artificial and, when it disappears, so will the domination of one colour group by another. The ANC has spent half a century fighting against racialism. When it triumphs it will not change that policy.

This then is what the ANC is fighting. Their struggle is a truly national one. It is a struggle of the African people, inspired by their own suffering and their own experience. It is a struggle for the right to live.

During my lifetime I have dedicated myself to this struggle of the African people. I have fought against white domination, and I have fought against black domination. I have cherished the ideal of a democratic and free society in which all persons live together in harmony and with equal opportunities. It is an ideal which I hope to live for and to achieve. But if needs be, it is an ideal for which I am prepared to die.

Steve Biko: "White Racism and Black Consciousness: The Totality of White Power in South Africa"[1]

Editor's Comment: Stephen Biko was an articulate leader of the Black Consciousness Movement in South Africa. Influenced in part by the teachings of African-American civil rights leaders in the United States, he became an important voice for the empowerment of Africans. Following his assassination in 1977, his funeral was attended by 10,000 people, highlighting his significance both nationally and internationally. What does he have to say about white liberal anti-apartheid groups and why is he critical of cooperation with them? How does Biko see the problems of South Africa as related to social structures and not just government alone? In his view, how does white privilege prevent the possibility of a complete investment by most whites in systemic reform? How does he think liberals should act and understand their role in resistance? What does Biko mean by "Black Consciousness"? Why did its emergence contrast and confront the traditional leadership of the ANC? How is Biko's articulation of Black Consciousness also a critique of colonialism?

"No race possesses the monopoly of beauty, intelligence, force, and there is room for all of us at the rendezvous of victory." I do not think Aimé Césaire was thinking about South Africa when he said these words. The whites in this country have placed themselves on a path of no return. So blatantly exploitative in terms of the mind and body is the practice of white racism that one wonders if the interests of blacks and whites in this country have not become so mutually exclusive as to exclude the possibility of there being "room for all of us at the rendezvous of victory."

---

1. Speech given to the Abe Bailey Institute, Cape Town, January 1971. Excerpt taken from Steve Biko, *I Write What I Like*, 2004 [1978]. Used by permission of the Steve Biko Foundation.

The white man's quest for power has led him to destroy with utter ruthlessness whatever has stood in his way. In an effort to divide the black world in terms of aspirations, the powers that be have evolved a philosophy that stratifies the black world and gives preferential treatment to certain groups. Further, they have built up several tribal cocoons, thereby hoping to increase inter-tribal ill-feeling and to divert the energies of the black people towards attaining false prescribed "freedoms." Moreover, it was hoped, the black people could be effectively contained in these various cocoons of repression, euphemistically referred to as "home-lands." At some stage, however, the powers that be had to start defining the sphere of activity of these apartheid institutions. Most blacks suspected initially the barrenness of the promise and have now realised that they have been taken for a big ride. Just as the Native Representative Council became a political flop that embarrassed its creators, I predict that a time will come when these stooge bodies will prove very costly not only in terms of money but also in terms of the credibility of the story the Nationalists are trying to sell. In the meantime, the blacks are beginning to realise the need to rally around the cause of their suffering—their black skin—and to ignore the false promises that come from the white world.

Then again the progressively sterner legislation that has lately filled the South African statute books has had a great effect in convincing the people of the evil inherent in the system of apartheid. No amount of propaganda on Radio Bantu or promises of freedom being granted to some desert homeland will ever convince the blacks that the government means well, so long as they experience manifesta-tions of the lack of respect for the dignity of man and for his property as shown during the mass removals of Africans from the urban areas. The unnecessary harassment of Africans by police, both in towns and inside townships, and the ruthless application of that scourge of the people, the pass laws, are constant reminders that the white man is on top and that the blacks are only tolerated—with the greatest restraints. Needless to say, anyone finding himself at the receiving end of such deliberate (though uncalled for) cruelty must ultimately ask himself the question: what do I have to lose? This is what the blacks are beginning to ask themselves.

. . . The flirtation between the Progressive Party and blacks was brought to a rude stop by legislation. . . . The Progressives have never been a black man's real hope. They have always been a white party at heart, fighting for a more lasting way of preserving white values in this southern tip of Africa. It will not be long before the blacks relate their poverty to their blackness in concrete terms. Because of the tradition forced onto the country, the poor people shall always be black people. It is not surprising, therefore, that the blacks should wish to rid themselves of a system that locks up the wealth of the country in the hands of a few. No doubt Rick Turner was thinking of this when he declared that "any black government is likely to be socialist," in his article on "The Relevance of Contemporary Radical Thought."

We now come to the group that has longest enjoyed confidence from the black world—the liberal establishment, including radical and leftist groups. The biggest mistake the black world ever made was to assume that whoever opposed apartheid was an ally. For a long time the black world has been looking only at the governing party and not so much at the whole power structure as the object of their rage. In a sense the very political vocabulary that the blacks have used has been inherited from the liberals. Therefore it is not surprising that alliances were formed so easily with the liberals.

Who are the liberals in South Africa? It is that curious bunch of non-conformists who explain their participation in negative terms; that bunch of do-gooders that goes under all sorts of names— liberals, leftists, etc. These are the people who argue that they are not responsible for white racism and the country's "inhumanity to the black man"; these are the people who claim that they too feel the oppression just as acutely as the blacks and therefore should be jointly involved in the black

man's struggle for a place under the sun; in short, these are the people who say that they have black souls wrapped up in white skins.

The liberals set about their business with the utmost efficiency. They made it a political dogma that all groups opposing the status quo must necessarily be non-racial in structure. They maintained that if you stood for a principle of non-racialism you could not in any way adopt what they described as racialist policies. They even defined to the black people what the latter should fight for.

With this sort of influence behind them, most black leaders tended to rely too much on the advice of liberals. For a long time, in fact, it became the occupation of the leadership to "calm the masses down," while they engaged in fruitless negotiation with the status quo. Their whole political action, in fact, was a programmed course in the art of gentle persuasion through protests and limited boycotts and they hoped the rest could be safely left to the troubled conscience of the fair-minded English folk.

Of course this situation could not last. A new breed of black leaders was beginning to take a dim view of the involvement of liberals in a struggle that they regarded as essentially theirs . . .

It never occurred to the liberals that the integration they insisted upon as an effective way of opposing apartheid was impossible to achieve in South Africa. It had to be artificial because it was being foisted on two parties whose entire upbringing had been to support the lie that one race was superior and others inferior. One has to overhaul the whole system in South Africa before hoping to get black and white walking hand in hand to oppose a common enemy. As it is, both black and white walk into a hastily organised integrated circle carrying with them the seeds of destruction of that circle—their inferiority and superiority complexes.

The myth of integration as propounded under the banner of the liberal ideology must be cracked and killed because it makes people believe that something is being done when in reality the artificially integrated circles are a soporific to the blacks while salving the consciences of the guilt-stricken white. It works from the false premise that, because it is difficult to bring people from different races together in this country, achievement of this is in itself a step towards the total liberation of the blacks. Nothing could be more misleading.

How many white people fighting for their version of a change in South Africa are really motivated by genuine concern and not by guilt? Obviously it is a cruel assumption to believe that all whites are not sincere, yet methods adopted by some groups often do suggest a lack of real commitment. The essence of politics is to direct oneself to the group which wields power. Most white dissident groups are aware of the power wielded by the white power structure. They are quick to quote statistics on how big the defence budget is. They know exactly how effectively the police and the army can control protesting black hordes—peaceful or otherwise. They know to what degree the black world is infiltrated by the security police. Hence they are completely convinced of the impotence of the black people. Why then do they persist in talking to the blacks? Since they are aware that the problem in this country is white racism, why do they not address themselves to the white world? Why do they insist on talking to blacks?

In an effort to answer these questions one has to come to the painful conclusion that the liberal is in fact appeasing his own conscience, or at best is eager to demonstrate his identification with the black people only so far as it does not sever all his ties with his relatives on the other side of the colour line. Being white, he possesses the natural passport to the exclusive pool of white privileges from which he does not hesitate to extract whatever suits him. Yet, since he identifies with the blacks, he moves around his white circles—white-only beaches, restaurants, and cinemas—with a lighter load, feeling that he is not like the rest. Yet at the back of his mind is a constant reminder that he is quite comfortable as things stand and therefore should not bother about change. Although he does not vote for the Nationalists (now that they are in the majority anyway), he feels secure under the protection offered by the Nationalists and subconsciously shuns the idea of change.

The limitations that have accompanied the involvement of liberals in the black man's struggle have been mostly responsible for the arrest of progress. Because of their inferiority complex, blacks have tended to listen seriously to what the liberals had to say. With their characteristic arrogance of assuming a "monopoly on intelligence and moral judgment," these self-appointed trustees of black interests have gone on to set the pattern and pace for the realisation of the black man's aspirations.

I am not sneering at the liberals and their involvement. Neither am I suggesting that they are the most to blame for the black man's plight. Rather I am illustrating the fundamental fact that total identification with an oppressed group in a system that forces one group to enjoy privilege and to live on the sweat of another, is impossible. White society collectively owes the blacks so huge a debt that no one member should automatically expect to escape from the blanket condemnation that needs must come from the black world. It is not as if whites are allowed to enjoy privilege only when they declare their solidarity with the ruling party. They are born into privilege and are nourished by and nurtured in the system of ruthless exploitation of black energy. For the 20-year-old white liberal to expect to be accepted with open arms is surely to overestimate the powers of forgiveness of the black people. No matter how genuine a liberal's motivations may be, he has to accept that, though he did not choose to be born into privilege, the blacks cannot but be suspicious of his motives.

The liberal must fight on his own and for himself. If they are true liberals they must realise that they themselves are oppressed, and that they must fight for their own freedom and not that of the nebulous "they" with whom they can hardly claim identification.

What I have tried to show is that in South Africa political power has always rested with white society. Not only have the whites been guilty of being on the offensive but, by some skilful manoeuvres, they have managed to control the responses of the blacks to the provocation. Not only have they kicked the black but they have also told him how to react to the kick. For a long time the black has been listening with patience to the advice he has been receiving on how best to respond to the kick. With painful slowness he is now beginning to show signs that it is his right and duty to respond to the kick in the way he sees fit.

Black Consciousness

"We Coloured men, in this specific moment of historical evolution, have consciously grasped in its full breath, the notion of our peculiar uniqueness, the notion of just who we are and what, and that we are ready, on every plane and in every department, to assume the responsibilities which proceed from this coming into consciousness. The peculiarity of our place in the world is not to be confused with anyone else's. The peculiarity of our problems which aren't to be reduced to subordinate forms of any other problem. The peculiarity of our history, laced with terrible misfortunes which belong to no other history. The peculiarity of our culture, which we intend to live and to make live in an ever realler manner." (Aimé Césaire, 1956, in his letter of resignation from the French Communist Party.)

At about the same time that Césaire said this, there was emerging in South Africa a group of angry young black men who were beginning to "grasp the notion of (their) peculiar uniqueness" and who were eager to define who they were and what. These were the elements who were disgruntled with the direction imposed on the African National Congress by the "old guard" within its leadership. These young men were questioning a number of things, among which was the "go slow" attitude adopted by the leadership, and the ease with which the leadership accepted coalitions with organisations other than those run by blacks. The "People's Charter" adopted in Kliptown in 1955 was evidence of this. In a sense one can say that these were the first real signs that the blacks in South Africa were beginning to realise the need to go it alone and to evolve a philosophy based on, and directed by, blacks. In other words, Black Consciousness was slowly manifesting itself.

. . . The emergence of SASO [South African Students' Organisation] and its tough policy of non-involvement with the white world set people's minds thinking along new lines. This was a challenge to the age-old tradition in South Africa that opposition to apartheid was enough to qualify whites for acceptance by the black world. Despite protest and charges of racialism from liberal-minded white students, the black students stood firm in their rejection of the principle of unholy alliances between blacks and whites. A spokesman of the new right-of-middle group, NAFSAS, was treated to a dose of the new thinking when a black student told him that "we shall lead ourselves, be it to the sea, to the mountain or to the desert; we shall have nothing to do with white students."

The importance of the SASO stand is not really to be found in SASO per se—for SASO has the natural limitations of being a student organisation with an ever-changing membership. Rather it is to be found in the fact that this new approach opened a huge crack in the traditional approach and made the blacks sit up and think again. It heralded a new era in which blacks are beginning to take care of their own business and to see with greater clarity the immensity of their responsibility.

The call for Black Consciousness is the most positive call to come from any group in the black world for a long time. It is more than just a reactionary rejection of whites by blacks. The quintessence of it is the realisation by the blacks that, in order to feature well in this game of power politics, they have to use the concept of group power and to build a strong foundation for this. Being an historically, politically, socially and economically disinherited and dispossessed group, they have the strongest foundation from which to operate. The philosophy of Black Consciousness, therefore, expresses group pride and the determination by the blacks to rise and attain the envisaged self. At the heart of this kind of thinking is the realisation by the blacks that the most potent weapon in the hands of the oppressor is the mind of the oppressed. Once the latter has been so effectively manipulated and controlled by the oppressor as to make the oppressed believe that he is a liability to the white man, then there will be nothing the oppressed can do that will really scare the powerful masters. Hence thinking along lines of Black Consciousness makes the black man see himself as a being, entire in himself, and not as an extension of a broom or additional leverage to some machine. At the end of it all, he cannot tolerate attempts by anybody to dwarf the significance of his manhood. Once this happens, we shall know that the real man in the black person is beginning to shine through.

. . . The growth of awareness among South African blacks has often been ascribed to influence from the American "Negro" movement. Yet it seems to me that this is a sequel to the attainment of independence by so many African states within so short a time . . . The fact that American terminology has often been used to express our thoughts is merely because all new ideas seem to get extensive publicity in the United States.

National consciousness and its spread in South Africa has to work against a number of factors. First there are the traditional complexes, then the emptiness of the native's past and lastly the question of black-white dependency. The traditional inferior-superior black-white complexes are deliberate creations of the colonialist. Through the work of missionaries and kind of god whose word could not be doubted. As Fanon puts it: "Colonialism is not satisfied merely with holding a people in its grip and emptying the Native's brain of all form and content; by a kind of perverted logic, it turns to the past of the oppressed people and distorts, disfigures, and destroys it." At the end of it all, the

blacks have nothing to lean on, nothing to cheer them up at the present moment and very much to be afraid of in the future.

The attitude of some rural African folk who are against education is often misunderstood, not least by the African intellectual. Yet the reasons put forward by these people carry with them the realisation of their inherent dignity and worth. They see education as the quickest way of destroying the substance of the African culture. They complain bitterly of the disruption in the life pattern, non-observation of customs, and constant derision from the nonconformists whenever any of them go through school. Lack of respect for the elders is, in the African tradition, an unforgivable and cardinal sin. Yet how can one prevent the loss of respect of child for father when the child is actively taught by his know-all white tutors to disregard his family's teachings? How can an African avoid losing respect for his tradition when in school his whole cultural background is summed up in one word: barbarism?

To add to the white-oriented education received, the whole history of the black people is presented as a long lamentation of repeated defeats. Strangely enough, everybody has come to accept that the history of South Africa starts in 1652. No doubt this is to support the often-told lie that blacks arrived in this country at about the same time as the whites . . .

Our culture must be defined in concrete terms. We must relate the past to the present and demonstrate an historical evolution of the modern African. We must reject the attempts by the powers that be to project an arrested image of our culture. This is not the sum total of our culture. They have deliberately arrested our culture at the tribal stage to perpetuate the myth that African people were near cannibals, had no real ambitions in life, and were preoccupied with sex and drink. In fact the wide-spread vice often found in the African townships is a result of the interference of the White man in the natural evolution of the true native culture. "Wherever colonisation is a fact, the indigenous culture begins to rot and among the ruins something begins to be born which is condemned to exist on the margin allowed it by the European culture." It is through the evolution of our genuine culture that our identity can be fully rediscovered.

We must seek to restore to the black people a sense of the great stress we used to lay on the value of human relationships; to highlight the fact that in the pre-Van Riebeeck days we had a high regard for people, their property and for life in general; to reduce the hold of technology over man and to reduce the materialistic element that is slowly creeping into the African character. "Is there any way that my people can have the blessings of technology without being eaten away by materialism and losing the spiritual dimension from their lives?" asks President Kaunda and then, talking of the typical tribal African community, he says:

> *Those people who are dependent upon and live in closest relationship with Nature are most conscious of the operation of these forces: the pulse of their lives beats in harmony with the pulse of the Universe; they may be simple and unlettered people and their horizons may be strictly limited, yet I believe that they inhabit a larger world than the sophisticated Westerner who has magnified his physical senses through invented gadgets at the price, all too often, of cutting out the dimension of the spiritual.*

. . . As the situation stands today, money from the black world tends to take a unidirectional flow to the white society. Blacks buy from white supermarkets, white greengrocers, white bottle stores, white chemists, and, to crown it all, those who can, bank at white-owned banks. Needless to say, they travel to work in government-owned trains or white-owned buses. If then we wish to make use of the little we have to improve our lot, it can only lead to greater awareness of the power we wield as a group. The "Buy Black" campaign that is being waged by some people in the Johannesburg area must not be scoffed at.

It is often claimed that the advocates of Black Consciousness are hemming themselves in into a closed world, choosing to weep on each other's shoulders and thereby cutting out useful dialogue with the rest of the world. Yet I feel that the black people of the world, in choosing to reject the legacy of colonialism and white domination and to build around themselves their own values, standards and outlook to life, have at last established a solid base for meaningful cooperation amongst themselves in the larger battle of the Third World against the rich nations. As Fanon puts it; "The consciousness of the self is not the closing of a door to communication. . . . National consciousness, which is not nationalism, is the only thing that will give us an international dimension." This is an encouraging sign, for there is no doubt that the black-white power struggle in South Africa is but a microcosm of the global confrontation between the Third World and the rich white nations of the world which is manifesting itself in an ever more real manner as the years go by.

Thus, in this age and day, one cannot but welcome the evolution of a positive outlook in the black world. . . . We have in us the will to live through these trying times; over the years we have attained moral superiority over the white man; we shall watch as time destroys his paper castles and know that all these little pranks were but frantic attempts of frightened little people to convince each other that they can control the minds and bodies of indigenous people of Africa indefinitely.

Statement by the UDF National Executive Committee on National Launching of UDF (1983)[1]

Editor's Note: The UDF was the largest antiapartheid organization operating in the 1980s, at a time when all other organizations had been banned and their leaders imprisoned or driven into exile. Largely an ANC front organization, the UDF presented itself as a

1. Used by permission of the ANC Archives.

coalition of local, grassroots, community and student organizations that shared opposition to the apartheid policies of President P. W. Botha. Botha attempted to put a friendly face on apartheid while painting its opponents as part of a communist "total onslaught" against South Africa. One of his projects was the Koornhof plan to create city councils in the townships and give them a veneer of being representative. They were intensely disliked by township residents, and much UDF protest was directed at these councils, who were regarded as puppets of the Botha regime.

The national executive committee of the United Democratic Front (UDF) met in Johannesburg on Saturday July 30 and Sunday July 31. It was decided that the UDF should be launched nationally in Cape Town at a People's rally on August 20. The executive meeting brought together the leadership of the Transvaal, Natal and Western Cape UDF's. The purpose of the meeting was to define a common approach and policy in resistance to the constitutional and Koornhof Bills. This meeting was the result of months of hard work, concerted efforts and mass consultations with organisations and individuals throughout the country.

Over the past six months a number of fully constituted units of the UDF have emerged. A UDF was launched in Natal in May, in the Transvaal in the same month, and in the Cape in July. This executive meeting therefore reflected the aspirations and expectations of the vast majority of the oppressed masses.

The strength of the UDF lies in the democratic nature of its composition. The central characteristic of the UDF is that it is made up of trade unions as well as community, women's student, religious, youth, sports, political, professional, and business organisations and interest groups. These organisations represent people of all colours and creeds from all strata of South African society.

All have clearly rejected the constitutional and Koornhof Bills. All of us have recognised that these manoeuvres of the state are designed to weaken the people's resistance by dividing them whilst entrenching apartheid. We have firmly and unanimously committed ourselves to the achievement of a democratic society under the banner of the UDF through the active participation of thousands of members of our organisations.

A declaration of policy and intent has evolved and is in the process of being finalised. The conscience and the moral impulse of all freedomloving people of South Africa have been aroused. People have been moved to reject these pernicious and evil laws which consolidate the heresy of apartheid.

Whilst the UDF articulates the viewpoint of the broad cross-section of people, we accept as fundamental that the main burden of exploitation and discrimination falls on the poor.

Accordingly, the main thrust of the organisation is directed towards the participation of working people in the workplace, in the communities and wherever they may be.

We call upon all democratic organisations who have not as yet identified with the UDF to join us and further unify the resistance to these new Bills.

The grand design of apartheid is to fragment our people's unity. And those who deliberately refrain from helping us to maximise this unity advance the cause of the enemy and delay the cause of democracy.

At this stage in constructing unity, hundreds of organisations are already an integral part of the UDF. This process continues.

The UDF draws inspiration from the overwhelming support and commitment of the people. And we announce the national launching of the UNITED DEMOCRATIC FRONT in CAPE TOWN on August 20 1983.

This historic event is the culmination of the first phase of this process. It is tangible manifestation of the indomitable will of the people and is a momentous step on the long road to freedom.

ISSUED BY: National Executive Committee of the United Democratic Front Johannesburg,

1 August 1983
  UDF Press Conference
  Khotso House, Johannesburg

List of Organisations which Support and Are Affiliates of the RegionalUDF

TRANSVAAL

Labour Organisations

- General and Allied Workers Union
- Municipal and General Workers' Union
- Council of Unions of South Africa
- South African Allied Workers Union
- Commercial and Catering Workers Union of South Africa
- SA Mine Workers Union
- Johannesburg Scooter Drivers' Association

Civic Organisations

- Soweto Civic Associations
- Huhudi Civic Association
- Mohalakeng Civic Association
- Kagiso Residents' Organisation
- Winterveld Action Committee
- East Rand People's Organisation
- Soweto Residents' Association
- Mamelodi Action Committee

Political

- Committee of Ten
- Transvaal Indian Congress
- Transvaal Anti-President's Council Committee
- Anti-Community Council Committee

Youth And Students

- Azanian Students' Organisation
- Congress of South African Students
- National Union of South African Students
- Young Christian Students
- Young Christian Workers
- Soweto Youth Congress
- Catholic Students Association

Church

- Witwatersrand Council of Churches
- Islamic Council of South Africa

Women

- Federation of South African Women

Others

- Detainees Aid Movement
- National Educational Union of South Africa
- Detainees' Parents Support Committee
- Khuvangano

NATAL

Labour

- South African Allied Workers Union
- Tin Workers
- African Workers Association
- National Federation of Workers
- Council of Unions of South Africa

Civic

- Joint Rent Action Committee
- Durban Housing Action Committee
- Phoenix Working Committee
- Newlands East Residents Association
- Chatsworth Housing Action Committee
- Joint Commuters Committee
- Tongaat Civic Association
- Pietermaritzburg Combined Ratepayers Association
- Reservoir Hills Ratepayers Association
- Verulam Housing Action Committee
- Merebank Ratepayers Association
- Greenwoodpark Ratepayers Association
- Asherville Housing Action Committee
- St Wendolins Welfare Committee
- Isulumusi Inanda

Church

- Diakonia
- Islamic Council of South Africa

Political
- Natal Indian Congress
- Release Mandela Committee
- Detainees Support Committee
- Black Sash
- Natal Anti-SAIC Committee

Youth and Student
- Azaso
- Univeristy of Natal, Durban, Student Representative Council
- COSAS
- Merebank Ex-Student Society
- MSRC (Medical Students Representative Council)
- University of Durban-Westville SRC
- Lamontville Youth Organisation

Women
- Women for Peaceful Change Now
- Durban Women's Group

UDF
- North Coast Region UDF
- Western Areas Region UDF

WESTERN CAPE
Civic
- The Cape Areas Housing Action Committee
- The Western Cape Civic Association

Women
- The United Women's Organisation

Student and Youth
- The Azanian Students' Organisation
- The Congress of South African Students
- The Cape Youth Congress
- The Inter-Church Youth
- The National Union of South African Students

Labour
- The Media Workers Association
- The South African Food and Canning Workers Union
- The Cape Town Municipality Workers Association
- The General Workers Union

Church
- The Muslim Judicial Council
- The Ecumenical Action Movement
- The Islamic Council of South Africa
- The Western Province Council of Churches

Traders
- The Western Cape Traders Association

Interim Publicity Secretary of the UDF
Zac Yacoob

The Kairos Document: Challenge to the Church (1985)

A Theological Comment on the Political Crisis in South Africa[1]

Editor's Note: One of the challenges faced by opponents to apartheid was the longstanding support that white supremacy had received from The Dutch Reformed Church and other Christian denominations. Signed by 156 theologians and ministers of different races and denominations, the Kairos Document provided the theological and religious critique of apartheid needed to strengthen resolve among antiapartheid activists, most of whom also were Christians, gain backing from world religious organizations, and weaken religious support inside South Africa for the National government and its policies. How does this document use Christian theology and biblical interpretation to discuss the nature of justice? How does the Kairos Document address the idea of reconciliation as a response to the injustices of the

1. Kairos Theologians, *Kairos Document: Challenge to the Church*, used by permission of South African History Online (www.sahistory.org.za).

apartheid system? What does this document from Christian denominations say about resistance and the use of violence and how does it rationalize its position on this issue?

The Kairos Document Preface

The Kairos Document is a Christian, biblical and theological comment on the political crisis in South Africa today. It is an attempt by concerned Christians in South Africa to reflect on the situation of death in our country. It is a critique of the current theological models that determine the type of activities the Church engages in to try to resolve the problems of the country. It is an attempt to develop, out of this perplexing situation, an alternative biblical and theological model that will in turn lead to forms of activity that will make a real difference to the future of our country.

Of particular interest is the way the theological material was produced. In June 1985 as the crisis was intensifying in the country, as more and more people were killed, maimed and imprisoned, as one black township after another revolted against the apartheid regime, as the people refused to be oppressed or to co-operate with oppressors, facing death by the day, and as the apartheid army moved into the townships to rule by the barrel of the gun, a number of theologians who were concerned about the situation expressed the need to reflect on this situation to determine what response by the Church and by all Christians in South Africa would be most appropriate.

A first discussion group met at the beginning of July in the heart of Soweto. Participants spoke freely about the situation and the various responses of the Church, Church leaders, and Christians. A critique of these responses was made and the theology from which these responses flowed was also subjected to a critical analysis. Individual members of the group were assigned to put together material on specific themes which were raised during the discussion and to present the material to the next session of the group.

At the second meeting the material itself was subjected to a critique and various people were commissioned to do more investigations on specific problematic areas. The latest findings with the rest of the material were collated and presented to the third meeting where more than thirty people, consisting of theologians, ordinary Christians (lay theologians) and some Church leaders.

After a very extensive discussion some adjustments and additions were made especially in regard to the section entitled "Challenge to Action." The group then appointed a committee to subject the document to further critique by various other Christian groupings throughout the country. Everybody was told that "this was a people's document which you can also own even by demolishing it if your position can stand the test of biblical faith and Christian experience in South Africa." They were told that this was an open-ended document which will never be said to be final.

The "Working Committee," as it was called, was inundated with comments, suggestions and enthusiastic appreciation from various groups and individuals in the country. By the 13th of September 1985 when the document was submitted for publication there were still comments and recommendations flowing in. The first publication therefore must be taken as a beginning, a basis for further discussion by all Christians in the country. Further editions will be published later.

—25 September 1985, Johannesburg

Chapter One

Editor's Comment: Keep in mind that the international context of the apartheid system and the responses to it was the Cold War struggle, which was often defined as a struggle between democratic capitalism and communist atheistic authoritarianism, a conceptual schism to which the National Party government often appealed in its search for both domestic and international support. What is the meaning of the term "Kairos," and why is it important to the authors of this document? How has apartheid

*created a crisis for Christian faith? How does the
document distinguish between different modes of
theology and why is that important for understanding
social and political forces? Why does the way that the
Bible is used and interpreted matter? What does the
document assert about the God of "State Theology,"
and how does this suggestion derive from concepts of
justice?*

THE MOMENT OF TRUTH

The time has come. The moment of truth has
arrived. South Africa has been plunged into a crisis
that is shaking the foundations and there is every
indication that the crisis has only just begun and
that it will deepen and become even more threatening in the months to come. It is the KAIROS or
moment of truth not only for apartheid but also for
the Church.

We as a group of theologians have been trying to
understand the theological significance of this
moment in our history. It is serious, very serious.
For very many Christians in South Africa this is the
KAIROS, the moment of grace and opportunity, the
favorable time in which God issues a challenge to
decisive action. It is a dangerous time because,
if this opportunity is missed, and allowed to pass
by, the loss for the Church, for the Gospel and for
all the people of South Africa will be immeasur-
able. Jesus wept over Jerusalem. He wept over the
tragedy of the destruction of the city and the
massacre of the people that was imminent, "and all
because you did not recognize your opportunity
(KAIROS) when God offered it" (Lk 19:44).

A crisis is a judgment that brings out the best in
some people and the worst in others. A crisis is a
moment of truth that shows us up for what we
really are. There will be no place to hide and no
way of pretending to be what we are not in fact. At
this moment in South Africa the Church is about to
be shown up for what it really is and no cover-up
will be possible.

What the present crisis shows up, although
many of us have known it all along, is that the
Church is divided. More and more people are now
saying that there are in fact two Churches in South
Africa—a White Church and a Black Church. Even
within the same denomination there are in fact
two Churches. In the life and death conflict
between different social forces that has come to a
head in South Africa today, there are Christians (or
at least people who profess to be Christians) on
both sides of the conflict—and some who are
trying to sit on the fence!

Does this prove that Christian faith has no real
meaning or relevance for our times? Does it show
that the Bible can be used for any purpose at all?
Such problems would be critical enough for the
Church in any circumstances but when we also
come to see that the conflict in South Africa is
between the oppressor and the oppressed, the
crisis for the Church as an institution becomes
much more acute. Both oppressor and oppressed
claim loyalty to the same Church. They are both
baptized in the same baptism and participate
together in the breaking of the same bread, the
same body and blood of Christ. There we sit in
the same Church while outside Christian policemen and soldiers are beating up and killing
Christian children or torturing Christian prisoners
to death while yet other Christians stand by and
weakly plead for peace.

The Church is divided and its Day of Judgment
has come.

The moment of truth has compelled us to
analyze more carefully the different theologies in
our Churches and to speak out more clearly and
boldly about the real significance of these theologies. We have been able to isolate three theologies
and we have chosen to call them "State Theology,"
"Church Theology," and "Prophetic Theology." In
our thoroughgoing criticism of the first and second
theologies we do not wish to mince our words. The
situation is too critical for that.

Chapter Two
CRITIQUE OF STATE THEOLOGY

The South African apartheid State has a theology of its own and we have chosen to call it "State

Theology." "State Theology" is simply the theological justification of the status quo with its racism, capitalism and totalitarianism. It blesses injustice, canonizes the will of the powerful and reduces the poor to passivity, obedience and apathy.

How does "State Theology" do this? It does it by misusing theological concepts and biblical texts for its own political purposes. In this document we would like to draw your attention to four key examples of how this is done in South Africa. The first would be the use of Romans 13:1–7 to give an absolute and "divine" authority to the State. The second would be the use of the idea of "Law and Order" to determine and control what the people may be permitted to regard as just and unjust. The third would be the use of the word "communist" to brand anyone who rejects "State Theology." And finally there is the use that is made of the name of God.

2.1 Romans 13:1–7   The misuse of this famous text is not confined to the present government in South Africa. Throughout the history of Christianity totalitarian regimes have tried to legitimize an attitude of blind obedience and absolute servility towards the state by quoting this text. The well-known theologian Oscar Cullman, pointed this out thirty years ago:

As soon as Christians, out of loyalty to the gospel of Jesus, offer resistance to a State's totalitarian claim, the representatives of the State or their collaborationist theological advisers are accustomed to appeal to this saying of Paul, as if Christians are here commended to endorse and thus to abet all the crimes of a totalitarian State. (The State in the New Testament, SCM 1957 p 56.)

But what then is the meaning of Rom 13:1–7 and why is the use made of it by "State Theology" unjustifiable from a biblical point of view?

"State Theology" assumes that in this text Paul is presenting us with the absolute and definitive Christian doctrine about the State, in other words an absolute and universal principle that is equally valid for all times and in all circumstances . . .

What has been overlooked here is one of the most fundamental of all principles of biblical interpretation: every text must be interpreted in its context. . . . Paul was writing to a particular Christian community in Rome, a community that had its own particular problems in relation to the State at that time and in those circumstances. That is part of the context of our text.

Many authors have drawn attention to the fact that in the rest of the Bible God does not demand obedience to oppressive rulers. Examples can be given ranging from Pharaoh to Pilate and through into Apostolic times. The Jews and later the Christians did not believe that their imperial overlords, the Egyptians, the Babylonians, the Greeks or the Romans, had some kind of divine right to rule them and oppress them. These empires were the beasts described in the Book of Daniel and the Book of Revelations. God allowed them to rule for a while but he did not approve of what they did. It was not God's will. His will was the freedom and liberation of Israel. Rom 13:1–7 cannot be contradicting all of this.

But most revealing of all is the circumstances of the Roman Christians to whom Paul was writing. They were not revolutionaries. They were not trying to overthrow the State. They were not calling for a change of government . . .

Paul is simply not addressing the issue of a just or unjust State or the need to change one government for another. He is simply establishing the fact that there will be some kind of secular authority and that Christians as such are not exonerated from subjection to secular laws and authorities. He does not say anything at all about what they should do when the State becomes unjust and oppressive. That is another question . . .

2.2 Law and Order   The State makes use of the concept of law and order to maintain the status quo which it depicts as "normal." But this law is the unjust and discriminatory laws of apartheid and this order is the organized and institutionalized disorder of oppression. Anyone who wishes to change this law and this order is made to feel that they are lawless and disorderly. In other words they are made to feel guilty of sin.

It is indeed the duty of the State to maintain law and order, but it has not divine mandate to maintain any kind of law and order. Something does not become moral and just simply because the State has declared it to be a law and the organization of a society is not a just and right order simply because it has been instituted by the State. We cannot accept any kind of law and any kind of order. The concern of Christians is that we should have in our country a just law and a right order.

In the present crisis and especially during the State of Emergency, "State Theology" has tried to re-establish the status quo of orderly discrimination, exploitation and oppression by appealing to the consciences of its citizens in the name of law and order. It tries to make those who reject this law and this order feel that they are ungodly.

2.3 The Threat of Communism We all know how the South African State makes use of the label "communist." Anything that threatens the status quo is labeled "communist." Anyone who opposes the State and especially anyone who rejects its theology is simply dismissed as a "communist." No account is taken of what communism really means. No thought is given to why some people have indeed opted for communism or for some form of socialism. Even people who have not rejected capitalism are called "communists" when they reject "State Theology." The State uses the label "communist" in an uncritical and unexamined way as its symbol of evil.

"State Theology" like every other theology needs to have its own concrete symbol of evil. It must be able to symbolize what it regards as godless behavior and what ideas must be regarded as atheistic. It must have its own version of hell. And so it has invented, or rather taken over, the myth of communism. All evil is communistic and all communist or socialist ideas are atheistic and godless. Threats about hell-fire and eternal damnation are replaced by threats and warnings about the horrors of a tyrannical, totalitarian, atheistic and terrorist communist regime—a kind of hell-on-earth. This is a very convenient way of frightening some people into accepting any kind of domination and exploitation by a capitalist minority.

The South African State has its own heretical theology and according to that theology millions of Christians in South Africa (not to mention the rest of the world) are to be regarded as "atheists." It is significant that in earlier times when Christians rejected the gods of the Roman Empire they were branded as "atheists"—by the State.

2.4 The God of the State The State in its oppression of the people makes use again and again of the name of God. Military chaplains use it to encourage the South African Defense Force, police chaplains use it to strengthen policemen and cabinet ministers use it in their propaganda speeches. But perhaps the most revealing of all is the blasphemous use of God's holy name in the preamble to the new apartheid constitution.

This god is an idol. It is as mischievous, sinister and evil as any of the idols that the prophets of Israel had to contend with. Here we have a god who is historically on the side of the white settlers, who dispossesses black people of their land and who gives the major part of the land to his "chosen people."

It is the god of superior weapons who conquered those who were armed with nothing but spears. It is the god of the casspirs and hippos,[1] the god of teargas, rubber bullets, sjamboks[2], prison cells and death sentences. Here is a god who exalts the proud and humbles the poor—the very opposite of the God of the Bible who "scatters the proud of heart, pulls down the mighty from their thrones and exalts the humble" (Lk 1:51–52). From a theological point of view the opposite of the God of the Bible is the devil, Satan. The god of the South African State is not merely an idol or false god, it is

1. Armored vehicles.
2. Heavy whips, often made of rhinoceros hide.

the devil disguised as Almighty God—the anti-christ.

The oppressive South African regime will always be particularly abhorrent to Christians precisely because it makes use of Christianity to justify its evil ways. As Christians we simply cannot tolerate this blasphemous use of God's name and God's Word. "State Theology" is not only heretical, it is blasphemous. Christians who are trying to remain faithful to the God of the Bible are even more horrified when they see that there are Churches, like the White Dutch Reformed Churches and other groups of Christians, who actually subscribe to this heretical theology. "State Theology" needs its own prophets and it manages to find them from the ranks of those who profess to be ministers of God's Word in some of our Churches. What is particularly tragic for a Christian is to see the number of people who are fooled and confused by these false prophets and their heretical theology.

Chapter Three

Editor's Comment: The ancient ambivalence of Christians toward how to deal with political injustice was grounded in the Bible itself, which at times seemed to accord legitimacy even to violent resistance (as in the case of David's struggle against Saul or Jesus's expulsion of the money changers at the Temple) but at other times affirmed rather forcefully that a personal decision to refrain from retribution was particularly virtuous (as in Jesus's teaching in the Beatitudes, his exhortation to pray for one's enemies, and the apostle Paul's recommendation to obey the government). This ambivalence has been manifest throughout Christian history and was especially pronounced in the Reformation of the sixteenth century, in which Martin Luther recommended unquestioning obedience, the Catholics pointed to Augustine's theory of "Just War," Mennonite Anabaptists insisted on radical nonviolence, and John Calvin and his Reformed successors maintained that violent resistance to tyranny was not just an option but a spiritual obligation. How does this

section of the Kairos Document deal with the idea of nonviolence (famously promoted by Mahatma Gandhi in South Africa and India and by Martin Luther King in the United States)? What is the document's position on the nature of forgiveness and its place in the problem of justice? How does this chapter deal with peacemaking and reconciliation, and how might these considerations provide a framework for moving society past the ills of apartheid? How is true justice contrasted with previous efforts to promote justice?

CRITIQUE OF "CHURCH THEOLOGY"

We have analyzed the statements that are made from time to time by the so-called "English-speaking" Churches. We have looked at what Church leaders tend to say in their speeches and press statements about the apartheid regime and the present crisis. What we found running through all these pronouncements is a series of inter-related theological assumptions. These we have chosen to call "Church Theology." We are well aware of the fact that this theology does not express the faith of the majority of Christians in South Africa today who form the greater part of most of our Churches. Nevertheless the opinions expressed by Church leaders are regarded in the media and generally in our society as the official opinions of the Churches. We have therefore chosen to call these opinions "Church Theology." The crisis in which we find ourselves today compels us to question this theology, to question its assumptions, its implications and its practicality.

In a limited, guarded and cautious way this theology is critical of apartheid. Its criticism, however, is superficial and counter-productive because instead of engaging in an in-depth analysis of the signs of our times, it relies upon a few stock ideas derived from Christian tradition and then uncritically and repeatedly applies them to our situation. The stock ideas used by almost all these Church leaders that we would like to examine here are: reconciliation (or peace), justice and non-violence.

3.1 Reconciliation "Church Theology" takes "reconciliation" as the key to problem resolution. It talks about the need for reconciliation between white and black, or between all South Africans. "Church Theology" often describes the Christian stance in the following way: "We must be fair. We must listen to both sides of the story. If the two sides can only meet to talk and negotiate they will sort out their differences and misunderstandings, and the conflict will be resolved." On the face of it this may sound very Christian. But is it?

The fallacy here is that "Reconciliation" has been made into an absolute principle that must be applied in all cases of conflict or dissension. But not all cases of conflict are the same. We can imagine a private quarrel between two people or two groups whose differences are based upon misunderstandings. In such cases it would be appropriate to talk and negotiate to sort out the misunderstandings and to reconcile the two sides. But there are other conflicts in which one side is right and the other wrong. There are conflicts where one side is a fully armed and violent oppressor while the other side is defenseless and oppressed. There are conflicts that can only be described as the struggle between justice and injustice, good and evil, God and the devil. To speak of reconciling these two is not only a mistaken application of the Christian idea of reconciliation, it is a total betrayal of all that Christian faith has ever meant. Nowhere in the Bible or in Christian tradition has it ever been suggested that we ought to try to reconcile good and evil, God and the devil. We are supposed to do away with evil, injustice, oppression and sin—not come to terms with it. We are supposed to oppose, confront and reject the devil and not try to sup with the devil.

In our situation in South Africa today it would be totally unChristian to plead for reconciliation and peace before the present injustices have been removed. Any such plea plays into the hands of the oppressor by trying to persuade those of us who are oppressed to accept our oppression and to become reconciled to the intolerable crimes that are committed against us. That is not Christian reconciliation, it is sin. It is asking us to become accomplices in our own oppression, to become servants of the devil. No reconciliation is possible in South Africa without justice.

What this means in practice is that no reconciliation, no forgiveness and no negotiations are possible without repentance. The Biblical teaching on reconciliation and forgiveness makes it quite clear that nobody can be forgiven and reconciled with God unless he or she repents of their sins. Nor are we expected to forgive the unrepentant sinner. When he or she repents we must be willing to forgive seventy times seven times but before that, we are expected to preach repentance to those who sin against us or against anyone. Reconciliation, forgiveness and negotiations will become our Christian duty in South Africa only when the apartheid regime shows signs of genuine repentance. The recent speech of PW Botha in Durban, the continued military repression of the people in the townships and the jailing of all its opponents is clear proof of the total lack of repentance on the part of the present regime.

There is nothing that we want more than true reconciliation and genuine peace—the peace that God wants and not the peace the world wants (Jn 14:27). The peace that God wants is based upon truth, repentance, justice and love. The peace that the world offers us is a unity that compromises the truth, covers over injustice and oppression and is totally motivated by selfishness . . .

It would be quite wrong to try to preserve "peace" and "unity" at all costs, even at the cost of truth and justice and, worse still, at the cost of thousands of young lives.

3.2 Justice It would be quite wrong to give the impression that "Church Theology" in South Africa is not particularly concerned about the need for justice. There have been some very strong and very sincere demands for justice. But the question we need to ask here, the very serious theological question is: What kind of justice? An examination of Church statements and pronouncements gives the distinct impression that the justice that is envisaged is the justice of reform, that is to say, a justice that is determined by the oppressor, by the white minority and that is offered to the people as a kind of concession. It does not appear to be the more radical justice that comes from below and is determined by the people of South Africa.

One of our main reasons for drawing this conclusion is the simple fact that almost all Church statements and appeals are made to the State or to the white community. The assumption seems to be that changes must come from whites or at least from people who are at the top of the pile . . .

At the heart of this approach is the reliance upon "individual conversions" in response to "moralizing demands" to change the structures of a society. It has not worked and it never will work. The present crisis with all its cruelty, brutality and callousness is ample proof of the ineffectiveness of years and years of Christian "moralizing" about the need for love. The problem that we are dealing with here in South Africa is not merely a problem of personal guilt, it is a problem of structural injustice. People are suffering, people are being maimed and killed and tortured every day. We cannot just sit back and wait for the oppressor to see the light so that the oppressed can put out their hands and beg for the crumbs of some small reforms. That in itself would be degrading and oppressive.

There have been reforms and, no doubt, there will be further reforms in the near future. And it may well be that the Church's appeal to the consciences of whites has contributed marginally to the introduction of some of these reforms. But can such reforms ever be regarded as real change, as the introduction of a true and lasting justice? Reforms that come from the top are never satisfactory. They seldom do more than make the oppression more effective and more acceptable. . . . True justice, God's justice, demands a radical change of structures. This can only come from below, from the oppressed themselves. God will bring about change through the oppressed as he did through the oppressed Hebrew slaves in Egypt. God does not bring his justice through reforms introduced by the Pharaoh's of this world.

Why then does "Church Theology" appeal to the top rather than to the people who are suffering? . . . An appeal to the conscience of those who perpetuate the system of injustice must be made. But real change and true justice can only come from below, from the people—most of whom are Christians.

3.3 Non-Violence The stance of "Church Theology" on non-violence, expressed as a blanket condemnation of all that is called violence, has not only been unable to curb the violence of our situation, it has actually, although unwittingly, been a major contributing factor in the recent escalation of State violence. Here again non-violence has been made into an absolute principle that applies to anything anyone calls violence without regard for who is using it, which side they are on or what purpose they may have in mind. In our situation, this is simply counter-productive.

The problem for the Church here is the way the word violence is being used in the propaganda of the State. The State and the media have chosen to call violence what some people do in the townships as they struggle for their liberation i.e. throwing stones, burning cars and buildings and sometimes killing collaborators. But this excludes the structural, institutional and unrepentant violence of the State and especially the oppressive and naked violence of the police and the army. These things are not counted as violence. And even when they are acknowledged to be "excessive," they are called "misconduct" or even "atrocities" but never violence. . . . That is how it is understood not only by the State and its supporters but also by the people who are struggling for their freedom. Violence, especially in our circumstances, is a loaded word.

It is true that Church statements and pronouncements do also condemn the violence of the police. They do say that they condemn all violence.

But is it legitimate, especially in our circumstances, to use the same word violence in a blanket condemnation to cover the ruthless and repressive activities of the State and the desperate attempts of the people to defend themselves? Do such abstractions and generalizations not confuse the issue? How can acts of oppression, injustice and domination be equated with acts of resistance and self-defense? Would it be legitimate to describe both the physical force used by a rapist and the physical force used by a woman trying to resist the rapist as violence?

Moreover there is nothing in the Bible or in our Christian tradition that would permit us to make such generalizations. Throughout the Bible the word violence is used to describe everything that is done by a wicked oppressor (e.g., Ps 72:12–14; Is 59:1–8; Jer 22:13–17; Amos 3:9–10, 6:3; Mic 2:2, 3:1–3; 6:12). It is never used to describe the activities of Israel's armies in attempting to liberate themselves or to resist aggression. When Jesus says that we should turn the other cheek he is telling us that we must not take revenge; he is not saying that we should never defend ourselves or others. There is a long and consistent Christian tradition about the use of physical force to defend oneself against aggressors and tyrants. In other words there are circumstances when physical force may be used. They are very restrictive circumstances, only as the very last resort and only as the lesser of two evils, or, as Bonhoeffer put it, "the lesser of two guilts." But it is simply not true to say that every possible use of physical force is violence and that no matter what the circumstances may be it is never permissible.

This is not to say that any use of force at any time by people who are oppressed is permissible simply because they are struggling for their liberation . . .

And finally what makes the professed non-violence of "Church Theology" extremely suspect in the eyes of very many people, including ourselves, is the tacit support that many-Church leaders give to the growing militarisation of the South African State. How can one condemn all violence and then appoint chaplains to a very violent and oppressive army? How can one condemn all violence and then allow young males to accept their conscription into the armed forces? Is it because the activities of the armed forces and the police are counted as defensive? That raises very serious questions about whose side such Church leaders might be on. Why are the activities of young blacks in the townships not regarded as defensive?

In practice what one calls "violence" and what one calls "self-defense" seems to depend upon which side one is on. To call all physical force "violence" is to try to be neutral and to refuse to make a judgment about who is right and who is wrong. The attempt to remain neutral in this kind of conflict is futile. Neutrality enables the status quo of oppression (and therefore violence) to continue. It is a way of giving tacit support to the oppressor.

3.4 The Fundamental Problem It is not enough to criticize "Church Theology" we must also try to account for it. What is behind the mistakes and misunderstandings and inadequacies of this theology?

In the first place we can point to a lack of social analysis. We have seen how "Church Theology" tends to make use of absolute principles like reconciliation, negotiation non-violence and peaceful solutions and applies them indiscriminately and uncritically to all situations. Very little attempt is made to analyze what is actually happening in our society and why it is happening. It is not possible to make valid moral judgment about a society without first understanding that society . . .

But we have still not pinpointed the fundamental problem. Why has "Church Theology" not developed a social analysis? Why does it have an inadequate understanding of the need for political strategies? And why does it make a virtue of neutrality and sitting on the sidelines?

The answer must be sought in the type of faith and spirituality that has dominated Church life for centuries. As we all know, spirituality has tended to be an other-worldly affair that has very little, if anything at all, to do with the affairs of this world. Social and political matters were seen as worldly affairs that have nothing to do with the spiritual concerns of the Church. Moreover, spirituality has also been understood to be purely private and individualistic. Public affairs and social problems were thought to be beyond the sphere of spirituality. And finally the spirituality we inherit tends to rely upon God to intervene in his own good time to put right what is wrong in the world. That leaves very little for human beings to do except to pray for God's intervention.

It is precisely this kind of spirituality that, when faced with the present crisis in South Africa, leaves so many Christians and Church leaders in a state of near paralysis.

. . . God redeems the whole person as part of his whole creation (Rom 8:18–24). A truly biblical spirituality would penetrate into every "aspect of human existence and would exclude nothing from God's redemptive will." Biblical faith is prophetically relevant to everything that happens in the world.

Chapter Four

Editor's Comment: Consider in this section the consistent biblical theme of God's preference for the poor and the oppressed. In Christian tradition, Christ (whom Christians believe to have been God incarnate) has often been used as a symbol of hope and promise of a better future for those who suffer presently. The key term for this is "redemption," the idea that God can turn what is evil to the benefit of the good. In this chapter, is "redemption" a term that reflects a distant hope in the afterlife or a term that suggests God's endorsement of human action? How does the chapter place the injustices of apartheid within the span of human experience? What does the existence of tyranny demand from Christians in response, and can any part of the system that promotes injustice be preserved?

TOWARDS A PROPHETIC THEOLOGY
Our present KAIROS calls for a response from Christians that is biblical, spiritual, pastoral and,

above all, prophetic. It is not enough in these circumstances to repeat generalized Christian principles. We need a bold and incisive response that is prophetic because it speaks to the particular circumstances of this crisis, a response that does not give the impression of sitting on the fence but is clearly and unambiguously taking a stand.

4.1 Social Analysis The first task of a prophetic theology for our times would be an attempt at social analysis or what Jesus would call "reading the signs of the times" (Mt 16:3) or "interpreting this KAIROS" (Lk 12:56). It is not possible to do this in any detail in the document but we must start with at least the broad outlines of an analysis of the conflict in which we find ourselves.

It would be quite wrong to see the present conflict as simply a racial war. The racial component is there but we are not dealing with two equal races or nations each with their own selfish group interests. The situation we are dealing with here is one of oppression. The conflict is between an oppressor and the oppressed. The conflict between two irreconcilable causes or interests in which the one is just and the other is unjust.

On the one hand we have the interests of those who benefit from the status quo and who are determined to maintain it at any cost, even at the cost of millions of lives. It is in their interests to introduce a number of reforms in order to ensure that the system is not radically changed and that they can continue to benefit from the system because it favors them and enables them to accumulate a great deal of wealth and to maintain an exceptionally high standard of living. And they want to make sure that it stays that way even if some adjustments are needed.

On the other hand we have those who do not benefit in any way from the system the way it is now. They are treated as mere labor units, paid starvation wages, separated from their families by migratory labor, moved about like cattle and dumped in homelands to starve—and all for the benefit of a privileged minority. They have no say in the system and are supposed to be grateful for the concessions that are offered to them like crumbs. It is not in their interests to allow this system to continue even in some "reformed" or "revised" form. They are determined to change the system radically so that it no longer benefits only the privileged few. And they are willing to do this even at the cost of their own lives. What they want is justice for all.

This is our situation of civil war or revolution. The one side is committed to maintaining the system at all costs and the other side is committed to changing it at all costs. There are two conflicting projects here and no compromise is possible. Either we have full and equal justice for all or we don't.

The Bible has a great deal to say about this kind of conflict, about a world that is divided into oppressors and oppressed.

4.2 Oppression in the Bible   When we search the Bible for a message about oppression we discover, as others throughout the world are discovering, that oppression is a central theme that runs right through the Old and New Testaments. The biblical scholars who have taken the trouble to study the theme of oppression in the Bible have discovered that there are no less than twenty different root words in Hebrew to describe oppression. As one author says, oppression is "a basic structural category of biblical theology" (T. D. Hanks, *God So Loved the Third World*, Orbis, 1983, p. 4).

Moreover the description of oppression in the Bible is concrete and vivid. The Bible describes oppression as the experience of being crushed, degraded, humiliated, exploited, impoverished, defrauded, deceived and enslaved. And the oppressors are described as cruel, ruthless, arrogant, greedy, violent and tyrannical and as the enemy. . . . But what made all the difference for this particular group of oppressed people was the revelation of Yahweh. God revealed himself as Yahweh, the one who has compassion on those who suffer and who liberates them from their oppressors.

. . . Throughout the Bible God appears as the liberator of the oppressed. He is not neutral. He does not attempt to reconcile Moses and Pharaoh, to reconcile the Hebrew slaves with their Egyptian oppressors or to reconcile the Jewish people with any of their late oppressors. Oppression is sin and it cannot be compromised with, it must be done away with. God takes sides with the oppressed. As we read in Psalm 103:6 (JB) "God who does what is right, is always on the side of the oppressed."

4.3 Tyranny in the Christian Tradition   There is a long Christian tradition relating to oppression, but the word that has been used most frequently to describe this particular form of sinfulness is the word "tyranny." According to this tradition once it is established beyond doubt that a particular ruler is a tyrant or that a particular regime is tyrannical, it forfeits the moral right to govern and the people acquire the right to resist and to find the means to protect their own interests against injustice and oppression. In other words a tyrannical regime has no moral legitimacy. It may be the de facto government and it may even be recognized by other governments and therefore be the de iure or legal government. But if it is a tyrannical regime, it is, from a moral and theological point of view, illegitimate. There are indeed some differences of opinion in the Christian tradition about the means that might be used to replace a tyrant but there has not been any doubt about our Christian duty to refuse to co-operate with tyranny and to do whatever we can to remove it.

. . . Of course everything hinges on the definition of a tyrant. At what point does a government become a tyrannical regime?

The traditional Latin definition of a tyrant is *hostis boni communis*—an enemy of the common good. The purpose of all government is the promotion of what is called the common good of the people governed. To promote the common good is to govern in the interests of, and for the benefit of, all the people. Many governments fail to do this at times. There might be this or that injustice done to some of the people. And such lapses would indeed have to be criticized. But occasional acts of injustice would not make a government into an enemy of the people, a tyrant.

To be an enemy of the people a government would have to be hostile to the common good in principle. Such a government would be acting against the interests of the people as a whole and permanently. . . . Such a government would be in principle irreformable. Any reform that it might try to introduce would not be calculated to serve the common good but to serve the interests of the minority from whom it received its mandate.

A tyrannical regime cannot continue to rule for very long without becoming more and more violent . . .

That leaves us with the question of whether the present government of South Africa is tyrannical or not? There can be no doubt what the majority of the people of South Africa think. For them the apartheid regime is indeed the enemy of the people and that is precisely what they call it: the enemy. In the present crisis, more than before, the regime has lost any legitimacy that it might have had in the eyes of the people. Are the people right or wrong?

Apartheid is a system whereby a minority regime elected by one small section of the population is given an explicit mandate to govern in the interests of, and for the benefit of, the white community. Such a mandate or policy is by definition hostile to the common good of all the people. In fact because it tries to rule in the exclusive interests of whites and not in the interests of all, it ends up ruling in a way that is not even in the interests of those same whites. It becomes an enemy of all the people. A totalitarian regime. A reign of terror.

This also means that the apartheid minority regime is irreformable. We cannot expect the apartheid regime to experience a conversion or change of heart and totally abandon the policy of apartheid . . .

A regime that is in principle the enemy of the people cannot suddenly begin to rule in the interests of all the people. It can only be replaced by another government—one that has been elected by the majority of the people with an explicit mandate to govern in the interests of all the people.

A regime that has made itself the enemy of the people has thereby also made itself the enemy of God. People are made in the image and likeness of God and whatever to the least of them we do to God (Mt 25:49, 45).

To say that the State or the regime is the enemy of God is not to say that all those who support the system are aware of this. On the whole they simply do not know what they are doing. Many people have been blinded by the regime's propaganda. They are frequently quite ignorant of the consequences of their stance. However, such blindness does not make the State any less tyrannical or any less of an enemy of the people and an enemy of God.

On the other hand the fact that the State is tyrannical and an enemy of God is no excuse for hatred. As Christians we are called upon to love our enemies (Mt 5:44). It is not said that we should not or will not have enemies or that we should not identify tyrannical regimes as indeed our enemies. But once we have identified our enemies, we must endeavor to love them. That is not always easy. But then we must also remember that the most loving thing we can do for both the oppressed and for our enemies who are oppressors is to eliminate the oppression, remove the tyrants from power and establish a just government for the common good of all the people.

4.4 A Message of Hope   At the very heart of the gospel of Jesus Christ and at the very center of all true prophecy is a message of hope. Nothing could be more relevant and more necessary at this moment of crisis in South Africa than the Christian message of hope.

Jesus has taught us to speak of this hope as the coming of God's kingdom. We believe that God is at work in our world turning hopeless and evil situations to good so that his "Kingdom may come" and his "Will may be done on earth as it is in heaven." We believe that goodness and justice and love will triumph in the end and that tyranny and oppression cannot last forever. One day "all tears will be wiped away" (Rev 7:17; 21:4) and "the lamb will lie down with the lion" (Is 11:6). True peace and true reconciliation are not only desirable, they are assured and guaranteed. This is our faith and our hope.

Why is it that this powerful message of hope has not been highlighted in "Church Theology," in the statements and pronouncements of Church leaders? Is it because they have been addressing themselves to the oppressor rather than to the oppressed? Is it because they do not want to encourage the oppressed to be too hopeful for too much?

As the crisis deepens day-by-day, what both the oppressor and the oppressed can legitimately demand of the Churches is a message of hope. Most of the oppressed people in South Africa today and especially the youth do have hope. They are acting courageously and fearlessly because they have a sure hope that liberation will come. Often enough their bodies are broken but nothing can now break their spirit . . .

On the other hand the oppressor and those who believe the propaganda of the oppressor are desperately fearful. They must be made aware of the diabolical evils of the present system and they must be called to repentance but they must also be given something to hope for. At present they have false hopes.

Chapter Five
CHALLENGE TO ACTION

5.1 God Sides with the Oppressed   To say that the Church must now take sides unequivocally and consistently with the poor and the oppressed is to overlook the fact that the majority of Christians in South Africa have already done so. By far the greater part of the Church in South Africa is poor and oppressed. . . . We are a divided Church precisely because not all the members of our Churches have taken sides against oppression. In other words not all Christians have united them-

selves with God "who is always on the side of the oppressed" (Ps 103:6). As far as the present crisis is concerned, there is only one way forward to Church unity and that is for those Christians who find themselves on the side of the oppressor or sitting on the fence, to cross over to the other side to be united in faith and action with those who are oppressed. Unity and reconciliation within the Church itself is only possible around God and Jesus Christ who are to be found on the side of the poor and the oppressed.

If this is what the Church must become, if this is what the Church as a whole must have as its project, how then are we to translate it into concrete and effective action?

5.2 Participation in the Struggle   Christians, if they are not doing so already, must quite simply participate in the struggle for liberation and for a just society. The campaigns of the people, from consumer boycotts to stayaways, need to be supported and encouraged by the Church. Criticism will sometimes be necessary but encouragement and support will also be necessary. In other words the present crisis challenges the whole Church to move beyond a mere "ambulance ministry" to a ministry of involvement and participation.

5.3 Transforming Church Activities   The Church has its own specific activities: Sunday services, communion services, baptisms, Sunday school, funerals and so forth. It also has its specific way of expressing its faith and its commitment i.e. in the form of confessions of faith. All of these activities must be re-shaped to be more fully consistent with a prophetic faith related to the KAIROS that God is offering us today. The evil forces we speak of in baptism must be named. We know what these evil forces are in South Africa today. The unity and sharing we profess in our communion services or Masses must be named. It is the solidarity of the people inviting all to join in the struggle for God's peace in South Africa. The repentance we preach must be named. It is repentance for our share of the guilt for the suffering and oppression in our country.

Much of what we do in our Church services has lost its relevance to the poor and the oppressed. Our services and sacraments have been appropriated to serve the need of the individual for comfort and security. Now these same Church activities must be reappropriated to serve the real religious needs of all the people and to further the liberating mission of God and the Church in the world.

5.4 Special Campaigns   Over and above its regular activities the Church would need to have special programmes, projects and campaigns because of the special needs of the struggle for liberation in South Africa today.

5.5 Civil Disobedience   Once it is established that the present regime has no moral legitimacy and is in fact a tyrannical regime certain things follow for the Church and its activities. In the first place the Church cannot collaborate with tyranny. It cannot or should not do anything that appears to give legitimacy to a morally illegitimate regime. Secondly, that Church should not only pray for a change of government, it should also mobilize its members in every parish to begin to think and work and plan for a change of government in South Africa. We must begin to look ahead and begin working now with firm hope and faith for a better future. And finally the moral illegitimacy of the apartheid regime means that the Church will have to be involved at times in civil disobedience. A Church that takes its responsibilities seriously in these circumstances will sometimes have to confront and to disobey the State in order to obey God.

5.6 Moral Guidance   The people look to the Church, especially in the midst of our present crisis, for moral guidance . . .

But the Church of Jesus Christ is not called to be a bastion of caution and moderation. The Church should challenge, inspire and motivate people. It has a message of the cross that inspires us to make sacrifices for justice and liberation. It has a message of hope that challenges us to wake up and to act with hope and confidence. The Church must preach this message not only in words and sermons and statements but also through its actions, programmes, campaigns and divine services.

Conclusion

As we said in the beginning, there is nothing final about this document. Our hope is that it will stimulate discussion, debate, reflection and prayer, but, above all, that it will lead to action.

Although the document suggests various modes of involvement it does not prescribe the particular actions anyone should take. We call upon all those who are committed to this prophetic form of theology to use the document for discussion in groups, small and big, to determine an appropriate form of action, depending on their particular situation, and to take up the action with other related groups and organizations.

The challenge to renewal and action that we have set out here is addressed to the Church. But that does not mean that it is intended only for Church leaders. The challenge of the faith and of our present KAIROS is addressed to all who bear the name Christian. None of us can simply sit back and wait to be told what to do by our Church leaders or anyone else. We must all accept responsibility for acting and living out our Christian faith in these circumstances. We pray that God will help all of us to translate the challenge of our times into action.

We are convinced that this challenge comes from God and that it is addressed to all of us. We see the present crisis or KAIROS as indeed a divine visitation.

And finally we also like to call upon our Christian brothers and sisters throughout the world to give us the necessary support in this regard so that the daily loss of so many young lives may be brought to a speedy end.

We, the undersigned, take joint responsibility for what is presented in this document, not as a final statement of the truth but as the direction in which God is leading us at this moment or our history.

[There follows a list of 156 signatories from over 20 South African denominations.]

SUPPLEMENTAL READINGS

Constitution of the African National Congress

Editor's Note: In 1991, not long after the release of Nelson Mandela and in response to gestures for cooperation by the National Party government of South Africa, the African National Congress met to ratify a newly revised constitutional vision. Why might the ANC embrace the confrontational language scattered throughout this document, and how might that language stand as an obstacle to dialogue with other interest groups? What sort of "new" South Africa do the stated goals of the ANC Constitution suggest that it is seeking? For the ANC, what are the most important or determinative features of democracy? Does gender have a significant place within this constitution and how might that affect the efforts of some members of the ANC in the postapartheid era? Are there elements of this constitution to which groups like IFP and Afrikaner organizations might reject? How might groups opposed to the ANC question its appropriateness for a role of political leadership in a postapartheid era?

As Adopted at the ANC National Conference, June 1991[1]

Preamble
Whereas the ANC was founded in 1912 to defend and advance the rights of the African people after the violent destruction of their independence and the creation of the white supremacist Union of South Africa; and

1. Used by permission of the ANC Archives.

Whereas in the course of fulfilling this historic aim, the ANC has emerged to lead the struggle of all democratic and patriotic forces to destroy the apartheid state and replace it with the united, non-racial, nonsexist and democratic South Africa in which the people as a whole shall govern and all shall enjoy equal rights; and

Whereas through the struggles and sacrifices of its members over the generations the ANC has come to be recognised as the central organiser and inspirer of a vast popular upsurge against apartheid, involving a great array of social, cultural, religious, trade union, professional and political organisations.

Now therefore, the Forty-Eighth National Conference of the ANC, duly constituted and assembled, cognisant of the historic mission of the ANC and of the need to build a mass based democratic structure to enable It to fulfill its historic mission, hereby adopts this constitution.

A. Name
The name of the organisation shall be the African National Congress, hereinafter referred to as the ANC.

B. Aims and Objectives
The aims and objectives of the ANC shall be

To unite all the people of South Africa, Africans in particular, for the complete liberation of the country from all forms of discrimination and national oppression.

To end apartheid in all its forms and transform South Africa as rapidly as possible into a united, non-racial, non-sexist and democratic country based on the principles of the Freedom Charter.

To defend the democratic gains of the people and advance towards a society in which the government is freely chosen by the people according to the principles of universal suffrage on a common voter's role.

To fight for social justice and eliminate the vast inequalities created by apartheid and the system of national oppression.

To build a South African nation with a common patriotism and loyalty in which the cultural, linguistic and religious diversity of the people is recognised.

To promote economic development for the benefit of all.

To support and advance the cause of national liberation, women's emancipation, development, world peace, disarmament and respect of the environment.

To support and promote the struggle for the rights of children.

C. Character of the ANC

The ANC is a non-racial and a democratic liberation movement.

The ANC is a democratic organisation whose policies are determined by the membership and whose leadership shall be accountable to the membership in terms of the procedures laid down in the Constitution.

The ANC shall in its composition and functioning be non-racial, anti-racist and anti-sexist and against any form of tribalistic exclusivism or ethnic chauvinism.

While striving for the maximum unity of purpose and functioning, the ANC shall respect the linguistic, cultural and religious diversity of its members.

The ANC shall support the emancipation of women, combat sexism and ensure that the voice of women is fully heard in the organisation and that women are properly represented at all levels.

The principles of freedom of speech and free circulation of ideas and information shall operate within the ANC.

Membership of all bodies of the ANC will be open to all men and women in the organisation without regard to race, colour or creed.

The ANC co-operates closely with religious bodies in the country and provides, on an inter-faith basis, for the recognition of the spiritual needs of its many members who are believers.

D. Membership

Membership of the ANC shall be open to all South Africans above the age of 18 years, irrespective of race, colour and creed, who accept its principles, policies and programmes and are prepared to abide by its Constitution and rules.

Spouses, or children of South Africans who have manifested a clear identification with the South African people and its struggle, may apply for membership.

All other persons who have manifested a clear identification with the South African people and their struggle are resident in South Africa, may apply for membership.

The NEC may, acting on its own or on the recommendation of branch or regional executive committees, grant honourary membership to those men and women who do not qualify for membership under Clause D1, 2 and 3, but who have demonstrated an unwavering commitment to the ANC and its programme.

Applications for membership shall be considered by the branch committee where such exists, and by the regional executive committee if no branch committee exists. The branch committee, the regional executive committee, or such interim structures as the REC or NEC may create from time to time to decide on applications, shall have the power to accept or refuse any application for membership provided such acceptance or refusal shall be subject to review by the next higher organ of the ANC.

Membership cards shall be issued to registered members of the ANC and to persons whose application for membership has been accepted, subject to review as aforesaid, and, in all cases, subject to payment of the prescribed subscription.

On being accepted in the ANC, a new member shall, in a language he or she knows well, make the following solemn declaration to the body or person who received the application:

I, . . . , solemnly declare that I will abide by the aims and objectives of the ANC as set out in the Constitution and the Freedom Charter, that I am joining the organisation voluntarily and without motives of personal gain or material advantage, and that I will participate in the life of the organisation as a loyal, active and disciplined member.

Members shall pay an annual subscription fee as determined by the National Executive Committee.

Non-earning members or those on reduced incomes will pay a flat fee at a low amount fixed by the NEC.

E. Rights and Duties of the Members

RIGHTS:

A member of the ANC shall have the right to:

Take a full and active part in the discussion, formulation and implementation of the policy of the ANC.

Receive and impart information on all aspects of ANC policy and activities.

Offer constructive criticism of any member, official, policy programme or activity of the ANC within its structures.

Take part in elections and be elected or appointed to any committee, structure, commission or delegation of the ANC.

Submit proposals or statements to the branch, region or NEC provided such proposals or statements are submitted through the appropriate structures.

DUTIES:

A member of the ANC shall:

Belong to and take an active part in the life of his or her branch.

Take all necessary steps to understand and carry out the aims, policy and programme of the ANC.

Explain the aims, policy and programme of the ANC to the people.

Deepen his or her understanding of the social, cultural, political and economic problems of the country.

Combat propaganda detrimental to the interests of the ANC and defend the policy aims and programme of the ANC.

Fight against racism, tribal chauvinism, sexism, religious and political intolerance or any other form of discrimination or chauvinism.

Observe discipline, behave honestly and carry out loyally decisions of the majority and decisions of higher bodies.

Inform his or her branch of movement to any other area and report to the branch committee secretary on arriving at any new area.

Refrain from publishing and/or distributing any media without authorisation which purports to be the view of any organised grouping, faction or tendency within the ANC.

F. Organisational Structure

The ANC shall consist of the following organs:

The National Conference which elects the NEC.

The Regional Conference which elects the regional executive committees.

The Regional General Councils.

The branch meetings which elect the branch committees.

Branches may be grouped together in zones and may be subdivided into small units such as street committees, and zones may be grouped into sub-regions.

The ANC Women's League shall be open to women who are members of the ANC and shall have the same basic structure, namely, national, regional and branch. Its objectives will be to defend and advance the rights of women, both inside and outside the ANC, against all forms of national, social and gender oppression and to ensure that women play a full role in the life of the organisation, in the peoples' struggle and in national life. The Women's League will function as an autonomous body within the overall structure of the ANC, of which it will be an integral part, with its own Constitution, Rules and Regulations, provided that these shall not be in conflict with the Constitution and policies of the ANC.

The ANC Youth League shall be open to all persons between the ages of 14 and 35. It will operate on a national, regional and branch basis. Its objectives will be to unite and lead young men and women in confronting and dealing with the problems that face the youth, and in ensuring that the youth make a full and rich contribution to the work of the ANC and the life of the nation. The Youth League will function as an autonomous body within the overall structure of the ANC, of which it will be an integral part, with its own Constitution, Rules and Regulations, provided that these shall not be in conflict with the Constitution and policies of the ANC.

Members of the Youth League over the age of 18, shall be expected to play a full part in the general political life of the ANC.

A member of the Youth League shall not be eligible for any position as office-bearer of the ANC or to attend ANC conferences, members' or executive meetings of the ANC (unless specially invited), unless he or she is a full member of the ANC.

G. Umkhonto We Sizwe (MK)

Pending the creation of a united defence force representing the whole of the South African nation and defending the principles of a new non-racial, non-sexist democratic constitution, Umkhonto we Sizwe (MK) shall continue as an honoured and integral part of the ANC under the political guidance and control of the NEC.

The NEC shall from time to time determine MK's tasks and functions.

Membership of MK shall be drawn from ANC structures and shall be on the basis of free and voluntary choice.

The NEC shall be responsible for the general welfare and interests of the cadres and, where appropriate, ex-cadres of MK who continue to be members of the ANC.

ANC Policy Guidelines for a Democratic South Africa Adopted at the National Conference, 28–31 May 1992[1]

(Excerpts)

Editor's Note: How does this document present the idea of political sovereignty? Of what is that sovereignty composed and how is it to be manifested in the constitutional ordering of society? How does this policy statement fit into the narrative of negotiations between the ANC and the NP between 1990 and 1993?

A Democratic Constitution for South Africa
BASIC PRINCIPLES

Sovereignty vests in the people of South Africa. Their will shall be expressed by their democratically elected representatives in periodic free and fair elections. These elected representatives will adopt a constitution which shall be the highest law of the land guaranteeing their basic rights.

The goal of the ANC, ever since it was formed in 1912, has been to give all the people of our country, the chance to choose their own government. That is why generations of our leaders and members have set their sights on the objective of a new and democratic constitution which would at last remove the colonial status of the African people, abolish all forms of discrimination, and recognise the basic equality of all South Africans.

We are proud of our role in pioneering democracy and constitutionalism in our land, especially through the Freedom Charter. None has fought harder for freedom and democracy than we have. The people will finally have won the right to choose their own government. At the same time they will have the right to remove any government through periodic elections.

Our constitution shall not only guarantee an accountable non-racial, non-sexist and democratic structure of government, but shall also empower

1. Used by permission of the ANC Archives.

all citizens to shape and share in the many aspects of life outside government.

Our constitution shall guarantee the space for civic bodies trade unions and the numerous other organisations which people create to deal with their everyday problems and aspirations. These are the institutions of civil society which are crucial if we are to have a deep and thorough democratic order.

Our task now is to rally all South African patriots around the principles for which we have always stood, namely, of equality, mutual respect, dignity and promotion of basic human rights. After so many decades of struggle and sacrifice, we must achieve a constitution that guarantees that oppression, discrimination, inequality and division will never stalk our land again.

We want a country that is unified, open, non-racial, non-sexist, democratic and free. We must abolish all forms of discrimination, domination, privilege or abuse. We must ensure that the basic rights and freedoms of all are respected. We must see to it that the religious, linguistic and cultural variety of our land is fully acknowledged, and that no person shall be subjected to any forms of oppression or abuse. We do not want new forms of tyranny to replace the old.

South Africa has never had good government for all. Government has until now always been used to harass, divide and humiliate the great majority of South Africans, while securing privilege and relatively high standards of service for the minority. We need a constitution that guarantees a high quality of government service for all. The public service must be based on the principles of representivity, competency, impartiality and accountability. For the first time we envisage a public service that is drawn from and serves the interests of the public as a whole.

AZAPO Constitution (Excerpts)[1]

Editor's Note: Formed in 1978 as a radical intellectual movement calling for a socialist South Africa, the

1. Used by permission.

Azanian People's Organisation was an offshoot of the Black Consciousness Movement of Steven Biko and Onkgopotse Tiro and was, because of its principles of economic justice, understood as indigenous to African culture. How do questions of identity shape the constitutional goals of AZAPO? What are the "anti-African" systems that the document identifies as the culprits in perpetuating tyranny, injustice, and oppression? What systemic goals does AZAPO identify as remedies for the suffering of Africans?

Chapter 1
PREAMBLE:
WHEREAS we, the Black people of AZANIA,

(a) Conscious of the adverse physical and psychological effects of centuries of oppression on Black people, and on Black workers in particular; and

(b) Aware of the determination of Black workers to gain freedom and justice, and their desire to occupy their rightful place in the land of their birth; and

(c) Realising that the system in Azania is based on white racism, capitalism and neo-colonialism; and

(d) Acknowledging that Black people in general, and Black workers in particular are responsible for the creation of the bulk of the wealth in Azania; and

(e) Mindful of the fact that the system seeks to render Black workers powerless and perpetually subservient by creating and utilising tactics of divide and rule; and

(f) Alive to the danger that the system shall always endeavour to divide and frustrate the liberation efforts of the people towards true emancipation; and

(g) Conscious of the desire of Black people to liberate themselves from the system; and

(h) Motivated and inspired by our individual and collective quest for liberation, return of the land to its rightful owners, justice, peace and equality of persons; and

Therefore Hereby Resolve

In active pursuit of the above, to found a National Liberation and Political Organisation.

Section 1

THE NAME

The name of the National Liberation and Political Organisation shall be the **AZANIAN PEOPLE'S ORGANISATION (AZAPO),** hereinafter called "the organization."

Section 2

AIMS AND OBJECTIVES

(i)   To organise, mobilise and lead the oppressed people of Azania towards the elimination of neo-colonialism, capitalism, imperialism and all other forms of oppression in our country.

(ii) To reconquer the land for fair and equitable distribution amongst all Azanians.

(iii) To recapture and restore political, economic and social power and control to all Azanians.

(iv) To establish a revolutionary national democracy in Azania.

(v)   To establish a democratic, socialist Republic of Azania.

(vi) To work towards the unity of all people in order to maximise efforts at the total liberation of all the oppressed and exploited.

(vii) In keeping with the above, employ all means at our disposal for the attainment of the aims, goals and objectives of the organisation.

Address by State President F. W. de Klerk, DMS, at the Opening of the Second Session of the Ninth Parliament of the Republic of South Africa

Friday, 2 February 1990

Editor's Note: Why does de Klerk think it was important to push for "drastic" constitutional change in South Africa? Does this admission confirm the validity of certain theories of resistance? Are the stated goals of the president similar or different from those of the ANC and other resistance organizations? What hints does he give about the impact of international conditions on the perpetuation or demise of apartheid? What key words and phrases does de Klerk use to address human rights that seek to allay the anxieties and concerns of multiple parties on various sides of the social and political tensions in South Africa? What "sacrifices" and developments will South Africans need to make, and why are these important for a new, more stable state? What "good faith" gestures does de Klerk make to confirm the seriousness of his intent to resistance movements, and how does he justify those gestures to defenders of the status quo? How does de Klerk seek to balance tensions related to security and dissent, and how do his comments regarding Nelson Mandela's release from prison mirror those tensions and the way he seeks to balance them?

Mr. Speaker, Members of Parliament.

The general election on September the 6th, 1989, placed our country irrevocably on the road of drastic change. Underlying this is the growing realization by an increasing number of South Africans that only a negotiated understanding among the representative leaders of the entire population is able to ensure lasting peace.

The alternative is growing violence, tension and conflict. That is unacceptable and in no-body's interest. The well-being of all in this country is linked inextricably to the ability of the leaders to come to terms with one another on a new dispensation. No-one can escape this simple truth.

On its part, the Government will accord the process of negotiation the highest priority. The aim is a totally new and just constitutional dispensation in which every inhabitant will enjoy equal rights, treatment and opportunity in every sphere of endeavor—constitutional, social and economic.

I hope that this new Parliament will play a

constructive part in both the prelude to negotiations and the negotiating process itself. I wish to ask all of you who identify yourselves with the broad aim of a new South Africa, and that is the overwhelming majority:

Let us put petty politics aside when we discuss the future during this session.

Help us build a broad consensus about the fundamentals of a new, realistic and democratic dispensation.

Let us work together on a plan that will rid our country of suspicion and steer it away from domination and radicalism of any kind.

During the term of this new Parliament, we shall have to deal, complimentary to one another, with the normal processes of legislation and day-to-day government, as well as with the process of negotiation and renewal.

Within this framework I wish to deal first with several matters more closely concerned with the normal process of government before I turn specifically to negotiation and related issues.

Foreign Relations

The Government is aware of the important part the world at large has to play in the realization of our country's national interests.

Without contact and co-operation with the rest of the world we cannot promote the well-being and security of our citizens. The dynamic developments in international politics have created new opportunities for South Africa as well. Important advances have been made, among other things, in our contacts abroad, especially where these were precluded previously by ideological considerations.

I hope this trend will be encouraged by the important change of climate that is taking place in South Africa.

For South Africa, indeed for the whole world, the past year has been one of change and major upheaval. In Eastern Europe and even the Soviet Union itself, political and economic upheaval surged forward in an unstoppable tide. At the same time, Beijing temporarily smothered with brutal violence the yearning of the people of the Chinese mainland for greater freedom.

The year 1989 will go down in history as the year in which Stalinist Communism expired.

These developments will entail unpredictable consequences for Europe, but they will also be of decisive importance to Africa.

Human Rights

Some time ago the Government referred the question of the protection of fundamental human rights to the South African Law Commission. This resulted in the Law Commission's interim working document on individual and minority rights. It elicited substantial public interest.

I am satisfied that every individual and organization in the country has had ample opportunity to make representations to the Law Commission, express criticism freely and make suggestions. At present, the Law Commission is considering the representations received. A final report is expected in the course of this year.

In view of the exceptional importance of the subject of human rights to our country and all its people, I wish to ask the Law Commission to accord this task high priority.

The whole question of protecting individual and minority rights, which includes collective rights and the rights of national groups, is still under consideration by the Law commission.

Therefore, it would be inappropriate for the Government to express a view on the details now. However, certain matters of principle have emerged fairly clearly and I wish to devote some remarks to them.

The Government accepts the principle of recognition and protection of the fundamental individual rights which form the constitutional basis of most Western democracies. We acknowledge, too, that the most practical way of protecting those rights is vested in a declaration of rights justifiable by an independent judiciary. However, it is clear that a system for the protection of the rights of individuals, minorities and national entities has to form a well-rounded and balanced whole. South Africa has its own national composition and our constitutional dispensation has to take this into account. The formal recognition of individual rights does not mean that the problems of a heterogeneous population will simply disappear. Any new constitution which disregards this reality will be inappropriate and even harmful.

Naturally, the protection of collective, minority and national rights may not bring about an imbalance in respect of individual rights. It is neither the Government's policy nor its intention that any group—in whichever way it may be defined—shall be favoured above or in relation to any of the others.

The Government is requesting the Law Commission to undertake a further task and report on it. This task is directed at the balanced protection in a future constitution of the human rights of all our citizens, as well as of collective units, associations, minorities and nations. This investigation will also serve the purpose of supporting negotiations towards a new constitution.

The terms of reference also include:

the identification of the main types and models of democratic constitutions which deserve consideration in the aforementioned context; an analysis of the ways in which the relevant rights are protected in every model; and possible methods by means of which such constitutions may be made to succeed and be safeguarded in a legitimate manner.

The Economy

A new South Africa is possible only if it is bolstered by a sound and growing economy, with particular emphasis on the creation of employment. With a view to this, the Government has taken thorough cognisance of the advice contained in numerous reports by a variety of advisory bodies. The central message is that South Africa, too, will have to make certain structural changes to its economy, just as its major trading partners had to do a decade or so ago.

The period of exceptionally high economic growth experienced by the Western world in the sixties, was brought to an end by the oil crisis in 1973. Drastic structural adaptations became inevitable for these countries, especially after the second oil crisis in 1979, when serious imbalances occurred in their economies. After considerable sacrifices, those countries which persevered with their structural adjustment programmes, recovered economically so that lengthy periods of high economic growth and low inflation were possible.

During that particular period, South Africa was protected temporarily by the rising gold price from the necessity of making similar adjustments immediately. In fact, the high gold price even brought prosperity with it for a while. The recovery of the world economy and the decline in the price of gold and other primary products, brought with them unhealthy trends. These included high inflation, a serious weakening in the productivity of capital, stagnation in the economy's ability to generate income and employment opportunities. All of this made a drastic structural adjustment of our economy inevitable.

The Government's basic point of departure is to reduce the role of the public sector in the economy and to give the private sector maximum opportunity for optimal performance. In this process, preference has to be given to allowing the market forces and a sound competitive structure to bring about the necessary adjustments.

Naturally, those who make and implement economic policy have a major responsibility at the same time to promote an environment optimally conducive to investment, job creation and economic growth by means of appropriate and properly co-ordinated fiscal and monetary policy. The Government remains committed to this balanced and practical approach.

By means of restricting capital expenditure in parastatal institutions, privatization, deregulation and curtailing government expenditure, substantial progress has been made already towards reducing the role of the authorities in the economy. We shall persist with this in a well-considered way.

This does not mean that the State will forsake its indispensable development role, especially in our particular circumstances. On the contrary, it is the precise intention of the government to concentrate an equitable portion of its capacity on these aims by means of the meticulous determination of priorities.

Following the progress that has been made in other areas of the economy in recent years, it is now opportune to give particular attention to the supply side of the economy.

Fundamental factors which will contribute to the success of this restructuring are:

- the gradual reduction of inflation to levels comparable to those of our principal trading partners;
- the encouragement of personal initiative and savings;
- the subjection of all economic decisions by the authorities to stringent financial measures and discipline;
- rapid progress with the reform of our system of taxation; and
- the encouragement of exports as the impetus for industrialisation and earning foreign exchange.

These and other adjustments, which will require sacrifices, have to be seen as prerequisites for a new period of sustained growth in productive employment in the nineties. The Government has also noted with appreciation the manner in which the Reserve Bank has discharged its special responsibility in striving towards our common goals.

The Government is very much aware of the necessity of proper co-ordination and consistent implementation of its economic policy. For this reason, the establishment of the necessary structures and expertise to ensure this co-ordination is being given preference. This applies both to the various functions within the Government and to the interaction between the authorities and the private sector.

This is obviously not the occasion for me to deal in greater detail with our total economic strategy or with the recent course of the economy.

I shall confine myself to a few specific remarks on one aspect of fiscal policy that has been a source of criticism of the Government for some time, namely State expenditure.

The Government's financial year ends only in two months' time and several other important economic indicators for the 1989 calendar year are still subject to refinements at this stage. Nonetheless, several important trends are becoming increasingly clear. I am grateful to be able to say that we have apparently succeeded to a substantial degree in achieving most of our economic aims in the past year.

In respect of Government expenditure, the budget for the current financial year will be the most accurate in many years. The financial figures will show:

- that Government expenditure is thoroughly under control;
- that our normal financial programme has not exerted any significant upward pressure on rates of interest; and
- that we will close the year with a surplus, even without taking the income from the privatization of Iscor into account.

Without pre-empting this year's main budget, I wish to emphasize that is it is also our intention to co-ordinate fiscal and monetary policy in the coming financial year in a way that will enable us to achieve the ensuing goals–namely:

- that the present downturn will take the form of a soft landing which will help to make adjustments as easy as possible;
- that our economy will consolidate before the next upward phase so that we will be able to grow from a sound base; and
- that we shall persist with the implementation of the required structural adaptations in respect, among other things, of the following: easing the tax burden, especially on

individuals; sustained and adequate generation of surpluses on the current account of the balance of payments; and the reconstruction of our gold and foreign exchange reserves.

It is a matter of considerable seriousness to the Government, especially in this particular period of our history, to promote a dynamic economy which will make it possible for increasing numbers of people to be employed and share in rising standards of living.

Negotiation

In conclusion, I wish to focus the spotlight on the process of negotiation and related issues. At this stage I am refraining deliberately from discussing the merits of numerous political questions which undoubtedly will be debated during the next few weeks. The focus, now, has to fall on negotiation.

Practically every leader agrees that negotiation is the key to reconciliation, peace and a new and just dispensation. However, numerous excuses for refusing to take part are advanced. Some of the reasons being advanced are valid. Others are merely part of [a] political chess game. And while the game of chess proceeds, valuable time is being lost.

Against this background I committed the Government during my inauguration to giving active attention to the most important obstacles in the way of negotiation. Today I am able to announce far-reaching decisions in this connection. I believe that these decisions will shape a new phase in which there will be a movement away from measures which have been seized upon as a justification for confrontation and violence. The emphasis has to move, and will move now, to a debate and discussion of political and economic points of view as part of the process of negotiation.

I wish to urge every political and community leader, in and outside Parliament, to approach the new opportunities which are being created, constructively. There is no time left for advancing all manner of new conditions that will delay the negotiating process.

The steps that have been decided are the following:

The prohibition of the African National Congress, the Pan Africanist Congress, the South African Communist Party and a number of subsidiary organizations is being rescinded.

People serving prison sentences merely because they were members of one of these organisations or because they committed another offence which was merely an offence because of prohibition on one of the organisations was in force, will be identified and released. Prisoners who have been sentenced for other offences such ad murder terrorism or arson are not affected by this.

The media emergency regulations as well as the education emergency regulations are being abolished in their entirety.

The security emergency regulations will be amended to still make provision for effective control over visual material pertaining to scenes of unrest.

The restrictions in terms of the emergency regulations on 33 organisations are being rescinded. The organizations include the following:

National Education Crisis Committee
South African National Students Congress
United Democratic Front
COSATU (Congress of South African Trade Unions)
Blanke Gevrydingsbeweging van Suid-Afrika (White Liberation Movement)

The conditions imposed in terms of the security emergency regulations on 374 people on their release, are being rescinded and the regulations which provide for such conditions are being abolished.

The period of detention in terms of the security

emergency regulations will be limited henceforth to six months. Detainees also acquire the right to legal representation and a medical practitioner of their own choosing.

These decisions by the Cabinet are in accordance with the Government's declared intention to normalize the political process in South Africa without jeopardizing the maintenance of the good order. They were preceded by thorough and unanimous advice by a group of officials which included members of the security community.

Implementation will be immediate and, where necessary, notices will appear in the Government Gazette from tomorrow.

The most important facets of the advice the Government received in this connection, are the following:

The events in the Soviet Union and Eastern Europe, to which I have referred already, weaken the capability of organizations which were previously supported strongly from those quarters.

The activities of the organizations from which the prohibitions are now being lifted, no longer entail the same degree of threat to internal security which initially necessitated the imposition of the prohibitions.

There have been important shifts of emphasis in the statements and points of view of the most important of the organizations concerned, which indicate a new approach and a preference for peaceful solutions.

The South African Police is convinced that it is able, in the present circumstances, to combat violence and other crimes perpetrated also by members of these organizations and to bring offenders to justice without the aid of prohibitions on organisations.

About one matter there should be no doubt. The lifting of the prohibition on the said organizations does not signify in the least the approval or condonation of terrorism or crimes of violence committed under their banner or which may be perpetrated in the future. Equally, it should not be interpreted as a deviation from the Government's principles, among other things, against their economic policy and aspects of their constitutional policy. This will be dealt with in debate and negotiation.

At the same time I wish to emphasise that the maintenance of law and order dare not be jeopardized. The Government will not forsake its duty in this connection. Violence from whichever source, will be fought with all available might. Peaceful protest may not become the springboard for lawlessness, violence and intimidation. No democratic country can tolerate that.

Strong emphasis will be placed as well on even more effective law enforcement. Proper provision of manpower and means for the police and all who are involved with the enforcement of the law, will be ensured. In fact, the budget for the coming financial year will already begin to give effect to this.

I wish to thank the members of our security forces and related services for the dedicated service they have rendered the Republic of South Africa. Their dedication makes reform in a stable climate possible.

On the state of emergency I have been advised that an emergency situation, which justifies these special measures which have been retained, still exists. There is still conflict which is manifesting itself mainly in Natal, but as a consequence of the countrywide political power struggle. In addition, there are indications that radicals are still trying to disrupt the possibilities of negotiation by means of mass violence.

It is my intention to terminate the state of emergency completely as soon as circumstances justify it and I request the co-operation of everybody towards this end. Those responsible for unrest and conflict have to bear the blame rot the continuing state of emergency. In the meantime, the state of emergency is inhibiting only those who use chaos and disorder as political instruments.

Otherwise the rules of the game under the state of emergency are the same for everybody.

Against this background the Government is convinced that the decisions I have announced are justified from the security point of view. However, these decisions are justified from a political point of view as well.

Our country and all its people have been embroiled in conflict, tension and violent struggle for decades. It is time for us to break out of the cycle of violence and break through to peace and reconciliation. The silent majority is yearning for this. The youth deserve it.

With the steps the Government has taken, it has proven its good faith and the table is laid for sensible leaders to begin talking about a new dispensation, to reach an understanding by the way of dialogue and discussion.

The agenda is open and the overall aims to which we are aspiring should be acceptable to all reasonable South Africans.

Among other things, those aims include a new, democratic constitution; universal franchise; no domination; equality before an independent judiciary; the protection of minorities as well as of individual rights; freedom of religion; a sound economy based on proven economic principles and private enterprise; dynamic pro- grammes directed at better education, health services, housing and social conditions for all.

In this connection Mr. Nelson Mandela could play an important part. The Government has noted that he has declared himself to be willing to make a constructive contribution to the peaceful politi- cal process in South Africa.

I wish to put it plainly that the Government has taken a firm decision to release Mr. Mandela unconditionally. I am serious about bringing this matter to finality without delay. The Government will take a decision soon on the date of his release. Unfortunately, a further short passage of time is unavoidable.

Normally, there is a certain passage of time between the decision to release and the actual release because of logistical and administrative requirements. In the case of Mr. Mandela there are factors in the way of his immediate release, of which his personal circumstances and safety are not the least. He has not been an ordinary prisoner for quite some time. Because of that, his case requires particular circumspection.

Today's announcements, in particular, go to the heart of what Black leaders—also Mr. Mandela— have been advancing over the years as their reason for having resorted to violence. The allegation has been that the Government did not wish to talk to them and that they were deprived of their right to normal political activity by the prohibition of their organizations.

Without conceding that violence has ever been justified, I wish to say today to those who argued in this manner:

The Government wishes to talk to all leaders who seek peace.

The unconditional lifting of the prohibition on the said organizations places everybody in a position to pursue politics freely.

The justification for violence which was always advanced, no longer exists.

These facts place everybody in South Africa before a fait accompli. On the basis of numerous previous statements there is no longer any reason- able excuse for the continuation of violence. The time for talking has arrived and whoever still makes excuses does not really wish to talk.

Therefore, I repeat my invitation with greater conviction than ever:

Walk through the open door, take your place at the negotiating table together with the Govern- ment and other leaders who have important power bases inside and outside of Parliament.

Henceforth, everybody's political points of view will be tested against their realism, their workabil- ity and their fairness. The time for negotiation has arrived.

To those political leaders who have always resisted violence I say thank you for your prin- cipled stand. These include all the leaders of parliamentary parties, leaders of important organizations and movements, such as Chief Minister Buthelezi, all of the other Chief Ministers and urban community leaders.

Through their participation and discussion they have made an important contribution to this moment in which the process of free political participation is able to be restored. Their places in the negotiating process are assured.

Conclusion

In my inaugural address I said the following:

"All reasonable people in this country–by far the majority–anxiously await a message of hope. It is our responsibility as leaders in all spheres to provide that message realistically with courage and conviction.

"If we fail in that, the ensuing chaos, the demise of stability and progress, will for ever be held against us

"History has thrust upon the leadership of this country the tremendous responsibility to turn our country away from its present direction of conflict and confrontation. Only we, the leaders of our peoples, can do it.

"The eyes of responsible governments across the world are focused on us. The hopes of millions of South Africans are centred around us. The future of Southern Africa depends on us. We dare not falter or fail."

This is where we stand:

Deeply under the impression of our responsibility.

Humble in the face of the tremendous challenges ahead.

Determined to move forward in faith and with conviction.

I ask Parliament to assist me on the road ahead. There is much to be done.

I call on the international community to re-evaluate its position and to adopt a positive attitude towards the dynamic evolution which is taking place in South Africa.

I pray that the Almighty Lord will guide and sustain us on our course through uncharted waters and will bless your labours and deliberations.

Mr. Speaker, Members of Parliament, I now declare this Second Session of the Ninth Parliament of the Republic of South Africa to be duly opened.

Joe Slovo: "Has Socialism Failed?"

Joe Slovo (South African Communist Party)

Editor's Note: Joe Slovo was born in 1926 in Lithuania to Jewish parents. The family emigrated to South Africa when he was eight years old. Slovo joined the South African Communist Party in 1942 and eventually became its leader. He was a member of the ANC and Umkhonto we Sizwe, was part of the Congress of Democrats that drew up the Freedom Charter, and lived in exile from 1963 to 1990. The context of this essay was the dramatic collapse of the Soviet communist system 1989 in the USSR, East Germany, and other eastern European states. These events drew enthusiastic responses from exponents of free market economics, who celebrated the "victory of capitalism." Many followers of the nineteenth-century economic philosopher Karl Marx found themselves on uncertain ground. Terminology has always been important to Marxism, so readers should be aware of concepts such as "means of production" (the industrial tools used to produce the goods of society), "bourgeoisie" (the capitalist middle class), and "proletariat" (the working class). "Capitalism" is understood as the common economic system of "the West" (meaning western Europe and America) that empowers the wealthy to assert power over the actual producers through unregulated markets and private monopolies. "Communism" is understood as a political and social system controlled by workers themselves and oriented toward eradicating economic disparity between social classes and establishing antiracial and anticolonial universal justice. Slovo is also quite intent on distinguishing "Stalinism," the form of rigid and brutal authoritarianism that was developed in the 1930s by Josef Stalin, from a true application of the goals of Karl Marx and Vladimir Lenin. Be attentive to Slovo's use of the terms "socialism" and "communism"—does he use these terms interchangeably or are they distinct? Is he always consistent in his use of terminology? How does Slovo understand the basic objectives of communism?

January 1990

1. Introduction

Socialism is undoubtedly in the throes of a crisis greater than at any time since 1917. The last half of 1989 saw the dramatic collapse of most of the communist party governments of Eastern Europe. Their downfall was brought about through massive upsurges which had the support not only of the majority of the working class but also a large slice of the membership of the ruling parties themselves. These were popular revolts against unpopular regimes; if socialists are unable to come to terms with this reality, the future of socialism is indeed bleak.

The mounting chronicle of crimes and distortions in the history of existing socialism, its economic failures and the divide which developed between socialism and democracy, have raised doubts in the minds of many former supporters of the socialist cause as to whether socialism can work at all. Indeed, we must expect that, for a time, many in the affected countries will be easy targets for those aiming to achieve a reversion to capitalism, including an embrace of its external policies.[1]

Shock-waves of very necessary self-examination have also been triggered off among communists both inside and outside the socialist world. For our part, we firmly believe in the future of socialism;

1. Marx used the term "primitive accumulation" to describe the original process of capitalist accumulation, which, he maintained, was not the result of abstinence but rather of acts (including brigandage) such as the expropriation of the peasantry as happened during the British Enclosures (Capital Volume 1, Part VII). Preobrazhensky in *The New Economics* (1926) talked about "primitive socialist accumulation" involving the expropriation of resources from the better-off classes to generate capital for socialist industrial development. Here, the term is used to describe the arbitrary measures taken against the Soviet peasantry to forcibly "enclose" them into collectives.

and we do not dismiss its whole past as an unmitigated failure. Socialism certainly produced a Stalin and a Ceaușescu, but it also produced a Lenin and a Gorbachev. Despite the distortions at the top, the nobility of socialism's basic objectives inspired millions upon millions to devote themselves selflessly to building it on the ground. And, no one can doubt that if humanity is today poised to enter an unprecedented era of peace and civilised international relations, it is in the first place due to the efforts of the socialist world.

But it is more vital than ever to subject the past of existing socialism to an unsparing critique in order to draw the necessary lessons.

2. Ideological Responses

Editor's comment: This section discusses the collapse of communist political authority in the USSR and Eastern European countries. How does it explain the demise of communism? How is the typical portrayal of communism skewed to create an incomplete picture? According to Slovo, what were the primary problems of Stalinism? How do Stalinism and capitalism relate differently to the principles of democracy? What are the core values and goals of Marxist communism?

The ideological responses to the crisis of existing socialism by constituents of what was previously known as the International Communist and Workers' movement (and among our own members) is still so varied and tentative that it is early days to attempt a neat categorisation. But at the risk of over-simplification, we identify a number of broad tendencies against which we must guard:

> Finding excuses for Stalinism
> Attributing the crisis to the pace of perestroika
> Acting as if we have declared a moratorium on socialist criticism of capitalism and imperialism and, worst of all,
> Concluding that socialist theory made the distortions inevitable.

A. STICKING TO STALINISM

The term "Stalinism" is used to denote the bureaucratic-authoritarian style of leadership (of parties both in and out of power) which denuded the party and the practice of socialism of most of its democratic content and concentrated power in the hands of a tiny, self-perpetuating elite.

While the mould for Stalinism was cast under Stalin's leadership it is not suggested that he bears sole responsibility for its negative practices. The essential content of Stalinism—socialism without democracy—was retained even after Stalin in the Soviet Union (until Gorbachev's intervention), albeit without some of the terror, brutality and judicial distortions associated with Stalin himself.

Among a diminishing minority there is still a reluctance to look squarely in the mirror of history and to concede that the socialism it reflects has, on balance, been so distorted that an appeal to its positive achievements (and of course there have been many) sounds hollow and very much like special pleading. It is surely now obvious that if the socialist world stands in tatters at this historic moment it is due to the Stalinist distortions . . .

Vigilance is clearly needed against the pre-perestroika styles of work and thinking which infected virtually every party (including ours) and moulded its members for so many decades. It is not enough merely to engage in the self-pitying cry: "we were misled." . . . In general, those who still defend the Stalinist model—even in a qualified way—are a dying breed; at the ideological level they will undoubtedly be left behind and they need not detain us here.

B. BLAMING GORBACHEV

. . . In the countries mentioned [Poland, Hungary, GDR, Czechoslovakia], despite the advantage of over 40 years of a monopoly of education, the media, etc., the parties in power could not find a significant section of the class they claimed to represent (or, for that matter, even a majority of their own membership) to defend them or their version of socialism. To blame perestroika and glasnost for the ailments of socialism is like blaming the diagnosis and the prescription for the illness. Indeed, the only way to ensure the future of socialism is to grasp the nettle with the political courage of a Gorbachev.

. . . In general, it is our view that the fact that the processes of perestroika and glasnost came too slowly, too little and too late in Eastern Europe did more than anything else to endanger the socialist perspective there. It is through these processes—and they must be implemented with all possible speed—that socialism has any hope of showing its essentially human face. When socialism as a world system comes into its own again—as it undoubtedly will—the "Gorbachev revolution" will have played a seminal role.

C. ABANDONING THE IDEOLOGICAL CONTEST

The transformations which have occurred in Poland, Hungary, the German Democratic Republic, Czechoslovakia and Bulgaria are revolutionary in scope. With the exception of Romania, is there another example in human history in which those in power have responded to the inevitable with such a civilised and pacific resignation?

We should remember De Gaulle's military response in 1968 when ten million workers and students filled the streets of Paris. It is not difficult to forecast how Bush or Thatcher would deal with millions in their streets supported by general strikes demanding the overthrow of their system of rule.

. . . whatever else may be happening in international relations, the ideological offensive by the representatives of capitalism against socialism is certainly at full blast.

The Western media gloat repeatedly with headlines such as "Communism—R.I.P." Professor Robert Heilbroner, a luminary of the New York New School, has already raised his champagne glass with a victory toast for capitalism. Asserting that the Soviet Union, China and Eastern Europe have proved that capitalism organises the material affairs of humankind more satisfactorily than socialism, he goes on to proclaim:

"Less than 75 years after it officially began, the contest between capitalism and socialism is over; capitalism has won . . . the great question now seems how rapid will be the transformation of socialism into capitalism, and not the other way around."[1]

. . . In the face of all this, it is no exaggeration to claim that, for the moment, the socialist critique of capitalism and the drive to win the hearts and minds of humanity for socialism have been virtually abandoned. The unprecedented offensive by capitalist ideologues against socialism has indeed been met by a unilateral ideological disarmament.

To the extent that this has come about through the need to concentrate on putting our own house in order it is, at least, understandable. But, in many cases, there is an inability to distinguish between socialism in general and the incorrect methods which were used to translate it on the ground. This has led to an unjustified flirtation with certain economic and political values of capitalism.

The perversion of democracy in the socialist experience is falsely contrasted to its practice in the capitalist West as if the latter gives adequate scope for the fulfillment of democratic ideals. The economic ravages caused by excessive centralisation and commandism under socialism seem also to have pushed into the background the basic socialist critique of capitalism that a society cannot be democratic which is ruled by profit and social inequality and in which power over the most vital areas of life is outside public control.

D: LOSING FAITH IN THE SOCIALIST OBJECTIVE

Some communists have been completely overwhelmed by the soiled image of socialism which they see in the mirror of history . . .

We believe, however, that the theory of Marxism, in all its essential respects, remains valid and provides an indispensable theoretical guide to achieve a society free of all forms of exploitation of

1. *The New Yorker*, 23 January 1989.

person by person. The major weaknesses which have emerged in the practice of socialism are the results of distortions and misapplications. They do not flow naturally from the basic concepts of Marxism whose core is essentially humane and democratic and which project a social order with an economic potential vastly superior to that of capitalism.

3. *Marxist Theory under Fire*

Editor's Note: Whereas during the Cold War Europeans and Americans often perceived communism as primarily a political system in competition with liberal democracy, Slovo and other communists preferred to point to the moral and ethical foundations of its ideology. What aspects of Marxist theory does Slovo stress as being central to the persistence of a healthy communism in the face of the collapse of the Soviet system?

Let us touch on some of the concepts which have come under fire in the post-perestroika polemics:

Marxism maintains that the class struggle is the motor of human history.[2] Some commentators in the socialist media are showing a temptation to jettison this theory merely because Stalin and the bureaucracy around him distorted it to rationalise tyrannical practices. But it remains valid both as an explanation of past social transformations and as a guide to the strategy and tactics of the struggle to win a socialist order; a struggle in which the working class plays the dominant role.

The economic stagnation of socialism and its poor technological performance as compared to the capitalist world sector cannot be attributed to the ineffectiveness of socialist relations of production but rather to their distortion. Socialist relations of production provide the most effective framework for maximising humanity's productive capacity

2. This must be understood as providing the immediate explanation of the way major social change manifests itself in a situation in which the relations of production have become obstacles to the development of productive forces.

and using its products in the interests of the whole society.

Marxist ethical doctrine sees no conflict between the contention that all morality is class-related and the assertion that working class values are concerned, above all, with the supremacy of human values.[1] The separation of these inter-dependent concepts (in later theory and practice) provided the context in which crimes against the people were rationalised in the name of the class. We continue to assert that it is only in a non-exploitative, communist, classless society that human values will find their ultimate expression and be freed of all class-related morality. In the meanwhile the socialist transition has the poten-tial of progressively asserting the values of the whole people over those of classes.

The great divide which developed between socialism and political democracy should not be treated as flowing naturally from key aspects of socialist doctrine. . . . We believe that Marxism clearly projects a system anchored in deep-seated political democracy and the rights of the individual which can only be truly attained when society as a whole assumes control and direction of all its riches and resources.

. . . In summary, we believe that Marxism is a social science whose fundamental postulates and basic insights into the historical processes remain a powerful (because accurate) theoretical weapon. But this is not to say that every word of Marx, Engels and Lenin must be taken as gospel; they were not infallible and they were not always correct in their projections.

Editor's Note: In this section, Slovo explains that in specific historical conditions socialism has been misapplied, but that those errors should not be attributed to the founding ideals and "science" of socialism. He is ready to acknowledge that Marx and Lenin were not always correct in their understanding of historical conditions, but he insists that these in no way undermine the interpretive power of the Marxist theory of class struggle. How does he explain the spread of communist systems that failed to uphold Marxist ideals?

Lenin, for example, believed that capitalism was about to collapse worldwide in the post-October period.

. . . Also, it could well be argued that the classical description of bourgeois democracy[2] was an over-simplification and tended to underesti-mate the historic achievements of working class struggle in imposing and defending aspects of a real democratic culture on the capitalist state; a culture which should not disappear but rather needs to be expanded under true socialism.

But we emphasise again that the fundamental distortions which emerged in the practice of existing socialism cannot be traced to the essential tenets of Marxist revolutionary science.

If we are looking for culprits, we must look at ourselves and not at the founders of Marxism.

The Fault Lies with us, not with Socialism . . .

We make no attempt here to answer the complex question of why so many millions of genuine socialists and revolutionaries became such blind worshippers in the temple of the cult of the person-ality. Suffice it to say that the strength of this conformism lay, partly, in an ideological convic-tion that those whom history had appointed as the custodians of humankind's communist future seemed to be building on foundations prepared by the founding fathers of Marxism. And there was not enough in classical Marxist theory about the

1. This type of formulation is preferred to the one occasionally used by Gorbachev, that there are certain universal human values which take priority over class values. This latter formulation tends to detract from the interdependence of working-class and human morality. It also perhaps goes too far in separating morality from its class connection, even though it is clear that the assertion of certain values can be in the mutual interests of otherwise contending classes.

2. See Lenin, "State and Revolution," in *Selected Works,* 203–4.

nature of the transition period to provide a detailed guide to the future.

4. Socialism and Democracy

Editor's Note: Slovo analyzes the relationship of socialism to democracy by examining both theoretical and historical developments. In the first section, he observes how Marx, Engels, Lenin, and Luxembourg stressed the importance of real freedom in contrast to the manipulated vision of the "Dictatorship of the Proletariat." The second and third sections deal with the historical emergence of one-party systems in communist countries and its negative consequences. The fourth section considers the complicated and mixed results of single-party states in Africa, observing that it has not been a strictly communist phenomenon, but that in all cases it results in the alienation of the majority of the people from governance. According to Luxembourg, how important is the presence of dissent to true proletarian democracy? Why does Slovo see a single-party political system as antithetical to socialist democracy? What are the implications of Slovo's discussion of a single-party system for his understanding of the situation of South Africa under apartheid, and how might this affect his consideration of the role of the ANC in a postapartheid state?

Marxist ideology saw the future state as "a direct democracy in which the task of governing would not be the preserve of a state bureaucracy" and as "an association in which the free development of each is a condition for the free development of all."[1] How did it happen that, in the name of this most humane and liberating ideology, the bureaucracy became so all-powerful and the individual was so suffocated?

To find, at least, the beginnings of an answer we need to look at four related areas:

The thesis of the "Dictatorship of the Proletariat" which was used as the theoretical rationalisation for unbridled authoritarianism.

1. *Communist Manifesto.*

The steady erosion of people's power both at the level of government and mass social organisations.

The perversion of the concept of the party as a vanguard of the working class, and

Whether, at the end of the day, socialist democracy can find real expression in a single-party state.

A. DICTATORSHIP OF THE PROLETARIAT

The concept of the "Dictatorship of the Proletariat" was dealt with rather thinly by Marx as "a transition to a classless society" without much further definition.[2]

. . . The concept of the "Dictatorship of the Proletariat" was elaborated by Lenin in State and Revolution in the very heat of the revolutionary transformation in 1917. Lenin quoted Engels approvingly when he said that "the proletariat needs the state, not in the interests of freedom but in order to hold down its adversaries, and as soon as it becomes possible to speak of freedom the state as such ceases to exist" (Engels, Letter to Bebel). In the meanwhile, in contrast to capitalist democracy which is "curtailed, wretched, false . . . for the rich, for the minority . . . the dictatorship of the proletariat, the period of transition to communism, will, for the first time, create democracy . . . for the majority . . . along with the necessary suppression of the exploiters, of the minority."[3]

. . . Rosa Luxemburg said, in a polemic with Lenin:

'Freedom only for the supporters of the government, only for the members of one party—however numerous they may be—is not freedom at all. Freedom is always and exclusively freedom for the one who thinks differently . . . its effectiveness vanishes when "freedom" becomes a special privilege.[4]

2. Letter to J. Wademeyer; see also "Critique of the Gotha Program," in *Selected Works*, p. 331.

3. *Selected Works*, Volume Two, pp. 302–3.

4. *The Russian Revolution*, p. 79, 14.

. . . The term "Dictatorship of the Proletariat" reflected the historical truth that in class-divided social formations state power is ultimately exercised by, and in the interests of, the class which owns and controls the means of production. It is in this sense that capitalist formations were described as a "dictatorship of the bourgeoisie" whose rule would be replaced by a "dictatorship of the proletariat" during the socialist transition period. In the latter case power would, however, be exercised in the interests of the overwhelming majority of the people and should lead to an ever-expanding genuine democracy—both political and economic.

D. THE SINGLE-PARTY STATE

Hegel coined the profound aphorism that truth is usually born as a heresy and dies as a superstition. With no real right to dissent by citizens or even by the mass of the party membership, truth became more and more inhibited by deadening dogma; a sort of catechism took the place of creative thought. And, within the confines of a single-party state, the alternative to active conformism was either silence or the risk of punishment as "an enemy of the people."

Is this suppression of the right to dissent inherent in the single-party state? Gorbachev recently made the point that:

"Developing the independent activities of the masses and prompting democratisation of all spheres of life under a one-party system is a noble but very difficult mission for the party. And a great deal will depend on how we deal with it."[1]

Gorbachev's thought has special relevance to many parts of our own continent where the one-party system abounds. It straddles both capitalist and socialist-oriented countries and in most of them it is used to prevent, among other things, the democratic organisation of the working people either politically or in trade unions.

This is not to say that all one-party states in our continent have in fact turned out to be authoritar-

1. *Pravda*, 26 November 1989, p. 18.

ian; indeed some of them are headed by the most humane leaders who passionately believe in democratic processes. Nor can we discuss the role they have played in preventing tribal, ethnic and regional fragmentation, combatting externally inspired banditry, and correcting some of the grave distortions we inherited from the colonial period.

In relation to the socialist perspective, it is sometimes forgotten that the concept of the single-party state is nowhere to be found in classical Marxist theory. And we have had sufficient experience of one-party rule in various parts of the world to perhaps conclude that the "mission" to promote real democracy under a one-party system is not just difficult but, in the long run, impossible.

But, in any case, where a single-party state is in place and there is not even democracy and accountability within the party, it becomes a short-cut to a political tyranny over the whole of society. And at different points in time this is what happened in most socialist states.

The resulting sense of political alienation of the great majority of the people was not the only negative feature of existing socialism. Of equal importance was the failure to overcome the sense of economic alienation inherited from the capitalist past.

5. Socialist Economic Alienation

Editor's Note: In this section, Slovo discusses the challenges facing real "socialization." His emphasis is on the need for full popular control over property and wealth. What is the role of democracy in establishing this deep connection between society and the de-alienation of objective wealth (i.e., wealth that is produced by workers but allocated to bourgeois powers for the perpetuation of exploitation of and injustice to the workers)?

The concept of alienation expressed "the objective transformation of the activity of man and of its results into an independent force, dominating him and inimical to him. . . ."[1] Alienation has its origins in class-dominated society based on private property. Under capitalism, in the course of the production process, the worker himself "always produces objective wealth, in the form of capital, an alien power that dominates and exploits him."[2] Thus, the exploited classes objectively create and recreate the conditions of their own domination and exploitation. Consciousness of this fuels the class struggle against capitalist relations of production.

The aim of communism is to achieve the complete mastery and control over social forces which humanity itself has generated but which, under capitalism, have become objectified as alien power which is seen to stand above society and exercises mastery over it. Communism, according to Marx, involves the creation of a society in which "socialised humanity, the associated producers, regulate their interchange with nature rationally, bringing it under their common control, instead of being ruled by it as by some blind power."[3]

The relevance of all this for our discussion is that only genuine socialist relations of production can begin the process which will lead to the de-alienation of society as a whole and generate the formation of a new "socialist person." The process of de-alienation—whose completion must await the stage of communism—cannot be advanced by education and ideology alone; conditions must be created which lead progressively to real participation and control by each individual (as part of "socialised humanity") over social life in all its aspects.

The destruction of the political and economic power of capital are merely first steps in the direction of de-alienation. The transfer of legal ownership of productive property from private capital to the state does not, on its own, create fully socialist relations of production, nor does it always significantly change the work-life of the producer.

The power to control the producers' work-life and to dispose of the products of labour is now in the hands of a "committee" rather than a board of directors. And if the "committee" separates itself from the producers by a bureaucratic wall without democratic accountability, its role is perceived no differently from that of the board of directors. It remains a force over which the producer has no real control and which (despite the absence of economic exploitation of the capitalist variety) dominates him as an alien power.

State property itself has to be transformed into social property. This involves reorganising social life as a whole so that the producers, at least as a collective, have a real say not only in the production of social wealth but also in its disposal. In the words of Gorbachev, what is required is "not only formal but also real socialisation and the real turning of the working people into the masters of all socialised production."[4]

De-alienation requires that the separation between social wealth creation and social wealth appropriation and distribution is ended and society as a whole is in control of all three processes. A degree of self-management (at the level of individual enterprises) is only one ingredient in the process of de-alienation; conditions must be created making possible full popular control over all society's institutions of power not just as a "constitutional right" but as a reality.

ALIENATION IN EXISTING SOCIALISM

Under capitalism economic compulsion sanctified by the rule of capital (threatened unemployment, etc.) plays an important role in providing the "incentive" for rising productivity despite alienation by[5] workers from the products of their labour. Capitalist economic levers based on the sanctity of private property are, at the end of the day, not over-concerned with the problems of alienation and more easily provide the incentive (in relation

1. Marx, *Capital*, Volume 1, p. 716, Penguin Books Edition.
2. A. P. Ogurtsov, *Soviet Encyclopedia of Philosophy*.
3. *Capital*, Volume 3, Chapter 48.

4. *Pravda*, 30 September 1989.
5. *Pravda*, 30 September 1989.

to the workers) that "he who does not work, neither shall he eat."

Under socialism guaranteed employment and the amount of remuneration did not always depend upon quality, productivity or efficiency, opening the way to parasitism at the point of production. Reward based on the socialist maxim of "to each according to his contribution" can obviously play a part in increasing productivity. But for socialist society as a whole to really come into its own requires an incentive based on the producer's real participation in the mechanisms of social control over the products of his/her labour; a feeling that the means of production and its products are his or hers as part of society. This incentive was too often absent and stood in the way of the process of de-alienation.

. . . But rectification of these areas alone would not establish the material and moral superiority of socialism as a way of life for humanity. Only the creation of real socialist relations of production will give birth to the socialist man and woman whose active participation in all the social processes will ensure that socialism reaches its full potential and moves towards a classless communist society. Under existing socialism alienation has persisted because of a less than full control and participation by the people in these processes.

In short, the way forward is through thorough-going democratic socialism; a way which can only be charted by a party which wins its support through democratic persuasion and ideological contest and not, as has too often happened up to now, by a claim of right.

6. A Look at Ourselves

Editor's Note: How does Slovo use a critique of past communist policy to reflect its strengths and potentialities? What key features of governance does the South African Communist Party endorse?

The commandist and bureaucratic approaches which took root during Stalin's time affected communist parties throughout the world, including our own. We cannot disclaim our share of the responsibility for the spread of the personality cult and a mechanical embrace of Soviet domestic and foreign policies, some of which discredited the cause of socialism. We kept silent for too long after the 1956 Khruschev revelations.

. . . We do not pretend that our party's changing postures in the direction of democratic socialism are the results only of our own independent evolution. Our shift undoubtedly owes a prime debt to the process of perestroika and glasnost which was so courageously unleashed under Gorbachev's inspiration. Closer to home, the democratic spirit which dominated in the re-emerged trade union movement from the early 1970's onwards, also made its impact.

But we can legitimately claim that in certain fundamental respects our indigenous revolutionary practice long ago ceased to be guided by Stalinist concepts. This is the case particularly in relation to the way the party performed its role as a working class vanguard, its relations with fraternal organisations and representatives of other social forces and, above all, its approach to the question of democracy in the post-apartheid state and in a future socialist South Africa.

THE PARTY AS A VANGUARD AND INNER-PARTY DEMOCRACY

We have always believed (and we continue to do so) that it is indispensable for the working class to have an independent political instrument which safeguards its role in the democratic revolution and which leads it towards an eventual classless society. But such leadership must be won rather than imposed. Our claim to represent the historic aspirations of the workers does not give us an absolute right to lead them or to exercise control over society as a whole in their name.

Our new programme asserts that a communist party does not earn the title of vanguard merely by proclaiming it. Nor does its claim to be the upholder of Marxism give it a monopoly of political wisdom or a natural right to exclusive control of the struggle. We can only earn our place as a vanguard force by superior efforts of leadership and devotion to the cause of liberation and socialism. And we can only win adherence to our ideology by demonstrating its superiority as a theoretical guide to revolutionary practice.

. . . Overall, despite the security risks involved in the clandestine conditions, the will of our membership finds democratic expression. This spirit of democracy also informs our relationship with fraternal political forces and our approach to the political framework of a post-liberation South Africa.

Relations with Fraternal Organisations . . .

We do not regard the trade unions or the national movement as mere conduits for our policies. Nor do we attempt to advance our policy positions through intrigue or manipulation. Our relationship with these organisations is based on complete respect for their independence, integrity and inner-democracy. In so far as our influence is felt, it is the result of open submissions of policy positions and the impact of individual communists who win respect as among the most loyal, the most devoted and ideologically clear members of these organisations.

Democracy and the Future   Our party's

programme holds firmly to a post-apartheid state which will guarantee all citizens the basic rights and freedoms of organisation, speech, thought, press, movement, residence, conscience and religion; full trade union rights for all workers including the right to strike, and one person one vote in free and democratic elections. These freedoms constitute the very essence of our national liberation and socialist objectives and they clearly imply political pluralism.

Both for these historical reasons and because experience has shown that an institutionalised one-party state has a strong propensity for authoritarianism, we remain protagonists of multi-party

post-apartheid democracy both in the national democratic and socialist phases, is desirable.

We believe that post-apartheid state power must clearly vest in the elected representatives of the people and not, directly or indirectly, in the administrative command of a party. The relationship which evolves between political parties and state structures must not, in any way, undermine the sovereignty of elected bodies.

We also believe that if there is real democracy in the post-apartheid state, the way will be open for a peaceful progression towards our ultimate objective—a socialist South Africa. This approach is consistent with the Marxist view—not always adhered to in practice—that the working class must win the majority to its side: as long as no violence is used against the people there is no other road to power.[1]

It follows that, in truly democratic conditions, it is perfectly legitimate and desirable for a party claiming to be the political instrument of the working class to attempt to lead its constituency in democratic contest for political power against other parties and groups representing other social forces. And if it wins, it must be constitutionally required, from time to time, to go back to the people for a renewed mandate. The alternative to this is self-perpetuating power with all its implications for corruption and dictatorship.

CONCLUSION
Editor's Note: How does Slovo articulate the humanitarian imperative of socialism? Why does a humane and just society need socialism?

We dare not underestimate the damage that has been wrought to the cause of socialism by the distortions we have touched upon. We, however, continue to have complete faith that socialism represents the most rational, just and democratic way for human beings to relate to one another.

Humankind can never attain real freedom until

1. Lenin, *Selected Works*, Volume 2, p. 36.

a society has been built in which no person has the freedom to exploit another person.

The bulk of humanity's resources will never be used for the good of humanity until they are in public ownership and under democratic control.

The ultimate aim of socialism to eliminate all class inequalities occupies a prime place in the body of civilised ethics even before Marx.

The all-round development of the individual and the creation of opportunities for every person to express his or her talents to the full can only find ultimate expression in a society which dedicates itself to people rather than profit.

The opponents of socialism are very vocal about what they call the failure of socialism in Africa.[1] But they say little, if anything, about Africa's real failure; the failures of capitalism. Over 90 percent of our continent's people live out their wretched and repressed lives in stagnating and declining capitalist-oriented economies. International capital, to whom most of these countries are mortgaged, virtually regards cheap bread, free education and full employment as economic crimes. Western outcries against violations of human rights are muted when they occur in countries with a capitalist orientation.

The way forward for the whole of humanity lies within a socialist framework guided by genuine socialist humanitarianism and not within a capitalist system which entrenches economic and social inequalities as a way of life. Socialism can undoubtedly be made to work without the negative practices which have distorted many of its key objectives.

But mere faith in the future of socialism is not enough. The lessons of past failures have to be learnt. Above all, we have to ensure that its funda-

mental tenet—socialist democracy—occupies a rightful place in all future practice.

The Birth of the Inkatha Freedom Party (IFP)[2]

Editor's Note: Mangosuthu Buthelezi, by birth of the Zulu aristocracy and educated at Harvard University, has long been the primary leader of the Zulus living in KwaZulu-Natal, though they also maintained a traditional kingship. In 1975, Buthelezi formed the Inkatha National Cultural Liberation Movement, which in 1990 evolved into the Inkatha Freedom Party. The party stressed the importance of Ubuntu-botho, meaning "I am, because you are," which symbolized an economic approach to empowering small businesses through stakeholder investment and cross-selling opportunities. How did Inkatha portray its role in the struggle against apartheid? How does it understand culture and the relationship of cultural expression to democracy?

On the 14th of July 1990 at a special conference in Ulundi the Inkatha Freedom Party (IFP) came into being. Dr. Mangosuthu Buthelezi was unanimously elected President of the IFP.

The guiding philosophy of the IFP remained Ubuthu-botho [sic]. The IFP's vision to solving the economic disenfranchisement of the majority of South Africans was that of a free market economy with a heavy influence on the social responsibility of the state in the light of the serious political, social and economic injustices of apartheid.

The IFP became the champion of federalism in South Africa. It argued that real power needed to be given to people to make decisions that affect their lives. Apartheid, argued the IFP, had proved to South Africa how a small minority of people could oppress the majority through the centralisation of power and that a fundamental and profound constitutional revolution needed occur to truly empower Black South Africans. The IFP remains convinced and committed to ensuring that federalism is implemented in South Africa . . .

---

1. They conveniently ignore the fact that most of the countries that tried to create conditions for the building of socialism faced unending civil war, aggression, and externally inspired banditry, a situation in which it is hardly possible to build any kind of stable social formation—capitalist or socialist.

2. http://www.ifp.org.za/.

At the July 1990 meeting at which Inkatha National Cultural Liberation Movement was transformed into the Inkatha Freedom Party it set itself the following tasks:

Task 1: To establish an open, free, non-racial, equal opportunity, reconciled society with democratic safeguards for all people.

Task 2: To harness the great resources of the country to fight the real enemies of the people, namely; poverty, hunger, unemployment, disease, ignorance, insecurity, homelessness and moral decay.

Task 3: To re-distribute the wealth of the country for the benefit of all people, and to establish political and economic structures that encourage enterprise and create the wealth all governments of the future will need.

Task 4: To ensure the maintenance of a stable, peaceful society in which all people can pursue their happiness, and realise their potential without fear or favour.

The Meaning of "Inkatha"

The name "Inkatha" has a deeply symbolic as well as practical meaning. In essence an "Inkatha" is a plaited coil or circle made of straws of grass, placed on the head to carry and alleviate the weight of a heavy burden. It is so powerfully woven together that it does not crumble and break. Neither does it slip and dislodge its burden.

Symbolically, therefore, the IFP feels a keen responsibility towards maintaining political balance and of assisting and protecting people from the heavy social and political burdens that they bear. As the circular shape of an Inkatha represents unity the IFP is committed to ensuring that no matter the diversity of the peoples South Africa becomes one nation.

Historical Background of the Inkatha Freedom Party

THE INKATHA NATIONAL CULTURAL LIBERATION MOVEMENT (1975)

The Inkatha National Cultural Liberation Movement was founded on the 21st March 1975 at KwaNzimela, in Northern KwaZulu. Inkatha emerged, along with the Black Consciousness Movement, to fill the vacuum in black politics caused by the banning of the ANC and PAC. Most of the founders of Inkatha had been either ANC office-bearers or activists. The most prominent example is that of Dr. M.G. Buthelezi, formerly a member of the ANC Youth League, who became the President of the Inkatha National Cultural Liberation Movement. Other prominent founding members of Inkatha were the late Rt. Rev. Bishop Dr. A.H. Zulu and Dr. Frank T. Mdlalose, among others.

Unlike King Solomon's Inkatha, the National Cultural Liberation Movement launched itself as an all-embracing national movement with its sights set on the liberation of all South Africans. Although established in KwaZulu, its membership was made open to all blacks—men, women and youth—and branches opened in KwaZulu, Natal, the Transvaal, the Orange Free State and the Western Cape.

The Inkatha National Cultural Liberation Movement did not claim to be the sole and authentic representative of the Black peoples of South Africa. Its aim was to work in a multi-strategy approach for the freedom of the people and for a united non-racial democratic country. Its emergence was a result of a desperate need at that time for black democratic forces to come to the fore and pick up the gauntlet of the black liberation struggle which had been left tragically destitute by so many others.

From the 1960's there had been no significant organised black political activity. The African National Congress (ANC) and the Pan Africanist Congress (PAC) had been banned and their leaders were either in jail, in exile or had "disappeared" into the underground movement. Wave after wave of repression by the South African Government had, by 1975, left black politics in disarray.

At the time of Inkatha's launch in 1975 the names of ANC leaders Nelson Mandela, Walter Sisulu, Goven Mbeki, Moses Mabhida and others including PAC leader Robert Sobukwe were being whispered in quiet corners. Dr. Buthelezi, from the beginning, spoke of them in his speeches and even quoted them, which was a punishable offence. He raised questions of their release and made their release conditional to any dialogue with the white racist Nationalist Party regime.

INKATHA AND THE ANC

When asked why he established Inkatha, Dr. Buthelezi said:

"I wanted democratic forces emerging in South Africa to accept a multi-strategy approach and offer to work in harmony with the ANC Mission in Exile. In 1974 when I set about gathering leaders together to establish Inkatha in 1975, I set about doing so with the clear intention NOT of subverting the ANC Mission in Exile—but of proving to them that democratic opposition to apartheid and non-violent tactics and strategies were still possible."

His attitude was that if the ANC Mission in Exile had (understandably) opted for violence, then it was incumbent on black South Africans to prove that democratic opposition could be productive. Dr. Buthelezi added: "I rallied black South Africans under the national colours of black South Africa—black, green and gold. I brought together a very considerable constituency, which had provided the old ANC with grass-root support while it was in the country. We sang old freedom songs and in every way identified with the ANC Mission in Exile. I told my people that they were our brothers and sisters and we should wage a struggle in harmony with them."

Dr. Buthelezi kept in contact with the ANC Mission in Exile and liaised with their offices in Swaziland. His emissaries had frequent meetings with the ANC Mission in Exile personnel. "I sent emissaries abroad charging them to argue the merits of a multi-strategy approach with them, and to offer co-operation in those projects where Inkatha's aims and objectives coincided with the ANC Mission in

Exile aims and objectives—and where tactics and strategies were not mutually hostile," said Buthelezi.

There was one issue about which Dr. Buthelezi made his views abundantly clear. He and Inkatha had never accepted the unilateral decision, which the ANC Mission in Exile had made, to commit black South Africa to the armed struggle as the primary means of bringing about change. He said: "I established Inkatha as a black liberation movement in the sincere hope that the dangerous divisions in black politics could be bridged. I could not side with the Black Consciousness Movement's rejection of the ANC Mission in Exile. I understood the grave difficulties, which the ANC Mission in Exile had been facing in the outside world. Both in South Africa and abroad I argued in public that the ANC had been driven underground by South African police brutality and that it was understandable that in an exiled position, where they were rejected by the West, the Mission in Exile should seek recourse in violence."

"I accepted that the ANC Mission in Exile having being rejected by the West, would naturally seek alliances elsewhere. It was for me understandable that they should start thinking in terms of the application of force against apartheid. I, however, never accepted the unilateral decision, which the ANC Mission in Exile made to commit black South Africa to the armed struggle as the primary means of bringing about change once they were in exile. They never consulted black South Africa about this very fundamental step. They made the decision unilaterally only after they had been in exile for some years."

In response to Dr. Buthelezi's and others questioning whether the armed struggle had a mandate from black South Africa, Mr. Joe Slovo, a member of the ANC Mission in Exile and the head of Umkhonto weSizwe, its military wing acknowledged: "The attempts, particularly in the West, to question this policy and to influence the ANC to consider the adoption of a "peaceful road to change" is nothing less than a recipe for submission and surrender of national liberation aims. We must bear in mind that the ANC was declared illegal long before it adopted a policy of armed struggle."

The decision of Dr. Buthelezi and the Inkatha National Cultural Liberation Movement, and later the Inkatha Freedom Party (IFP) not to support and adopt the ANC Mission in Exile's armed struggle would later be one the greatest points of conflict between the ANC and Inkatha. This conflict would result in the tragic loss of lives on both sides.

Inkatha under the leadership of Dr. M.G. Buthelezi, however, remained firm in their rejection of the armed struggle.

THE LONDON MEETING

After four years of sending emissaries abroad the time seemed ripe for a top-level meeting between Inkatha and the ANC. The first such meeting took place in Stockholm in the early part of 1979. That meeting was used as a consultative meeting to establish a summit conference between Inkatha and the ANC Mission in Exile, which took place in October 1979. Mr Oliver Tambo attended the meeting (which was chaired by Dr. A.H. Zulu, the Speaker of the KwaZulu Legislative Assembly).

Dr. Buthelezi later reflected: "I went to London determined to seek reconciliation and determined to bring about a working relationship between the ANC Mission in Exile and Inkatha. I was aware of the fact that Mr. Oliver Tambo was having difficulties with some elements of his organisation. Those with a firm commitment to violence did not want any evidence that non-violent strategies were viable in South Africa." In all his discussions with the ANC Mission in Exile Dr. Buthelezi was adamant that Inkatha should remain Inkatha and that it should remain committed to the Black popular will which expressed itself in Inkatha's massive membership, which had doubled in 1977 and again doubled in 1978. Inkatha rightly interpreted this massive increase of membership as a rejection by Black South Africans of the armed struggle.

Dr. Buthelezi later noted: "It was Inkatha's growing prominence, even in the early years of its existence, and the evidence of its mass support which was frightening to the militants in the ANC Mission in Exile. They wanted Inkatha crushed if it could not be subdued into being subservient to the Mission in Exile."

By the time the 1979 London meeting between Inkatha and the ANC Mission in Exile took place the militant elements in the ANC could no longer be controlled by Mr. Oliver Tambo. After the London meeting, for the first time in his career Mr. Tambo began criticising Buthelezi and Inkatha publicly. He had sided with those in his ranks who saw Inkatha as a threat and who wanted no evidence that black democratic opposition and black non-violent tactics and strategies were powerful forces for bringing about change.

The 1979 London meeting would prove to be a pivotal point in the relationship between the two organisations. It became the basis for ANC anti-Inkatha propaganda, until a meeting between both the organisations in Durban in 1991 where the IFP was vindicated of ANC allegations that Inkatha and Dr. Buthelezi had leaked confidential information to the press. At that meeting the ANC informant was named.

The Inkatha National Cultural Liberation Movement had well-articulated aims and objectives and from its very inception instilled within its supporters the need for self-reliance and self-help. Towards the end of the 70's Inkatha had made the realisation that the constitutional problems of South Africa would be best served by a federal, democratic form of government. This is still the view of the IFP today.

INKATHA AND THE KWAZULU GOVERNMENT

Inkatha and Dr. Buthelezi became the targets of a campaign of vilification waged by people who often did not know enough about the strategies underpinning Inkatha's liberation struggle. Many of those detractors, both in South Africa and abroad, did not know of the close relationship between Dr. Buthelezi and the ANC leadership, who had in 1953 urged Buthelezi to take up his traditional leadership as Inkosi of the Buthelezi Clan. In order to so do Buthelezi had to abandon his plans to do his law articles under Rowley Arenstein, a member of the South African Communist Party and the longest banned person in South Africa.

It was with the agreement of the ANC leadership at that time that Dr. Buthelezi assumed office in the government-created Territorial Authority in 1970 because it was believed to be in the best interests of the liberation struggle. So too, with counsel and agreement of the ANC leadership did Buthelezi accept the Chieftancy of the KwaZulu Government. He, however, refused to lead the KwaZulu Government into nominal independence because he realised that acceptance of the independence of KwaZulu would lead to the completion of the South African Government's institutional scheme of apartheid. His refusal is now recognised as a major cause of the failure of apartheid. Former President F. W. de Klerk later admitted that Buthelezi's refusal to accept independence of KwaZulu made them change their minds about apartheid.

INKATHA AND THE DISINVESTMENT CAMPAIGN

The disinvestment campaign, which fast gathered momentum in the West, would prove to be yet another strategy on which Inkatha and the ANC Mission in Exile would take divergent views. Inkatha argued that it could not accept as its own a strategy that had been determined with no or very little consultation with Black South Africans living in the country at the time. It argued that the disinvestment campaign did not serve the best short or long-term interests of the Blacks as it would simply add to the already heavy burden that Black people in South Africa were already carrying and completely destroy the economy, which Black South Africa hoped to inherit.

Inkatha prophesied that the disinvestment campaign would leave millions of black South Africans without work, food and would lead to a militancy that would severely strain and test the quality of any future democracy in South Africa, as it would render the future economy of South Africa unproductive. Inkatha believed strongly that other peaceful options needed to be sought to bring about change in the country.

By 1994 a "lost generation" of about 4 million Black South Africans, which can be directly attributed to the South African Government apartheid policy and indirectly to the disinvestment campaign, had evolved. While the disinvestment campaign did manage to play its role in putting pressure on the South African apartheid government at the time, it must also accept responsibility for the role it played in robbing many Black South African children of homes, food and an education. As a consequence the South African economy and work force have been rendered uncompetitive and major steps have now (2000) to be taken to redress the economic imbalances of apartheid, which were exacerbated by the disinvestment campaign.

THE INKATHA APPROACH TO TRADE UNIONISM

From its very inception in 1975 Inkatha was a supporter of the need for a strong Trade Union Movement in South Africa and recognised the right of workers to organise their labour. Inkatha, however, believed very strongly in the existence of a "natural" tension between the government of the day and the Trade Union Movement.

Inkatha noted that the then apartheid government had adopted the wrong approach because its Trade Unions served only the best interests of the small white minority. Inkatha also noted, though, the danger in the approach of the ANC in submerging itself totally within the Trade Union Movement because it knew that this relationship could not be sustained over a long period of time, in the best interests of the whole of South Africa, as the interests of government and of the trade union movement were not always compatible.

AIMS AND OBJECTIVES OF THE INKATHA CULTURAL LIBERATION MOVEMENT

To foster the spirit of unity among black people throughout South Africa and to keep alive the traditions of the people;

To help promote and encourage the development of the Black people spiritually, economically, educationally and politically;

To establish contact and liaise with cultural groups in Southern Africa with a view to the establishment of a common society;

To stamp out all forms of corruption, exploitation and intimidation;

To ensure acceptance of the principles of equal opportunity and equality opportunity for all peoples in all walks of life;

To co-operate with any movement or organisation for the improvement of the conditions of the people and to secure the most efficient production and equitable distribution of the wealth of the nation in the best interests of the people;

To abolish all forms of discrimination and segregation based on tribe, clan, sex, colour or creed;

To promote and support worthy indigenous customs and cultures;

To protect, encourage and promote trade, commerce, and industry. Agriculture and conservation of natural resources by all means in the interests of the people and encourage all citizens to participate in all sectors of the economy;

To give effect to the principles approved from time to time by the appropriate organs of the Movement;

To ensure observance of the fundamental freedoms and human rights;

To inculcate and foster a vigorous consciousness of patriotism and a strong sense of national unity based on a common and individual loyalty and devotion to our land;

To co-operate locally and internationally with all progressive African and other nationalist movements and political parties which work for the complete eradication of all forms of colonialism, racialism, neo-colonialism, imperialism and discrimination and to strive for the attainment of African Unity; and

To carry on any other activities which in the opinion of the Movement are conducive to the attainment of the aims and objectives of the national Movement and to do such things as are incidental to the attainment of the above objectives.

STATEMENT OF BELIEFS OF THE INKATHA NATIONAL CULTURAL LIBERATION MOVEMENT

We believe that respect for individuals and the value placed on cultural and large groups is synonymous with progress towards a politically stable society.

We believe that political rights of all national groups should be protected within constitutional framework, which outlaws discrimination, based on colour, sex or creed.

We believe in individual equality before the law, equality of opportunity and equality of benefits from the institutions of the State.

We believe that the identity of an individual within a particular cultural mile is essential to his identity as a South African, but we believe also that culture belongs to all and that no social, economic or political impediments which hinder the free movement of individuals from one cultural milieu to another are in any respect justified.

We recognise that there are privileged communities and under-privileged communities and we believe that it is the very social duty of the State to provide the opportunities and back those opportunities with resources to enable every individual who is under-privileged to develop to the maximum of his/her ability.

We believe that the resources of the country and the wealth which has already been created which is controlled by the State, belongs to all the people of South Africa, and we believe that the resources and the wealth of the country should be utilised for the greatest good of the greatest number.

We believe that we are facing a grave crisis in which the poor are threatened with greater poverty and we believe that it is essential that all people join hands and enter into a partnership.

We believe that fiscal control is essential to regulate the quantity and flow of money and *near* money, and we also believe that State control by equivalents of the Reserve Bank are essential for the utilisation of land, water and power in the interests of the economy and in the interests of developing underprivileged areas and populations.

We believe in the elimination of secrecy in public administration and we believe individuals should have rights of appeals to the courts to protect his or her privacy in the pursuit of that which is lawful.

We believe that practices acceptable in civilised nations should characterise the methods and the procedures used by the police in the enforcement of law.

We believe that the enforcement of law is devoid of meaning outside of the rule of law, and we believe that there should be both a criminal code and a justice code in which rights to appeal to the highest courts of the land are the rights of all persons, and we believe that upon pronouncement of an impartial law society, that the state should bear the costs of appeal where the appellant pursues a course of action to protect his individual rights.

We believe that in living the good life in a just society an individual should be free to attend any educational institution in which he has entry qualifications, reside where he wishes, own ground where he wishes, become qualified in any trade or profession for which he has the required degree of competence.

We believe that the development of trade unions, guilds and associations should be encouraged by the enactment of enabling legislation and courts of arbitration.

We believe that the accumulated injustices of the past and the injustice now present the institutions of our country have created bitterness and anger among the underprivileged sections of our populations, and we believe that growing fears of this anger and bitterness makes the privileged sections of our population intransigent in the face of the need for change.

We believe therefore that the transition from an unjust society to a just society will be difficult.

We believe that in this eleventh hour of South Africa, responsible leadership must publicly declare its commitment to bring about a just society within the foreseeable future, and we believe that leadership must meet the demands of responsibility by taking whatever steps remain from time to time to avoid a race war.

We believe that the mobilisation of constituency protest and a refusal to act within the restrictive confines of race exclusivity holds a promise we dare not abandon.

Buthelezi: "The Future of South Africa Should Be Determined by All Its Citizens"[1]

Editor's Note: In this letter to the Editor of the New York Times, Buthelezi directly challenges allegations made against him by the ANC, the UDF, and international media. How does he challenge the charges of collaboration with the white power structure? What does he assert is the main agenda of the ANC? Does he use language and images intended to encourage mistrust of the ANC? What, according to Buthelezi, is the political and constitutional intent of Inkatha?

To the Editor:

Your article on clashes between the black South African forces of the United Democratic Front and Inkatha, the organization I lead (front page, Jan. 21), discusses at length the appalling violence in the Pietermaritzburg area and its implications.

You allege that of all the major black groups, Inkatha is considered "the most politically accommodating" to whites. In "a transition to black rule" there are prospects, you say, that Inkatha would "provide special protection for whites."

What does this imply? That we believe all South

1. *New York Times*, 13 February 1988.

Africans—black and white—should share power? Or, that we are prepared to deal with our political oppressors behind black South Africa's back?

Inkatha, with 1.5 million paid-up members, is adamant that the future of this country should be determined by all its citizens. A post-apartheid constitution will have to be written by the people, and no organization can claim to be the sole and authentic representative (as the African National Congress does) of the majority of South Africans.

You do not mention that the pro-violence African National Congress (which receives arms and ammunition from the Soviet Union and elsewhere) is active in Pietermaritzburg. It is the stated policy of the A.N.C. to make South Africa ungovernable. The A.N.C. propagates a Socialist-Marxist one-party-state scenario rejected by many, including Inkatha, which believes our only workable option is to support a multiparty, free-enterprise system of government.

Precisely these issues lie at the heart of the violence in this country and specifically in Pietermaritzburg. Inkatha has no intention of being annihilated. This is not a war of our making. I want the bloodshed to stop, and I will continue to do whatever I can to quell the violence.

The "battle," you say, is one in which the urban-based United Democratic Front is trying to sway the loyalties of "traditional" rural Zulus. Besides being incorrect, this fails to articulate the aims and objectives of the front beyond that of being an "anti-apartheid" coalition and makes no mention of the support it receives from the A.N.C.

Inkatha loathes apartheid too, but the issue cannot be summed up so simply. You say that my "proposals for reshaping the country would build upon" my "tribal base" and that a "blueprint for Natal's future, drawn up by Inkatha, would allow for a powerful white role." This is rubbish.

The proposals to which you refer (accepted only in principle by Inkatha) are the result of a regional initiative, of months of negotiation and deliberation by black and white organizations, of which Inkatha was one. These proposals sought ways

blacks and whites could democratically share power in Natal-KwaZulu.

Ultimately, the people must decide what they want. I can merely keep on trying to create mechanisms for them to come together and talk about the future. Inkatha has its own aims and objectives, tactics and strategies.

Finally, you describe the assassination of the family of an Inkatha member, Phillip Thabethe, who was badly wounded in an attack. This man lost his wife, two sons and his mother, and still cannot work after he was struck by eight bullets from a Soviet-made Tokarev automatic pistol.

With no proof, an unnamed welfare worker is quoted as saying Mr. Thabethe is "one of the top Inkatha killers." This is defamation of the worst order, no matter that the hideous and untruthful allegation was denied. Do you think nothing of damning a man as a "killer"? Or is it all right if that person is a black bus driver in KwaZulu who has little chance of legally defending himself against being presented to the world as a butcher?

—MANGOSUTHU G. BUTHELEZI, Chief Minister of KwaZulu and President of Inkatha Ulundi, KwaZulu, Jan. 29, 1988

Negotiation Agreements

Editor's Note: A series of negotiation agreements were produced as the National Party, led by F. W. de Klerk, the ANC, led by Nelson Mandela, and others moved toward a postapartheid South Africa. At talks known as CODESA I and CODESA II, efforts to reach a national consensus failed and led to the Multi-Party Negotiating Process as a last attempt to find a compromise. What do these agreements reveal about the challenges in forming a consensus? How do the agreements attempt to navigate issues of security and political participation, and deal with political prisoners and multi-party tensions? Is it possible that smaller political parties saw in these agreements reasons to distrust the National Party and the ANC? Do these agreements introduce principles that are essential for the shaping of a new South Africa? If so, what challenges are these principles likely to face when implemented? See also the Groote Schuur Minute (http://www.sahistory.org.za/archive /document-17-groote-schuur-minute) and the Pretoria Minute (http://www.sahistory.org.za/archive/document -18-pretoria-minute) at South African History Online (http://www.sahistory.org.za/).

National Peace Accord

14 September 1991

To signify our common purpose to bring an end to political violence in our country and to set out the codes of conduct, procedures and mechanisms to achieve this goal

We, participants in the political process in South Africa, representing the political parties and organisations and governments indicated beneath our signatures, condemn the scourge of political violence which has afflicted our country and all such practices as have contributed to such violence in the past, and commit ourselves and the parties, organisations and governments we represent to this National Peace Accord.

The current prevalence of political violence in the country has already caused untold hardship, disruption and loss of life and property in our country. It now jeopardises the very process of peaceful political transformation and threatens to leave a legacy of insurmountable division and deep bitterness in our country. Many, probably millions, of citizens live in continuous fear as a result of the climate of violence. This dehumanising factor must be eliminated from our society.

In order to achieve some measure of stability and to consolidate the peace process, a priority shall be the introduction of reconstruction actions aimed at addressing the worst effects of political violence at a local level. This would achieve a measure of stability based on common effort thereby facilitating a base for broader socio-economic development.

Reconstruction and developmental actions of the communities as referred to above, shall be conducted within the wider context of socio-economic development.

In order to effectively eradicate intimidation and violence, mechanisms need to be created which shall on the one hand deal with the investigation of incidents and the causes of violence and intimidation and on the other hand actively combat the occurrence of violence and intimidation.

The police force, which by definition shall include the police forces of all self-governing territories, has a central role to play in terminating the violence and in preventing the future perpetration of such violence. However, the perception of the past role of the police has engendered suspicion and distrust between the police and many of the affected communities. In recognition of the need to promote more effective policing, a commitment to sound policing practices and a co-operative relationship between the police and the communities are necessary.

This Accord is intended to promote peace and prosperity in violence-stricken communities. The right of all people to live in peace and harmony will be promoted by the implementation of this Accord.

The Accord is of such a nature that every peace-loving person can support it. The Accord reflects the values of all key players in the arena of negotiation and reconciliation.

The implementation and monitoring of the Peace Accord represents a crucial phase in the process to restore peace and prosperity to all the people of South Africa.

Noting that the majority of South Africans are God-fearing citizens, we ask for His blessing, care and protection upon our Nation to fulfil the trust placed upon us to ensure freedom and security for all.

Bearing in mind the values which we hold, be these religious or humanitarian, we pledge ourselves with integrity of purpose to make this land a prosperous one where we can all live, work and play together in peace and harmony.

The signatories have agreed upon:

a Code of Conduct for political parties and
organisations to be followed by all the
political parties and organisations that are
signatories to this Accord;
a Code of Conduct to be adhered to by every
police official
to the best of his or her ability, as well as a
detailed agreement on the security forces;
the guidelines for the reconstruction and
development of the communities;
the establishment of mechanisms to implement
the provisions of this Accord.

The signatories acknowledge that the provisions of
this Peace Accord are subject to existing laws, rules
and procedures and budgetary constraints. New
structures should not be created where appropriate
existing structures can be used.

This Accord will not be construed so as to
detract from the validity of bilateral agreements
between any of the signatories.

*We, the signatories, accordingly solemnly bind
ourselves to this accord and shall ensure as far as
humanly possible that all our members and supporters will comply with the provisions of this accord
and will respects its underlying rights and values
and we, the government signatories, undertake to
pursue the objectives of this accord and seek to give
effect to its provisions by way of the legislative,
executive and budgeting procedures to which we
have access.*

CHAPTER 1
Principles

1.1 The establishment of a multi-party democracy
in South Africa is our common goal. Democracy
is impossible in a climate of violence, intimidation and fear. In order to ensure democratic
political activity all political participants must
recognise and uphold certain fundamental rights
described below and the corresponding responsibilities underlying those rights.

1.2 These fundamental rights include the right of
every individual to:

freedom of conscience and belief;
freedom of speech and expression;
freedom of association with others;
peaceful assembly;
freedom of movement;
participate freely in peaceful political activity.

1.3 The fundamental rights and responsibilities
derive from established democratic principles
namely:

democratic sovereignty derives from the people,
whose right it is to elect their government and
hold it accountable at the polls for its conduct
of their affairs;
the citizens must therefore be informed and
aware that political parties and the media
must be free to impart information and
opinion;
there should be an active civilsociety with
different interest groups freely participating
therein;
political parties and organisations, as well as
political leaders and other citizens, have an
obligation to refrain from incitement to
violence and hatred.

1.4 The process of reconstruction and socio-
economic development aimed at addressing the
causes of violent conflict, must be conducted in a
non-partisan manner, that is, without being
controlled by any political organisation or being to
the advantage of any political group at the expense
of another.

1.5 Reconstruction and developmental projects
must actively involve the affected communities.
Through a process of inclusive negotiations
involving recipients, experts and donors, the
community must be able to conceive, implement
and take responsibility for projects in a co-ordinated
way as close to the grassroots as possible. In

addition, reconstruction and development must facilitate the development of the economic and human resources of the communities concerned.

1.6 The initiatives referred to in 1.4 and 1.5 above, should in no way abrogate the right and duty of governments to continue their normal developmental activity, except that in doing so they should be sensitive to the spirit and contents of any agreement that may be reached in terms of 1.5 above.

1.7 The parties to this process commit themselves to facilitating the rapid removal of political, legislative and administrative obstacles to development and economic growth.

1.8 The implementation of a system to combat violence and intimidation will only succeed if the parties involved have a sincere commitment to reach this objective. Only then will all the people of South Africa be able to fulfil their potential and create a better future.

1.9 It is clear that violence and intimidation declines when it is investigated and when the background and reasons for it is (sic) exposed and given media attention. There is, therefore, need for an effective instrument to do just that. It is agreed that the Commission established by the Prevention of Public Violence and Intimidation Act, 1991, be used as an instrument to investigate and expose the background and reasons for violence, thereby reducing the incidence of violence and intimidation.

1.10 Since insufficient instruments exist to actively prevent violence and intimidation and regional and local levels, it is agreed that committees be appointed at regional and local levels to assist in this regard. Peace bodies are therefore to be established at both regional and local levels to be styled "Regional Dispute Resolution Committees" (RDRC) and "Local Dispute Resolution Committees" (LDRC) respectively. These bodies will be guided and co-ordinated at a national level by a National Peace Secretariat. At the local level the bodies will be assisted by Justices of the Peace.

1.11 The Preparatory Committee has played a crucial role in the process of bringing the major actors together to negotiate a Peace Accord. There is still much to be done to implement the Accord and establish the institutions of peace. To assist in this regard, a National Peace Committee shall be established.

1.12 There should be simple and expeditious procedures for the resolution of disputes regarding transgressions of the Code for Political Parties and Organisation by political parties and organisations who are signatories to the National Peace Accord. These disputes should wherever possible, be settled at grassroots level, through participation of the parties themselves; and by using the proven methods of mediation, arbitration and adjudication.

1.13 An effective and credible criminal judicial system requires the swift and just dispensation of justice. This in turn will promote the restoration of peace and prosperity to communities, freeing them of the ravages of violence and intimidation. Special attention should be given to unrest related cases by setting up Special Criminal Courts specifically for this purpose.

Meeting between the State President of the Republic of South Africa and the President of the African national Congress

(Held at the World Trade Centre on the 26 September, 1992)

1. **The attached Record of Understanding was agreed to.**
2. **On the way forward:**
   - The two delegations agreed that this summit has laid a basis for the resumption of the negotiation process.
   - To this end the ANC delegation advised the South African Government that it would recommend to its National Executive Committee that the process of negotiation be resumed, whereafter extensive bilateral discussions will be held.

- It was agreed that the practicalities with regard to bilateral discussions will be dealt with through the existing channel.

1. Since 21 August 1992 a series of meetings was held between Mr Roelf Meyer, Minister of Constitutional Development and Mr Cyril Ramaphosa, Secretary General of the African National Congress.

   These meetings entailed discussions with a view to remove obstacles towards the resumption of negotiations and focused on the identification of steps to be taken to address issues raised in earlier memoranda. The discussions took note of various opposing viewpoints on the relevant issues and obstacles. It was decided that these issues should not be dealt with exhaustively in the understanding. This document reflects the understanding reached at the conclusion of the discussions regarding these obstacles and issues.

2. The understandings on issues and obstacles included the following, although it was observed that there are still other important matters that will receive attention during the process of negotiation:

   (a) The Government and the ANC agreed that there is a need for a democratic constitution assembly/constitution-making body and that for such a body to be democratic it must:
   - be democratically elected;
   - draft and adopt the new constitution, implying that it should sit as a single chamber;
   - be bound only by agreed constitutional principles;
   - have a fixed time frame;
   - have adequate deadlock breaking mechanisms;
   - function democratically i.e. arrive at its decisions democratically with certain agreed-to majorities; and
   - be elected within an agreed predetermined time period.

   Within the framework of these principles, detail would have to be worked out in the negotiation process.

   (b) The Government and the ANC agreed that during the interim/transitional period there shall be constitutional continuity and so constitutional hiatus. In consideration of this principle, it was further agreed that:
   - the constitution-making body/constituent assembly shall also act as the interim / transitional Parliament;
   - there shall be an interim/transitional government of national unity;
   - the constitution-making body/constituent assembly cum interim/transitional Parliament and the interim/transitional government of national unity shall function within a constitutional framework/transitional constitution which shall provide for national and regional government during the period of transition and shall incorporate guaranteed justiciable fundamental rights and freedoms. The interim/transitional Parliament may function as a one- or two-chambered body.

   (c) The two parties are agreed that all prisoners whose imprisonment is related to political conflict of the past and whose release can make a contribution to reconciliation should be released.

The Government and the ANC agreed that the release of prisoners, namely, those who according to the ANC fall within the guidelines defining political offences, but according to the Government do not, and who have committed offences with a political motive on or before 8 October 1990 shall be carried out in stages *(as reflected in a separate document:* IMPLEMENTATION PROGRAMME: RELEASE OF PRISONERS*)* and be completed before 15

November 1992. To this end the parties have commenced a process of identification. It is the Government's position that all who have committed similar offences but who have not been charged and sentenced should be dealt with on the same basis. On this question no understanding could be reached as yet and it was agreed that the matter will receive further attention.

As the process of identification proceeds, releases shall be effected in the above-mentioned staged manner. Should it be found that the current executive powers of the State do not enable it to give effect to specific releases arising from the above identification the necessary legislation shall be enacted.

(d) The Goldstone Commission has given further attention to hostels and brought out an urgent report on certain matters and developments on this regard. The commission indicated that the problem is one of criminality and that it will have to investigate which localities are affected.

In the meantime some problematic hostels have been identified and the Government has undertaken as a matter of urgency to address and deal with the problem in relation to those hostels that have been associated with violence. Further measures will be taken, including fencing and policing to prevent criminality by hostel dwellers and to protect hostel dwellers against external aggression. A separate document (Implementation Programme: Hostels) records the identification of such hostels and the security measures to be taken in these instances.

Progress will be reported to the Goldstone Commission and the National Peace Secretariat. United Nations observers may witness the progress in co-operation with the Goldstone Commission and the National Peace Secretariat.

(e) In the present volatile atmosphere of violence the public display and carrying of dangerous weapons provokes further tension and should be prohibited. The Government has informed the ANC that it will issue a proclamation within weeks to prohibit countrywide the carrying and display of dangerous weapons at all public occasions subject to exemptions base on guidelines being prepared by the Goldstone Commission. The granting of exemptions shall be entrusted to one or more retired judges. On this basis, the terms of the proclamation and mechanism for exemption shall be prepared with the assistance of the Goldstone Commission.

(f) The Government acknowledges the right of all parties and organisations to participate in peaceful mass action in accordance with the provisions of the National Peace Accord and the Goldstone Commissions' recommendations. The ANC for its part reaffirms its commitment to the provisions of the Code of Conduct for Political Parties arrived at under the National Peace Accord and the agreement reached on 16 July 1992 under the auspices of the Goldstone Commission as important instruments to ensure democratic political activity in a climate of free political participation. The two parties also commit themselves to the strengthening of the Peace Accord process, to do everything in their power to calm down tensions and to finding ways and means of promoting reconciliation in South Africa. In view of the progress made in this summit and the progress we are likely to make when negotiations are resumed, the ANC expresses its intention to consult its constituency on a basis of urgency with a view to examine the current programme of mass action.

3. The two parties agreed to hold further meetings in order to address and finalise the following matters which were not completed at the summit:

- Climate of free political activity.
- Repressive/security legislation.
- Covert operations and special forces.
- Violence.

Agreed to at Johannesburg on 26 September 1992:
  Nelson Mandela
  F. W. de Klerk

Nelson Mandela Speeches

Editor's Note: After spending twenty-seven and a half years as a political prisoner, Mandela was released on 11 February 1990 at the order of South African President F. W. de Klerk. The national and international celebration of this event was legendary. What goals does Mandela set out for South Africa? Did his public addresses position Mandela to assume the role as South Africa's leader? What elements of his message, if any, might make the ANC's political opponents nervous or might challenge the ANC's allies?

Nelson Mandela's Address to Rally in Cape Town on His Release from Prison[1]

11 February 1990

Friends, comrades and fellow South Africans.

I greet you all in the name of peace, democracy and freedom for all.

I stand here before you not as a prophet but as a humble servant of you, the people. Your tireless and heroic sacrifices have made it possible for me to be here today. I therefore place the remaining years of my life in your hands.

On this day of my release, I extend my sincere and warmest gratitude to the millions of my compatriots and those in every corner of the globe who have campaigned tirelessly for my release.

I send special greetings to the people of Cape Town, this city which has been my home for three

1. Used by permission of the Nelson Mandela Foundation.

decades. Your mass marches and other forms of struggle have served as a constant source of strength to all political prisoners.

I salute the African National Congress. It has fulfilled our every expectation in its role as leader of the great march to freedom.

I salute our President, Comrade Oliver Tambo, for leading the ANC even under the most difficult circumstances.

I salute the rank and file members of the ANC. You have sacrificed life and limb in the pursuit of the noble cause of our struggle.

I salute combatants of Umkhonto we Sizwe, like Solomon Mahlangu and Ashley Kriel who have paid the ultimate price for the freedom of all South Africans.

I salute the South African Communist Party for its sterling contribution to the struggle for democracy. You have survived 40 years of unrelenting persecution. The memory of great communists like Moses Kotane, Yusuf Dadoo, Bram Fischer and Moses Mabhida will be cherished for generations to come.

I salute General Secretary Joe Slovo, one of our finest patriots. We are heartened by the fact that the alliance between ourselves and the Party remains as strong as it always was.

I salute the United Democratic Front, the National Education Crisis Committee, the South African Youth Congress, the Transvaal and Natal Indian Congresses and COSATU and the many other formations of the Mass Democratic Movement.

I also salute the Black Sash and the National Union of South African Students. We note with pride that you have acted as the conscience of white South Africa. Even during the darkest days in the history of our struggle you held the flag of liberty high. The large-scale mass mobilisation of the past few years is one of the key factors which led to the opening of the final chapter of our struggle.

I extend my greetings to the working class of our country. Your organised strength is the pride of our movement. You remain the most dependable force in the struggle to end exploitation and oppression.

I pay tribute to the many religious communities who carried the campaign for justice forward when the organisations for our people were silenced.

I greet the traditional leaders of our country—many of you continue to walk in the footsteps of great heroes like Hintsa and Sekhukune.

I pay tribute to the endless heroism of youth, you, the young lions. You, the young lions, have energised our entire struggle.

I pay tribute to the mothers and wives and sisters of our nation. You are the rock-hard foundation of our struggle. Apartheid has inflicted more pain on you than on anyone else.

On this occasion, we thank the world community for their great contribution to the anti-apartheid struggle. Without your support our struggle would not have reached this advanced stage. The sacrifice of the frontline states will be remembered by South Africans forever.

My salutations would be incomplete without expressing my deep appreciation for the strength given to me during my long and lonely years in prison by my beloved wife and family. I am convinced that your pain and suffering was far greater than my own.

Before I go any further I wish to make the point that I intend making only a few preliminary comments at this stage. I will make a more complete statement only after I have had the opportunity to consult with my comrades.

Today the majority of South Africans, black and white, recognise that apartheid has no future. It has to be ended by our own decisive mass action in order to build peace and security. The mass campaign of defiance and other actions of our organisation and people can only culminate in the establishment of democracy. The destruction caused by apartheid on our sub-continent is in-calculable. The fabric of family life of millions of my people has been shattered. Millions are homeless and unemployed. Our economy lies in ruins and our people are embroiled in political strife. Our resort to the armed struggle in 1960 with the formation of the military wing of the ANC, Um-khonto we Sizwe, was a purely defensive action against the violence of apartheid. The factors which necessitated the armed struggle still exist today. We have no option but to continue. We express the hope that a climate conducive to a negotiated settlement will be created soon so that there may no longer be the need for the armed struggle.

I am a loyal and disciplined member of the African National Congress. I am therefore in full agreement with all of its objectives, strategies and tactics.

The need to unite the people of our country is as important a task now as it always has been. No individual leader is able to take on this enormous task on his own. It is our task as leaders to place our views before our organisation and to allow the democratic structures to decide. On the question of democratic practice, I feel duty bound to make the point that a leader of the movement is a person who has been democratically elected at a national conference. This is a principle which must be upheld without any exceptions.

Today, I wish to report to you that my talks with the government have been aimed at normalising the political situation in the country. We have not as yet begun discussing the basic demands of the struggle. I wish to stress that I myself have at no time entered into negotiations about the future of our country except to insist on a meeting between the ANC and the government.

Mr. de Klerk has gone further than any other Nationalist president in taking real steps to normalise the situation. However, there are further steps as outlined in the Harare Declaration that have to be met before negotiations on the basic demands of our people can begin. I reiterate our call for, inter alia, the immediate ending of the State of Emergency and the freeing of all, and not only some, political prisoners. Only such a normalised situation, which allows for free political activity, can allow us to consult our people in order to obtain a mandate.

The people need to be consulted on who will negotiate and on the content of such negotiations.

Negotiations cannot take place above the heads or behind the backs of our people. It is our belief that the future of our country can only be determined by a body which is democratically elected on a non-racial basis. Negotiations on the dismantling of apartheid will have to address the overwhelming demand of our people for a democratic, non-racial and unitary South Africa. There must be an end to white monopoly on political power and a fundamental restructuring of our political and economic systems to ensure that the inequalities of apartheid are addressed and our society thoroughly democratised.

It must be added that Mr. de Klerk himself is a man of integrity who is acutely aware of the dangers of a public figure not honouring his undertakings. But as an organisation we base our policy and strategy on the harsh reality we are faced with. And this reality is that we are still suffering under the policy of the Nationalist government.

Our struggle has reached a decisive moment. We call on our people to seize this moment so that the process towards democracy is rapid and uninterrupted. We have waited too long for our freedom. We can no longer wait. Now is the time to intensify the struggle on all fronts. To relax our efforts now would be a mistake which generations to come will not be able to forgive. The sight of freedom looming on the horizon should encourage us to redouble our efforts.

It is only through disciplined mass action that our victory can be assured. We call on our white compatriots to join us in the shaping of a new South Africa. The freedom movement is a political home for you too. We call on the international community to continue the campaign to isolate the apartheid regime. To lift sanctions now would be to run the risk of aborting the process towards the complete eradication of apartheid.

Our march to freedom is irreversible. We must not allow fear to stand in our way. Universal suffrage on a common voters' role in a united democratic and non-racial South Africa is the only way to peace and racial harmony.

In conclusion I wish to quote my own words during my trial in 1964. They are true today as they were then:

"I have fought against white domination and I have fought against black domination. I have cherished the ideal of a democratic and free society in which all persons live together in harmony and with equal opportunities. It is an ideal which I hope to live for and to achieve. But if needs be, it is an ideal for which I am prepared to die."

Nelson Mandela's Address to Rally in Durban[1]
25 February 1990

Editor's Note: Durban is a large Indian Ocean port city in Natal. Here, the struggle for freedom in South Africa dates back to the anti-pass movement of Mahatma Gandhi in the early twentieth century. The speech refers to Natal legend Albert John Mvumbi Luthuli, a deeply religious Christian and teacher who turned to politics in midlife. Luthuli was appointed Chief of the Groutville reserve in 1935 and there managed tribal affairs for seventeen years. He became president of the ANC in 1952 and was persistently active in the nonviolent campaign resisting apartheid policies. He was imprisoned several times and was eventually the first African to be awarded the Nobel Peace Prize, in 1960. Why does Mandela center so much of his speech on Chief Luthuli, in this location especially? How does Mandela handle the issue of Zulu cultural identity? What is the implied subtext of his description of his interaction with Inkatha and its leadership? To what other ethnic group does Mandela pay tribute, and what is their connection to the liberation struggle?

Text in italics indicates where the address was delivered in Zulu.

Friends, comrades, and the people of Natal, I greet you all. I do so in the name of peace, the peace that is so desperately and urgently needed in this region.

In Natal, apartheid is a deadly cancer in our

1. Used by permission of the Nelson Mandela Foundation.

midst, setting house against house, and eating away at the precious ties that bound us together. This strife among ourselves wastes our energy and destroys our unity. My message to those of you involved in this battle of brother against brother is this: take your guns, your knives, and your pangas[1], and throw them into the sea. Close down the death factories. End this war now!

We also come together today to renew the ties that make us one people, and to reaffirm a single united stand against the oppression of apartheid. *We have gathered here to find a way of building even greater unity than we already have. Unity is the pillar and foundation of our struggle to end the misery which is caused by the oppression which is our greatest enemy. This repression and the violence it creates cannot be ended if we fight and attack each other.*

The people of Natal have fought a long struggle against oppression. The victory of the army of King Cetshwayo kaMpande at the Battle of Isandlwana in 1879 has been an inspiration for those of us engaged in the struggle for justice and freedom in South Africa. At Isandlwana, disciplined Zulu regiments, armed only with shields and spears, but filled with courage and determination, thrust back the guns and cannon of the British imperialists. When the British finally managed to defeat the Zulu kingdom, they divided it into 13 new chiefdoms. Later, they annexed the area and gave the land to white farmers. In 1906, in the reign of Dinizulu kaCetshwayo, the colonialists introduced the Poll Tax (Head Tax) and other regulations designed to force Africans to work for wages on white farms. The Zulu people, led by Chief Bambatha, refused to bow their proud heads and a powerful spirit of resistance developed, which, like the battle of Isandlwana, inspired generations of South Africans.

The ANC pays tribute to these heroic struggles of the Zulu people to combat oppression. And we are very proud that from the ranks of the Zulu people have emerged outstanding cadres of the ANC and national leaders like Dube,[2] Seme,[3] Luthuli. We remember another son of Natal, the young and talented Communist Party organiser, Johannes Nkosi, who, with three others, was brutally murdered in 1930, when he led a march into Durban to protest against the hated pass laws.

Another strand in the struggle against oppression began with the formation, right here in Natal, of the first black political organisation in Africa. The Natal Indian Congress, founded in 1894, began a tradition of extra-parliamentary protest that continues into the present. The next decade saw the increasing radicalisation of Indian politics under the leadership of Mahatma Gandhi.

In 1906, at the time when Bambatha led sections of Africans in a war to destroy the Poll Tax, our brothers who originated from India, led by Mahatma Gandhi, fought against the oppression of the British Government. In 1913, we see Indian workers striking in the sugar-cane plantations and in the coal mines. These actions show the oppressed of South Africa waging a struggle to end exploitation and oppression, mounting an important challenge to the repressive British rule.

In the passive resistance campaign of 1946, over 2,000 Indians went to jail, many for occupying land reserved for whites. The campaign made clear the common nature of Indian and African oppression and the necessity of united resistance. In 1947, this led to the Xuma-Naicker-Dadoo Pact, and to the joint action of Africans and Indians in the Defiance Campaign of 1952. We remind the people of Natal of this long and proud tradition of cooperation between Africans and Indians against racial discrimination and other forms of injustice and oppression. We are extremely disturbed by recent acts of violence against our Indian compatriots. The perpetrators of these acts are enemies of the liberation movement.

2. Rev. John Langalibelele Dube, first president of the ANC.

3. Pixley ka Isaka Seme, ANC founding member and its president between 1930 and 1937.

1. Machetes, widely used in Natal's sugar-growing areas for cutting cane.

Another great struggle in Natal has been that of the workers. In 1926, the Durban branch of the ICU powerfully voiced the grievances of migrant workers on the docks, railways and local industries. In the 1970s Durban workers led the country in a movement to organise and fought for workers' rights. In January 1973, 2,000 workers at the Coronation Brick and Tile factory in Durban came out on strike. They were followed by workers all over Durban. Out of these strikes grew a host of new union federations and, eventually COSATU, the biggest and most powerful labour organisation in our history. We recognise that battles won in industrial disputes can never be permanently secure without the necessary political changes. Our Defiance Campaign has succeeded in forcing the government to scrap discriminatory laws and has brought us to the point where we are to glimpse the outlines of a new South Africa. The Mass Democratic Movement stands as testimony to the powerful alliance of workers and progressive political organisations.

Whites, too, have made a contribution to the struggle in Natal. It began with the lonely voices of Bishop Colenso and his daughters who denounced imperialist injustices against the Zulu people and who campaigned vigorously for the freedom of their leaders. The Natal Liberal Party waged steadfast campaigns against removals, and its work has been continued into the present by people like Peter Brown. Whites also contributed significantly to the resurgence of labour struggles in the 1970s through the Wages Commission and the Trade Unions Advisory and Coordinating Council.

Our struggle has won the participation of every language and colour every stripe and hue in this country. These four strands of resistance and organisation have inspired all South Africans, and provide the foundations of our struggle today. We salute your proud and courageous history. *No people can boast more proudly of having ploughed a significant field in the struggle than the people of Natal.*

The past is a rich resource on which we can draw in order to make decisions for the future, but it does not dictate our choices. We should look back at the past and select what is good, and leave behind what is bad. The issue of chiefship is one such question. Not only in Natal, but all through the country, there have been chiefs who have been good and honest leaders who have piloted their people through the dark days of oppression with skill. These are the chiefs who have looked after the interests of their people and who enjoy the support of their people. We salute these traditional leaders. But there have been many bad chiefs who have profited from apartheid and who have increased the burden on their people. We denounce this misuse of office in the strongest terms. There are also chiefs who have collaborated with the system, but who have since seen the error of their ways. We commend their change of heart. Chiefly office is not something that history has given to certain individuals to use or abuse as they see fit. Like all forms of leadership, it places specific responsibilities on its holders. As Luthuli, himself a chief, put it: "A chief is primarily a servant of the people. He is the voice of his people."

The Zulu royal house continues today to enjoy the respect of its subjects. It has a glorious history. We are confident that its members will act in ways that will promote the well-being of all South Africans.

The ANC offers a home to all who subscribe to the principles of a free, democratic, non-racial and united South Africa. We are committed to building a single nation in our country. Our new nation will include blacks and whites, Zulus and Afrikaners, and speakers of every other language. ANC President-General Chief Luthuli said: "I personally believe that here in South Africa, with all of our diversities of colour and race, we will show the world a new pattern for democracy. I think that there is a challenge to us in South Africa, to set a new example for the world." This is the challenge we face today.

To do this we must eliminate all forms of factionalism and regionalism. We praise organisations which have fought to retain the dignity of our people. Although there are fundamental differences between us, we commend Inkatha for their demand over the years for the unbanning of the ANC and the release of political prisoners, as well as for their stand of refusing to participate in a negotiated settlement without the creation of the necessary climate. This stand of Inkatha has contributed in no small measure to making it difficult for the regime to implement successive schemes designed to perpetuate minority rule.

The 1986 Indaba[1] solution proposed for Natal broke new ground in so far as it addressed the question of the exclusion from political power of the African population of Natal and sought to make regional change pioneer national change. But we are now on the threshold of a very different scenario for national change. We are on the edge of a much greater step forward, for all our people throughout South Africa. There can be no separate solution for Natal under these conditions, nor can it be argued any longer that there is a need. We believe Inkatha and all the people of Natal would genuinely welcome a unitary, nonracial democratic South Africa, the goal of millions throughout the country. Our call is, "One nation, one country." *We must be one people across the whole of South Africa!*

Yet even now as we stand together on the threshold of a new South Africa, Natal is in flames. Brother is fighting brother in wars of vengeance and retaliation. Every family has lost dear ones in this strife. In the last few years of my imprisonment my greatest burden, my deepest suffering, was caused by reports which reached me of the terrible things which were happening here. *All of us are bereft of loved ones. All of us are aggrieved. Your tears are mine. What has happened has happened and must be accepted by you* [*the people of this region* (here Mandela evoked the terms of traditional praise songs in addressing the people)]. I extend my condolences to all of you who have lost your loved ones in this conflict.

It is my duty to remind you, in the middle of our great sufferings, of the responsibility which we

bear today. If we do not bring a halt to this conflict, we will be in a grave danger of corrupting the proud legacy of our struggle. We endanger the peace process in the whole of the country.

Apartheid is not yet dead. Equality and democracy continue to elude us. We do not have access to political power. We need to intensify our struggle to achieve our goals. But we cannot do this as long as the conflict amongst ourselves continues. Vigilantes, thugs and gangs like the notorious Sinyoras, have taken advantage of the hardships experienced by our people to profit and gain for themselves. We can stop them, and the descent into lawlessness and violence only by ceasing our feuds. We recognise that in order to bring war to an end, the two sides must talk. We are pleased to inform you that we are presently preparing for a meeting in the near future, between ourselves and the present Zulu monarch, King Zwelithini Goodwill kaBhekuzulu. It is my earnest wish that the meeting will establish a basis on which we can build a real peace.

Repeating the call made by Comrade Walter Sisulu at the Conference for a Democratic Future, we extend the hand of peace to Inkatha and hope that it might one day be possible for us to share a platform with its leader, Chief Mangosuthu Gatsha Buthelezi. We recognise the right of all organisations which are not racist to participate in political life. We commend the actions of those who have involved themselves actively in the search for peace in Natal. We commend the joint UDF–COSATU team. We also commend Dr Dhlomo, Dr Mdlalose, and Messrs Nkheli, Ndlovu and Zondi from Inkatha, as well as the churches in Natal, and certain business sectors, notably the Pietermaritzburg Chamber of Commerce. Our search for peace is a search for strength.

As a result of our historic struggles we, in the Mass Democratic Movement and in the ANC, are the premier political force in the country. This preeminence confers on us responsibilities over and above the concerns of power politics. We have a duty to look beyond our own ranks and our

1. A proposal for a change in the structure of regional government in Natal.

immediate concerns. We must strive more earnestly to unite all the people of our country and to nurture that unity into a common nationhood. Wherever divisions occur, such as in the strife here in Natal, it is a reflection against us and our greater societal goals. We need to look critically and candidly at aspects of our own practices which may not be acceptable or wise. We need to be rigorous in identifying our own contribution to the escalation of violence where it may occur. We have a greater purpose than the defeat of rival oppressed groups. It is the creation of a healthy and vibrant society.

We condemn, in the strongest possible terms, the use of violence as a way of settling differences amongst our people. *Great anger and violence can never build a nation. The apartheid regime uses this strife as a pretext for further oppression.*

We would like to see in members of all seasoned political organisations the total absence of intolerance towards those who differ from us on questions of strategy and tactics. Those who approach problems with intolerant attitudes are no credit to the struggle: they actively endanger our future.

The youth have been the shock troops of our struggle. We salute them for the ground which they have gained. Only through commitment have these victories been won; only through discipline can they be consolidated and made to last. *The youth must be like the warriors who fought under Shaka, the son of Senzangakhona, fighting with great bravery and skill. These heroes obeyed the commands of their commanders and their leaders. Today the community says, the world says, and I say: end this violence. Let us not be ruled by anger.* Our youth must be ready to demonstrate the same perfect discipline as the armies of King Shaka. If they do not, we will lose the ground which we have gained at such great cost.

The parties to the conflict in Natal have disagreed about a great deal. We have reached a stage where none of the parties can be regarded as right or wrong. Each carries a painful legacy of the past few years. But both sides share a common enemy: the enemy is that of inadequate housing, forced removals, lack of resources as basic as that of water, and rising unemployment. The Freedom Charter asserts that there should be houses, security and comfort for all. We demand that the government provides these basic necessities of life. *The shortage of housing, water and work opportunities, the forced removal of people and the destruction of their houses: these are our problems. They must not make us enemies. We must take lessons from what happened in Lamontville when they said: Asinamali*[1]—We have no money!—*they were expressing collectively the problems of the whole community.*

It is thus vital that we end the conflict in Natal, and end it now. Everyone must commit themselves to peace. Women of Natal, in the past and at crucial moments, you have shown greater wisdom than your menfolk. It was you who, in 1929 and again in 1959, identified and struck out at one of the roots of our oppression. You launched powerful campaigns against beer halls. *Women such as Dorothy Nyembe, Gladys Manzi and Ruth Shabane showed sharpness of mind by closing down the beer halls when the men were rendered useless by alcohol and families were being broken up. I hope that the women will again stand up and put their shoulders to the wheel together with the community to end the strife and violence.* More recently, the women of Chesterville arranged all-night vigils to protect their children. Mothers, sisters and daughters of Natal, it falls to you once again to intervene decisively.

I call on the women of Natal. *Each and every one of you must play your part!* I charge you with a special responsibility here today. It is you, in your wisdom now, who must begin the work of bringing peace to Natal. Tell your sons, your brothers, and your husbands, that you want peace and security. It is you who must show them the real enemy. *All women know of mass poverty and homelessness, of children dying from diseases caused by hunger,*

1. A slogan of the 1983 campaign against rent increases in Durban townships.

poverty and repression. We must therefore end the strife and the fighting and the misunderstanding in the community so that we defeat our common enemy, the apartheid regime. Open the cooking pots and ask the men why there is so little food inside. When the rains come into your homes, place the hands of your men in the pools on the floor, and ask them, why? When your child ails, and you have no money to take it to a doctor, ask them, why? There is only one answer, and that answer is our common deprivation. Go out and meet the women on the other side. Their story is the same. Then take your men with you. I want to hear from you. From each and every community, I want a report. I want to hear the story of how you made the peace. We place our trust in you.

Viva our mothers!

Viva our sisters!

Viva the women of our land!

I call on the people of Inanda. Join hands. All of you from Clermont, join hands; Hambanathi, Hammarsdale, Chesterville and Mpophomeni, join hands. People of Ashdown, Esikhaweni, Mbali, and Trustfeed, join hands. Those of you who are from Maphumulo's area, you too. Residents of Durban and Pietermaritzburg, it is your turn. Those from strife-torn Umlazi and tragic KwaMashu, join hands also. I know each one of these names from my time in prison. I know each as an explosion of conflict. And those of you whose homes I have not named, you too should join hands. We are many thousands gathered here in this stadium today. Let us now pledge ourselves to peace and to unity. Join hands all of you and raise them up for all to see.

A great deal of energy has been wasted by our people in violent actions across the towns and villages of this province. If we could channel this energy towards the real enemy of the people, apartheid, we could be free within days. We have already waited for our freedom for far too long. We can wait no longer. Join forces, Indians, Coloureds, Africans and freedom-loving Whites, to give apartheid its final blow. In the process, let us develop active democracy. Democratic structures which serve the people must be established in every school, township, village, factory and farm.

Since my release, I have become more convinced than ever that the real makers of history are the ordinary men and women of our country; their participation in every decision about the future is the only guarantee of true democracy and freedom. Undue reliance should not be placed on a white minority regime concerned to protect white minority rights as far as it can. Nor should our reliance be placed on the abilities of the statesmen amongst us and our political leaders to negotiate an acceptable settlement. It is only the united action of you, the people, that will ensure that freedom is finally achieved. I call, therefore, for an all-round intensification of our struggle. *Together we shall conquer!*

MAYIBUYE iAFRIKA

AMANDLA!

Nkosi Sikelel' iAfrika

Editor's Note: Originally written in 1897 in the Xhosa language, as early as the 1920s this text was adopted as a national anthem by many organizations and groups involved in ending South African segregation and apartheid. Its spiritual references were meaningful to people from many religions—Christianity, Islam, traditional African religions, and Hinduism. How do the words of the song correspond to the objectives and values of antiapartheid activists?

Nkosi Sikelel' iAfrika
Maluphakanyisw' uphondo lwayo
Yiva imathandazo yethu
Nkosi Sikelela Nkosi Sikelela
Nkosi Sikelel' iAfrika
Maluphakanyisw' uphondo lwayo
Yiva imathandazo yethu
Nkosi Sikelela
Thina lusapho lwayo.

CHORUS

Yihla moya, yihla moya
Yihla moya oyingcwele

Nkosi Sikelela

Thina lusapho lwayo.

(Repeat)

Lord, bless Africa.

May her spirit rise high up.

Hear thou our prayers.

Lord bless us.

Lord, bless Africa

May her spirit rise high up

Hear thou our prayers

Lord bless us Your family.

CHORUS

Descend, O Spirit

Descend, O Holy Spirit

Lord bless us

Your family.

(Repeat)

Violence: The Role of the Security Forces

Presenter: Jacques Pauw

Editor's Note: Jacques Pauw was an Afrikaner investigative journalist who reported on the criminal activities of the South African underworld and on atrocities committed by governments throughout Africa. He was also the founder of an Afrikaans antiapartheid newspaper, Vrye Weekblad. This 1992 address helped to expose the secretive "Third Force" in South Africa as a major source of violence beginning in 1990. Koevoet and Vlakplaas were paramilitary counterinsurgency units notorious for their brutality. Hermanus du Plessis and Eugene de Kock (sometimes known as "Prime Evil") were officers in the South African Security Force who established notorious reputations for their "counterinsurgency" work in the 1980s in Namibia and in the early 1990s in South Africa. What, according to Pauw, is the "Third Force"? What charges against official South African institutions does Pauw make? Why does he point to du Plessis and de Kock as important examples? Does Pauw think that the security forces in South Africa are reliable in their mission to protect citizens?

Date: **27 May 1992**

Venue: **University of the Witwatersrand, Johannesburg, South Africa**

As I stand before you, there are people out there dying in the townships. In the Madala Hostel in Alexandra, an Inkatha warlord may be urging his impis to yet again attack innocent township residents, while in an ANC stronghold in Phola Park, disillusioned Umkhonto we Sizwe members may be planning a revenge attack on Inkatha impis.[1]

In the past week, newspapers reported that a former hostel dweller has provided the Goldstone Commission with a direct link between Inkatha leaders and township violence and train attacks and that renegade members of the ANC's military wing in Phola Park have been involved in murders, armed robberies and attacks on security force members.

But I do not want to talk today about the complicity of Inkatha and the ANC in political violence. I want to introduce you to another dimension of this violence which has claimed the lives of 923 people in the first four months of this year and a staggering 12 867 people since September 1984.

Let us move to Police Headquarters in Pretoria where a senior police officer may be studying an intelligence report on a possible Inkatha attack. Instead of activating a special investigations or peacekeeping unit, he looks at the gold Rolex watch he received after 25 years of meritorious service, sees that it is 16h30, packs his briefcase, goes home and tells his wife about the bloody blacks killing each other again.

This may be Lieutenant-Colonel Hermanus "Boep" du Plessis, previously a member of the Port Elizabeth Security Branch, before being transferred to the newly-formed Crime Combatting and Investigation force in Pretoria.

Du Plessis is a man with a dirty and murderous past. He has been implicated in the brutal murder of activist Sizwe Kondile in 1981. Kondile was

1. *Impis* were armed bands of Zulu warriors, traditionally equipped with spears or gnarled walking sticks and a shield.

captured, interrogated and tortured by the Port Elizabeth Security Branch. He fell through a window, and to avoid a second "Steve Biko" incident, he had to be killed. He was transported by du Plessis and other security policemen to Komatipoort in the Eastern Transvaal where he was shot and burnt. It was proved in the Johannesburg Supreme Court last year that du Plessis sent false telex messages to Security Branch headquarters in Pretoria to conceal the real whereabouts of Kondile.

Du Plessis was also in charge of the interrogation of youth activist, Siphiwo Mtimkulu, who disappeared in 1982 and was never heard of again. He is alleged to have been killed by security police after instituting a claim for torture and poisoning against the Minister of Police.

And yet, despite the evidence against him, du Plessis remains a member of the South African Police. No action has ever been taken against him. I have seen du Plessis twice in my life, once at the Harms Commission of Inquiry where he was assisting the Commission with their investigation into death squads, and the second time as one of the investigating officers into the death squad allegations of a former member of the Vlakplaas counter-insurgency force.

I want to talk to you today about men like Hermanus du Plessis. Why do I specifically single him out? Because I believe that men like du Plessis are members of what is known today as the "Third Force."

I do not believe in the existence of a special force set up specifically to disrupt the peace process and kill anti-apartheid activists. What I do believe in, is in a unique and very special culture existing in the South African Police. Let us call it the Total Onslaught Ideology culture.

This culture is at least partly responsible for clear evidence of police complicity in acts of violence and their unwillingness to act against Inkatha and other forces opposed to the ANC.

I believe that this culture is alive and well and living in a rather large number of policemen, especially former security policemen. Men like Lieutenant-Colonel Hermanus du Plessis. Discredited, bent policemen, whose mission in life has been to destroy the ANC and its allies, and uphold apartheid through repressive legislation. Their past experiences have taught them that most black people are inferior, untrustworthy and have a strange tendency towards Communism.

As members of the Security Branch, performing illegal operations inside and outside the borders of the Republic of South Africa, du Plessis and his colleagues enjoyed a special protection. This enabled them to operate above the laws of the country and above the rules and regulations of the South African Police. The security police's culture, their techniques, skills and methods had much in common with those of a gang of ordinary thugs. What distinguishes them from common criminals was that they believed themselves to be involved in a kind of "Jihad"—a holy war against the total onslaught.

Then suddenly, on February 2, 1990, the South African political situation changed dramatically. The ANC and the South African Communist Party were no longer the enemy. There was no longer a total onslaught against Christianity or civilised norms. Since that day in February 1990, the SAP's Directorate of Public Relations would like to tell you, Hermanus du Plessis has suddenly become just a bobby on the beat. With the stroke of a pen, this once terrifying security policeman is now your friendly neighbourhood cop, catching thieves and fighting crime.

To prove this, and in an effort to get the support of the general public, Minister of Law and Order Adriaan Vlok disbanded the Security Police and declared: "This step would remove the police from the political playing field."

But has it really? No, it has not, and let us look at what happened. When Dirk Coetzee and Generals Jan Viktor and Jac Buchner started the Vlakplaas counter-insurgency unit in 1981, there were sixteen policemen. In 1990, this unit has grown to 120 men and later in the same year we discovered that the very notorious Koevoet unit has been brought from Namibia and integrated with the Vlakplaas unit.

In the same year, death squad commander Eugene de Kock was promoted from the rank of Major to Lieutenant-Colonel and Brigadier Nick van Rensburg was transferred from Port Elizabeth to Pretoria to head the Vlakplaas Unit. I have mentioned four names—Buchner, Viktor, de Kock and van Rensburg. Let's look at them.

Eugene de Kock has been implicated in various acts of atrocities, inside and outside of South Africa. He was transferred from the Koevoet unit to take over Vlakplaas in 1983. In June 1986, he was implicated in the killing of four young activists in Chesterville in Natal when his squad fired 88 rounds at the unarmed youths. In June 1988, his squad shot another four activists near Piet Retief in the South-eastern Transvaal. There was no evidence that the infiltrators were armed. It was the stock explanation: ANC infiltrators were frequently mowed down by the police in acts of "self-defence."

Former security policeman and self-confessed hitman Almon Nofemela claimed before the Harms Commission that de Kock point-blank shot security guard Japie Maponya to prevent identifying Nofemela afterwards. Judge Louis Harms rejected Nofemela's evidence, but a magistrate ruled afterwards that it was possible that Nofemela had been telling the truth. Maponya was never seen again.

To make things worse, de Kock is not even a good policeman. According to evidence before the Harms Commission, the counter-insurgency unit had not arrested more than 20 infiltrators between 1982 and 1990—an average of just more than two every year.

Brigadier Nick van Rensburg is alleged to have been involved in various death squad atrocities in the seventies and eighties. He was Ermelo Security Branch commander in the seventies and is alleged to have been involved in a break-in into the United Nations office in Swaziland and acts of violence in which various people were injured and killed. He then became head of Security Police in Port Elizabeth, where he is alleged to have been involved in the killing of Sizwe Kondile. Evidence was lead in the Rand Supreme Court in 1990 that van Rensburg gave the command to kill Kondile.

General Jan Viktor is Commissioner of Police in the Ciskei. He was the founder of the Vlakplaas hit squad unit where he was implicated in various atrocities and the killing of anti-apartheid activists. According to reports, he has "purged" the Ciskei police of those against the Ciskei Government or sympathetic towards the ANC and has reinstalled former Ciskei policemen who were kicked out of the police force after being jailed for the murder of Eric Mntonga.

Major-General Jac Buchner is Commissioner of KwaZulu Police. Previously, Buchner was the security police chief in Pietermaritzburg and was regarded as one of the SAP's experts on the ANC. He spent seven years in Rhodesia as an intelligence officer for the SAP during the bush war. Thereafter he was for many years based at Section C (Vlakplaas) where he was chief interrogator of captured ANC and PAC guerillas. He was the architect of using "turned" guerillas against the ANC and masterminded the raids on Matola in Maputo and Maseru in the early eighties. He is described by the ANC as an "efficient killing machine." Various members of his police force have been implicated and jailed for atrocities. There is evidence that officers under his command bought and provided arms to Inkatha.

How is it possible that these men can still serve in the South African Police, and how can the Government expect South Africa to have faith in its security forces when de Kock and his askaris still roam the townships and the SAP's architects of black-on-black violence still serve in the security forces?

Over the past two-and-a-half years, a succession of allegations against the security forces, which at first seemed incredible, have proved to be true. The allegations of hit squads seemed fantastic, but turned out to be true. The allegation of police collusion with Inkatha seemed far-fetched, and proved to be true. The idea that military officers would defy President de Klerk by concealing and destroying military evidence seemed incredible, and proved true. So did the police's complicity in the Trust Feed massacre and the subsequent cover-up, the involvement of the SADF's Chief of Military Intelligence in the killing of the Cradock Four, and the secret bases from where undercover and faceless policemen plan attacks on the ANC. The dirty tricks laundry list goes on and on.

The South African Police, and to a lesser extent the South African Defence Force, has become a degenerate organisation, a haven for gangsters like Hermanus du Plessis, Eugene de Kock, Nick van Rensburg, Jan Viktor and Jac Buchner.

These policemen, and many others, I believe, constitute South Africa's "Third Force." How can you expect a man to one day defend a specific set of norms and laws and the next day make a 180 degree turnaround? The Total Onslaught Ideology has been too deeply embedded in them.

Listen again to what Brian Mitchell said in the Trust Feed Massacre trial: "We attacked the UDF because we regarded them as the enemy and Inkatha as an ally."

The white public has had an enormous problem accepting the new political realities of South Africa. They might have voted "yes" in the referendum, but still deeply distrust the ANC and its Communist allies. This explains why the Inkatha Freedom Party enjoys such huge support in the northern suburbs of Johannesburg. Why would the attitude of the average South African policeman be that different?

Major Dolf Odendaal, second-in-command of the Peninsula Riot Squad, had to testify in 1988 in the Cape Supreme Court why the police did not act against a vigilante group burning down houses and driving out inhabitants. He said: "If black people decided to fight, there is nothing I can do. You do not know black people when they decide to fight." Odendaal told the court that he believed it would be a solution if, in unrest situations, police were by law allowed to shoot anyone holding a stone.

Why, I ask myself, would Odendaal's attitude suddenly have changed after February 1990? Yet, he still serves in the force and has recently been promoted to the rank of Lieutenant-Colonel.

Does this attitude not explain, perhaps, the police's unwillingness to act against Inkatha impis attacking ANC supporters, Casspir armoured vehicles guarding the "Rooidoeke" vigilante group, the unwillingness of a police general and brigadier to investigate the Trust Feed Massacre and the Commissioner of Police rushing to court to prevent the Weekly Mail from exposing an undercover police operation?

Respected UNISA criminologist, Irma Labuschagne, who testified on behalf of Brian Mitchell, has identified a new psychological disorder in South Africa; she calls it the Total Onslaught Ideology disorder. According to Labuschagne, South African policemen have been brutalised to such an extent by the Total Onslaught, that it should be recognised in our courts as a recognised disorder. She says that she believes that Brian Mitchell is a decent person, but was turned into a monster by this ideology. She says that many, many policemen are in dire need of psychological treatment before they can continue their policing activities. Her theory is fully supported by, amongst others, University of Cape Town psychologist, Prof. Don Foster, who also believes that South African policemen should undergo a healing process after being brutalised by four decades of apartheid rule.

What a shame that the South African Government and Police do not admit the crisis in their midst. Two weeks ago, there was a programme on police training on Radio 702 during which a Brigadier Chetty (the highest-ranking non-white police officer) was asked how the SAP was retraining Koevoet. Chetty replied that he was not aware of the existence of Koevoet in the SAP.

Let me first of all say that in my investigations over the past three years, I have come across many decent, professional and ethical policemen. The SAP is today a force consisting of 110 000 policemen. Members of the force are getting killed at an alarming rate and South Africa must be an extremely difficult country to police.

In many quarters of the SAP—and the SADF—there have been major changes and I often sense new attitudes and an acceptance of new political realities. But the top brass in the armed forces and the responsible politicians should realise that a culture cannot be terminated by new rules and regulations. Or change a monster into a dove. There has been no effort by the State to clean up the security forces and help create a new culture more conducive to peace and stability.

With the continued presence in the force of policemen implicated in atrocities and dirty tricks and the continued existence of former hit squad units like Vlakplaas, it is unthinkable that the South African Police can ever be acceptable to the majority of South Africans.

Unless the authorities remove the Hermanus du Plessis's from the force, disband units like Vlakplaas and start a healing process among policemen emerging from the previous era, the deep distrust in the SAP and their complicity in the violence will continue. And so will the existence of this faceless, silent "Third Force" that has driven basically decent human beings into committing ghastly atrocities.

Founding of COSATU*, November 1985[1]

(*Congress of South African Trade Unions)
Editor's Note: Skilled black workers, many of whom supported the African National Congress, the South African Communist Party, and other antiapartheid political organizations, formed unions to fight racial discrimination in the workplace. By the mid-1980s, they had earned a number of victories, including the right to bargain collectively. Their determination to force the largest corporations into affording better working conditions and wage scales, in turn pressed some industrial and manufacturing leaders to encourage the National Government to make political reforms. What organizational principles and actions did COSATU establish in order to build its movement? What does the document say about African leadership? What changes did COSATU leaders call for?

A Lion Has Been Born

Durban was typically hot and humid as 760 delegates from 33 unions, representing over 460,000 workers, moved into the hall. Many were singing. Behind the platform hung a banner proclaiming "Workers of the World Unite!," and an enormous panelled painting produced by Fosatu's[2] Port Elizabeth local stood to one side.

Cyril Ramaphosa, the convenor of the launching congress, shared the platform with two recording secretaries. In the foyer latecomers registered . . . each delegate was handed a cheap portable radio and headphones, used to allow simultaneous translation into four languages—Zulu, Sotho, English and Afrikaans.

Worker marshals struggled to keep a large contingent from the local and foreign media at bay. The mood was excited but nervous . . . there was a sense of urgency and widespread belief that the time was right to launch a new federation. In the townships, mass mobilisation and uprisings continued despite the government's declaration of a partial state of emergency only months before. The union movement needed a vehicle, a federation, to respond to these developments effectively.

At 11 A.M. on 30 November 1985, the launching congress opened with the singing of South Africa's unofficial national anthem, Nkosi Sikelel' iAfrika.

—*Excerpts from COSATU's own account*

A Giant Has Risen

Born in the midst of a state of emergency, township uprisings and tensions between divergent

---

1. Excerpt from Jeremy Baskin, *Striking Back* (Routledge, 1991). Used by permission of COSATU.

2. That is, the Federation of South African Trade Unions.

union traditions, COSATU's launch was a working class victory. On the last weekend of November 1985, worker delegates gathered at the sports hall of the University of Natal to launch the Congress of South African Trade Unions.

Unity talks had started informally in 1979, become more formal in 1981 and continued up to the launch. Although the talks had covered many issues, there were still many unresolved differences and underlying tensions. But unionists felt the differences could be debated endlessly. Decisions had to be made and the best place for this to happen was within the democratic structures of a federation. Thus the 760 delegates from 33 unions were at once excited and apprehensive. No one really knew what this meeting, or the future would hold.

Cyril Ramaphosa, then Num general secretary, earlier chosen as the convenor of the launching congress, set the tone with a short opening address: "The formation of this Congress represents an enormous victory for the working class in this country . . . In the next few days . . . we will be putting our heads together, not only to make sure we reach Pretoria, but also to make a better life for us workers in this country. What we have to make clear is that a giant has risen and will confront all that stand in its way."

With that, delegates set about fulfilling their first task—the adoption of a constitution.

A Constitution

The congress spent much of its time debating the federation's constitution, even though agreement on a draft had been reached during unity talks. There was lengthy and heated debate around the addition of an assistant general secretary, revealing tensions and unresolved issues.

A constitution, which determined the federation's basic structures, was finally agreed on. COSATU would be a disciplined and active federation with structures at national, regional and local levels. All structures should contain a majority of worker delegates. This was aimed at preventing union officials from dominating structures and was central to ensuring mass participation in decision making.

Structures would include a national congress every two years, a central executive committee (CEC) meeting every three months and an executive committee (Exco) which would meet every month.

Regional congresses would be held every four months and the regional executive committee would meet every month. Ten COSATU regions were established at the launch, but this was later changed to nine.

COSATU locals would be set up to unite workers from particular towns or townships. They would be open to all shop-stewards living or working in the area and were seen as COSATU's basic unit of organisation which would advance the federation's interests at grassroots level.

These structures have remained largely unchanged since COSATU's formation in 1985, apart from the restructuring of the executive committee in 1987. At the launch, the Exco comprised elected office bearers plus four additional members of the CEC. The 1987 Congress changed this to elected office bearers plus two delegates from each affiliate. This structure had been the original intention during unity talks, but was impractical due to the large number of affiliates joining COSATU at the launch. Once a programme of mergers was underway, it became more feasible.

Policies

The congress called for one union to be established in each industry within six months. Delegates voted for the launch of an education programme and a newspaper.

Another resolution examined exploitation and discrimination against women. Some of the issues it dealt with were women's access to "a limited range of occupations," that they had to do "boring and repetitive work with low and often unequal pay," sexual harassment in the workplace and women losing their jobs when they fell pregnant.

The congress decided that COSATU should take up these problems.

The right to strike and picket was another resolution and it called for the CEC to determine a national living wage. The congress condemned the bantustan system and the "super exploitation occurring in these areas." Delegates stated their determination to "organise in plants based within the Bantustans," even though it was very difficult to do so. The congress resolved that the migrant labour system, "including pass laws and influx control" should be scrapped and that workers had the right to live in "proper housing" with their families "near their place of work."

Other resolutions including a call for the lifting of the state of emergency, the withdrawal of troops from the townships, the release of political prisoners and the unbanning of all restricted individuals and organisations.

Delegates also decided that all forms of international pressure, "including disinvestment or the threat of disinvestment" were essential and should be supported—even though it was illegal at the time to make such calls.

Elections

The issue of elections was a difficult one. COSATU's leadership would be faced with enormous challenges. While the organisation had been launched, it still had to be built. This task would fall on the new leadership which had to be capable of weaving together the different strands of the union movement which came together to form COSATU. To do this effectively, the leadership would need overwhelming support. Any hint of acrimony would inhibit their ability to fulfill their tasks. So the elections were extensively caucused outside the congress hall to make sure that consensus was reached. Union delegates huddled together outside the hall, discussing prospective candidates, with emissaries moving from one caucus to another trying to reach common agreement.

After much discussion, Elijah Barayi was elected

president. He took to the podium saying, "You must know that a lion has been born." Chris Dlamini was elected vice-president, Makhulu Ledwaba second vice-president, Jay Naidoo general secretary and Sydney Mufamadi assistant general secretary. All except Ledwaba, who stood against Saawu's Robert Gqweta, were elected unopposed. All were men.

The Rally

The second day of the congress included a workers' rally at Kings Park stadium in Durban. Insufficient work had gone into the planning of the rally and so attendance was disappointing—only 10,000 workers gathered for the event. But the crowd that gathered was enthusiastic and responded warmly to the elected office bearers as they were introduced.

Barayi's speech stood out. Speaking in Xhosa, with his well-known wit and sharp tongue, he launched an attack on all homeland leaders, labelling them "puppets," and he called for the release of the people's "real leader" Nelson Mandela.

Barayi also called on the government to scrap the pass laws within six months or COSATU would call on people to burn their passes. While his comments did not reflect the issues agreed on at the congress, his tone reflected the spirit of the launch and was well received by the crowd.

The federation had been launched. And, while differences, debate and tension would continue to be a feature of COSATU meetings for years to come, the new structures would provide the framework for them to be ironed out, and policies developed.

COSATU was launched with an unambiguous political stamp and thousands of workers were jubilant about the launch. It gave them hope. It was their achievement. And, as delegates reported back to workers throughout the country, one particular song was to be heard wherever workers gathered. It was composed by Ccawusa members and it assumed for a time, the status of the "official"

COSATU song: *iCosatu sonyuka nayo/masingen' enkululekweni* ran the refrain—COSATU is rising up/let us go with it to freedom.

Constitution of the South African Communist Party

Adopted at the 8th Party Congress in December 1991[1]

(*Excerpts*)

Editor's Note: The South African Communist Party (SACP) had a long history in South Africa, and its longtime leader, Joe Slovo, was an outspoken opponent of apartheid. Why did the SACP decide to write a party constitution in 1991? How does the constitution reflect changing conditions in the South African and international contexts? What are the implicit notions of justice embedded in this document?

3. Aims

3.1 The Communist Party seeks to be the leading political force of the South African working class whose basic interests it advances in the struggle for national liberation and socialism

3.2 The SACP shall pursue this by means of educating, organising and mobilising the working class and its allies in support of our Party and its objectives of national liberation and socialism.

3.3 The Party shall strive to win acceptance as a vanguard by democratic means and in ideological contest with other political parties.

3.4 The ultimate aim of the Party is the building of a communist society in which all forms of exploitation of person by person will have ended and in which all the products of human endeavour will be distributed according to need. The attainment of such a society will require an interim socialist formation in which reward will be measured by contribution.

3.5 At all stages the Party commits itself to a

1. http://www.sacp.org.za/main.php?include=docs/history/1991/constitution7.html.

social order which will respect completely the cultural, language and religious rights of all sections of our society and the democratic rights of the individual. It will recognise the right to independence of all social organisations and political parties. This implies a multi-party political framework in which there will be regular open and free elections. Within such a framework the SACP will primarily dedicate itself to advancing the interests of the working class and its allies in democratic contest with other political forces

4. Guiding Principles

In leading the working class towards national and social emancipation the Party is guided by those principles of Marxism/Leninism which have proven universal validity by historical experience. The foundations for these principles were laid by Karl Marx, Friedrich Engels and Lenin and enriched by other great revolutionaries. In applying the general principles of Marxism/Leninism the SACP is, in the first place, concerned with their indigenous elaboration and application to the concrete realities of our own developing situation. More particularly the Communist Party will work:

4.1 To end the system of capitalist exploitation in South Africa and establish a socialist society based on the common ownership of, and participation in, and control by the producers of the key means of production. Such a society will respect and protect all personal non-exploitative property and such other private property as may be necessary for effective economic development and growth.

4.2 To organise, educate and lead our working class in pursuit of this strategic aim and the more immediate aim of winning the objectives of the national democratic revolution which is inseparably linked to it. The main content of the national democratic revolution is the national liberation of the African people in particular, and the black people in general, the destruction of the economic and political power of the racist ruling class, and the establishment of one united state of peoples power in which working class interests will be dominant and in which economic conditions will be created making it possible to move steadily towards social emancipation and, eventually, the total abolition of the exploitation of person by person.

4.3 To participate in and strengthen the liberation alliance of all classes and strata whose interests are served by the immediate aims of the national democratic revolution. This alliance is expressed through the liberation front headed by The African National Congress.

4.4 To spread the widest possible understanding of our basic ideology and its application to South African conditions, particularly among the working class.

4.5 To combat racism, tribalism, sex discrimination, regionalism, chauvinism and all forms of narrow nationalism.

4.6 To encourage an ongoing national and international dialogue with all organisations committed to peace, democracy and preservation of our environment.

4.7 To promote the ideas of proletarian internationalism and the unity of the workers of South Africa and the world, and to encourage an ongoing international dialogue with all organisations which are committed to a socialist future, and to act in solidarity with all struggles for liberation and social emancipation.

Significance of the African and Indian Joint Struggle

E. S. Reddy, 1987[1]

Editor's Note: Enuga Sreenivasulu Reddy was born in India in 1924 and became interested in liberation struggles in India and South Africa while he was a university student. A member of the United Nations secretariat for thirty-five years until his retirement in 1985, he dealt primarily with South Africa and was for

1. Used by permission of the ANC Archives.

a long time the official in charge of UN action against apartheid. How does he describe the impact of the ongoing legacy of colonialism in countries like India and South Africa? How does he see the struggles of Africans and Indians as linked? What is Reddy's concern regarding the Black Consciousness movement, and why does he see the term "Black" as ambivalent? How does he understand what it means to be "Black" and what are the implications of his understanding? During apartheid, what was the official status of Indians in relation to Africans, Coloureds, and Whites, and how did the government's attitude towards Indians make their status even more uncertain? What challenges and opportunities lie ahead for the liberation movement and how does Reddy see the Indian community's role in that? Do you think there may be new significance to this document for Indians in South Africa in 1993 that Reddy may or may not have anticipated in 1987 (consider especially the expected shift in power relations in the country)?

The struggle for liberation in South Africa—especially the development of the alliance between the African and Indian people in that struggle—became the base for the building of a powerful united democratic front to destroy apartheid and establish a non-racial democratic society . . .

This is a silver jubilee year for that liberation struggle.

In 1961, the racist regime proclaimed a so-called republic and suppressed, by a massive show of force, the national protest led by Nelson Mandela. The liberation movement then made the momentous decision to abandon its strict adherence to non-violence, and to combine peaceful resistance with armed struggle.

On December 16, this year, it will be the twenty-fifth anniversary of the dramatic appearance on the scene of Umkhonto we Sizwe ("Spear of the Nation")—the military wing of the African National Congress—led by Nelson Mandela and including combatants of all the racial groups in the country, African, Coloured, Indian and White.

A Personal Note

I became interested in the struggle for freedom in South Africa in my student days, especially in 1946. That was the year when the Indian people in South Africa launched a passive resistance movement against the "Ghetto Act"—the year when India imposed a trade embargo against South Africa and complained to the United Nations about racial discrimination in that country, thereby internationalising the South African problem.

It was also the year of the first strike of African mineworkers—which was suppressed brutally by the government of General Smuts, which did not hesitate to massacre the strikers on the streets and to force the miners down the pits, level by level, at gunpoint until they resumed work.

It was the year when the African National Congress and the Indian Congresses of Natal and Transvaal sent a joint delegation to the United Nations in the first joint action of the two communities. India was still under colonial rule at that time. Our generation saw our struggle for freedom as but a part of the struggle of all colonial peoples for emancipation.

We in India appreciated the support we received, in difficult days, from the great Pan-African leaders—like Dr. DuBois and Paul Robeson, to name but two—and from the Pan-African movement to which Trinidadians like Henry Sylvester-Williams and George Padmore made a great contribution.

I would also like to recall that in its resolution on South Africa, the Manchester Congress recognised that Africans are not the only victims of racialism and that Indians also suffered similar discrimination. It demanded "justice and human equality for the Indian community in South Africa."

We too tried to do our share—for instance by action to prevent the dispatch of Indian and colonialist troops to reconquer Indonesia and the nations of Indo-China which had declared independence in August 1945 in the wake of the Japanese surrender.

Personal Involvement

. . . I have . . . been increasingly inspired by the great liberation struggle in South Africa—a struggle that has united African, Indian and other peoples in that country, a struggle that has espoused a non-racial and international outlook similar to that of the Pan-African movement and our own national movement in India, with courage and consistency.

People's History

The first Pan-African Conference, convened in London by Henry Sylvester-Williams, barrister from Trinidad, said in its "Address to the Nations of the World" drafted by Dr. W.E.B. DuBois: "The problem of the twentieth century is the problem of the colour line—the relation of the darker to the lighter races of men in Asia and Africa, in America and the islands of the seas."

At that time, the British government was carrying on a war against the Boers and one of the causes of the war, as defined by it, was the ill-treatment by the Boer Republics of the indigenous African people as well as Her Majesty's Indian subjects. Both the Africans and Indians were, of course, to be betrayed soon after the end of the war and handed over to the tender mercies of the white settlers in one of a series of acts of perfidy.

But the words of the Pan-African Conference have proved prophetic, as our peoples struggled to destroy the colour line and build a community of humankind.

Since the end of the Second World War, a hundred nations have freed themselves from colonialism at the cost of millions of lives and now constitute a majority of the international community.

The map of the world has changed its colours. A shameful era in human history, spanning four or five centuries, is nearing its end, with the last battles being fought in South Africa and Namibia.

History has begun to be rewritten more truthfully. Africa, for instance, is no more the dark continent without a history, but the continent with a heritage of great kingdoms and civilisations.

We must acknowledge with gratitude and respect the contributions of historians of Africa, Asia and the Caribbean, as well as black scholars like Dr. W.E.B. Dubois.

The time has come, indeed, to conceive of a people's history of the world—a history in which the majority of the people, with darker skins, are not mere victims but actors.

Nightmare of Humanity

The period since the European navigators went in search of the wealth of the Indies and discovered Africa on the way or sailed by mistake to the Caribbean, the era when the European powers despoiled three continents, should not be romanticised as a story of European adventure, conquest and supremacy but treated as a long nightmare of humanity.

We must delve into our common experiences and the struggles our peoples have waged from the very beginning of European conquest and enslavement, and our march to redemption.

. . . Little is said of the extensive international contacts developed by the Indian national movement, especially under the leadership of Pandit Jawaharlal Nehru, with the freedom movements in Africa and elsewhere. These have had a great impact not only on the policy of independent India but also on the progress of the colonial revolution since the Second World War. They have led India to champion the cause of freedom in South Africa, Namibia and other African nations in the United Nations and other fora, at the cost of the hostility of major Western powers and thereby lay the foundations of the Non-Aligned Movement in which Africa has played an increasing role since the independence of Ghana in 1957.

Post-Slavery Period

One subject that deserves fuller study is "post-slavery," the replacement of slavery by new forms of bondage and servitude, humiliation and exploitation of human beings as mere beasts of burden—the systems of indentured labour, colonialism, neo-colonialism and their variants, not to speak of genocide.

. . . Soon after the abolition of slavery, Africa was carved up and almost the entire continent brought under colonial rule so that oppression extended from the coastal regions to the heart of the continent.

At the same time, the indentured labour system was invented to continue the supply of cheap and rightless labour, under conditions of semi-slavery, to South Africa and the Western hemisphere.

Indentured Labour

India—ravaged in the nineteenth century by famines, both natural calamities and tragedies created or aggravated by colonial plunderers—became the main victim of this system.

Indians were first brought to South Africa to work on sugar plantations in the Natal in the 1860s as the Zulu people were unwilling to work for the planters. More were brought later to work in the coal mines.

The Indian workers organised the first strike in South Africa, more than a century ago.

As the need for cheap labour increased with the discovery of diamond and gold mines, thousands of Chinese workers were brought in and there was even a move to bring some workers from the Caribbean. But that was not sufficient—and Africans were forced by the hut tax, the poll tax and other measures to labour in the mines, on the white farms and later in factories.

Coming after the dispossession of the Africans from most of their ancestral land in a century of so-called "kaffir wars," this forced labour system set the pattern for the inhuman oppression of the African people.

Apartheid was not an exclusive invention of the

Afrikaners, who trekked to the north in protest against the abolition of slavery. It was equally the creation of the mine owners—the British and American interests among them—in collusion with the local authorities.

Gold was discovered on the Witwatersrand in 1886. South Africa became prosperous but that brought no comfort to the indigenous people of that country but only immense sorrow and suffering.

This year, in a sense, marks the centenary of apartheid and must make us recall that prosperity has always made the racists more greedy and enabled them to invest more in reinforcing the chains that bound the black people and to shoot them.

Not Reform but Elimination of Racism

Even today, in the vast literature on South Africa, most writers continue to contend that the oppression of the black people was mainly the crime of the Afrikaners, that peaceful evolution toward equality would have taken place if the coalition of General Smuts and the English-speaking people had remained in power, that apartheid began with the coming to power of the National Party in 1948 and that our task is to beg for so-called reforms so as to return to that course of gradual evolution.

. . . But the Indians had experienced worst racism—though sometimes camouflaged—at the hands of the English-speaking Whites in the Natal. It was in the Natal, not in Bloemfontein, that as late as 1946, European clubs carried the sign "Indians and dogs not allowed."

General Smuts, extolled in the West as a liberal, was, in fact, the architect of much of the racist legislation in South Africa.

. . . The struggle in South Africa today is not for a change of racist masters, not for the replacement of apartheid by camouflaged racism, but for the total elimination of racism and the building of a non-racial society in which all the people will enjoy equal rights in all fields and no one will suffer the slightest humiliation because of the colour of his or her skin.

It is in that context that I wish to deal with the development and significance of the alliance of the African and Indian peoples in their common struggle against racism, the role of this alliance in building a united democratic front of all the black people and the democratic whites, and the wider implications of this great struggle in South Africa.

The Parallel Struggles

1946 was a landmark in the development of unity in the struggle of Africans and Indians in South Africa.

Africans and Indians have, of course, struggled for their rights for decades before 1946 but their struggles had been parallel rather than united.

The first modern mass movement in South Africa was the Indian movement led by Mohandas Karamchand Gandhi from 1894 to 1913. It was confined to the Indian community and had hardly any contact with the Africans.

. . . Gandhi, for his part, was experimenting and learning in South Africa. He saw his mission as defence of the honour and redress of the grievances of the Indians in a part of the British empire to which he owed allegiance. He felt that identification with the cause of the African majority would only scare the Whites into greater hysteria and endanger the Indians.

. . . In 1946, he was to declare that "there is a real bond between Asiatics and Africans" which "will grow as time passes." (*Harijan*, February 24, 1946). Asking Indians in South Africa to associate with the Africans, he said, the slogan today "is no longer 'Asia for the Asiatics' or 'Africa for the Africans' but the unity of all the exploited races of the earth."

As I said, the Indian and African movements in South Africa early in this century were parallel movements.

. . . There were already some efforts to bring the African, Indian and Coloured people together to deal with the common problem of racist oppression by the white minority.

. . . But these were only early beginnings and did not carry the mainstreams of the black communities.

Three Doctors' Pact

. . . In the Indian community, a very important role was played by Dr. Yusuf Dadoo, a Marxist, who was in the leadership of many joint struggles, facing repeated imprisonment and persecution. He advocated that the Indian people should link their destiny with that of the African majority and join with the Africans in the struggle against racism.

His approach coincided with that of Jawaharlal Nehru and other leaders of the Indian National Congress who advised Indians abroad to identify themselves with the indigenous people.

. . . In June 1946 the two Indian Congresses launched a passive resistance movement against the "Ghetto Act" which prohibited Indians from acquiring any more land. More than two thousand Indians, including 300 women, went to jail and many of them were brutally beaten up by white hooligans while the police stood by. Some members from other racial groups joined the campaign as an act of solidarity.

. . . The Government of India then broke all trade relations with South Africa and lodged a complaint against South Africa before the United Nations, thereby internationalising the issue of racism in South Africa. The Indian leaders also persuaded Dr. A.B. Xuma, President-General of the African National Congress, to lead a multi-racial delegation to the United Nations and collected funds for the purpose.

Out of this co-operation came the "Three Doctors' Pact" of 1947—an agreement signed by Dr. Xuma, Dr. Dadoo and Dr. Naicker—for co-operation between the ANC and the Indian Congresses in the struggle for equal rights in conformity with the United Nations Charter.

Unity Forged in Struggle

The members of the African Youth League, espousing African nationalism, were initially rather hesitant about any alliance with other racial groups. But experience in the struggle removed their apprehensions and reservations.

The Youth League was impressed by the participation of Indians in the May Day work stoppage in 1950 in protest against the ruthless measures by the apartheid regime, which came to power in 1948. Eighteen Africans were killed and scores were injured when police fired at African crowds.

The African National Congress, the Indian Congresses and the Communist Party then organised a huge demonstration of mourning and protest on June 26, 1950. That date has since become the South Africa Freedom Day and the occasion for the launching of major campaigns.

. . . Until that time, some people in South Africa and abroad feared or insinuated that the African people were incapable of non-violent resistance. But if passive resistance was a gift of Indians, the African people in South Africa and then the black people of the United States have developed and enriched it into a potent weapon, at a certain stage of the struggle for freedom, even against the most inhuman oppressor.

Freedom Charter

In June 1955, on the initiative of the African National Congress, a Congress of the People was convened in Kliptown, near Johannesburg, to draw up a Freedom Charter for a democratic South Africa of the future. It brought together 3,000 delegates from all racial groups and from all over the country and was the largest multi-racial conference in South African history.

At that Conference, the ANC presented its highest honour—*Isitwalandwe*—to Chief Albert J. Luthuli, President-General of the ANC, Dr. Yusuf Dadoo, President of the South African Indian Congress, and Father Trevor Huddleston, now President of the Anti-Apartheid Movement in Britain.

The Freedom Charter proclaimed that "South Africa belongs to all who live in it" and laid down the guidelines for the South Africa of the future. It was subsequently endorsed by each of the Congresses and is still the banner of their common struggle. The alliance of all racial groups in the struggle for the abolition of racism and the establishment of a non-racial democratic society was cemented by this Charter.

Before the end of the year, the apartheid regime arrested 156 leaders of the movement in pre-dawn raids all over the country and charged them with treason. The treason trial which dragged on until March 1961, when it collapsed and all the accused were acquitted, further reinforced the alliance.

"Umkhonto we Sizwe"

Another milestone in unity was after the Sharpeville massacre, the banning of the ANC and the beginning of armed struggle.

With the escalation of repression, and the suppression of protests against the establishment of a White Republic in 1961 by a massive show of force, Nelson Mandela and others became convinced that they had to abandon strict adherence to non-violence and prepare for an armed struggle.

The *Umkhonto we Sizwe* ("Spear of the Nation"), the military wing of the ANC—which made its dramatic appearance on December 16, 1961—was a multi-racial organisation. Among its leaders were many Indians, Coloured people and Whites.

Black Consciousness

The emergence of the black consciousness movement in South Africa in the late 1970s has generated some misunderstanding and confusion. Some of the literature on the movement engaged in mysticism and it was often portrayed as anti-white and almost a black version of apartheid.

The movement had several strands but its essence and historic significance was in forging a firmer unity among the oppressed people in fighting the collaborators—the chiefs and others in the black community who tried to take advantage of the repression against the liberation movement by accepting the apartheid caste system and the crumbs from the oppressors—and in facilitating

the revival of the liberation struggle with greater force.

Successive racist regimes had tried to maintain their domination by dividing the black people by a sort of caste system. The Indians were, however, in a peculiar position—on the one hand as a class between the Coloured people and the African majority and on the other as a totally insecure community since the regime did not even accept the permanence of the community until the 1960s.

After the National Party came to power in 1948 with its apartheid policy, it enforced stricter segregation among the racial groups but by humiliating the Coloured people and the Indians, as well as the African majority, facilitated a greater unity of the oppressed people.

There has been some confusion about the use of the term "Black" to denote all the oppressed people of South Africa—and the regime has tried to compound the confusion by changing the official designation of the African majority from "Native" to "Bantu" and then "Black."

But to me, "Black" is not meant to define the colour of the skin any more than "red" defines the skin colour of Communists or "yellow" the colour of stoolpigeons. "Black" today denotes those fighting against colonialism and racism.

. . . The relaxations of some discriminatory measures against the Coloured people and Indians in an effort to entice them have been welcomed by the Reagan administration and hailed in apartheid propaganda as reforms. But these are really contemptible manoeuvres by the racists.

Soweto and After

By mid-1970s, the liberation movement recovered from the severe blows it had suffered in 1963–64, and there was an upsurge of workers, students and others.

The response of the regime was, as always, an escalation of repression—the massacre of African schoolchildren in Soweto on June 16, 1976, and the indiscriminate killing and maiming of students and youth all over the country for several years.

But repression and violence now only fueled resistance, and the people resorted to mass defiance of the police, making many repressive laws inoperable.

It is, for instance, against the law to carry an ANC flag but when tens of thousands of people began marching with the ANC flag, the police could not stop them and the law was neutralised.

Thousands of young people went abroad to join the freedom fighters. Armed struggle escalated—deliberately restricted by the liberation movement to attacks on symbols of apartheid and carefully chosen targets like police stations, military bases, the nuclear reactor and the oil-from-coal plant—while taking great precautions to avoid killing of civilians. The initiative was thus seized by the people.

Faced with a political and economic crisis, the Botha regime tried, on the one hand, to counter the armed struggle by blackmailing and destabilising the frontline states and, on the other, by attempting to divide the oppressed people.

But when it staged elections for the South African Indian Council in 1981, offering some crumbs to the Indian community, the Natal Indian Congress and the Transvaal Indian Congress revived their activities and called for a boycott. There was a 90 percent boycott.

Then the apartheid regime proposed a new constitution offering separate chambers of parliament to the Coloured people and Indians, and excluding the African majority.

That only provoked widest opposition among the Black people.

It was at the conference of the Transvaal Indian Congress in January 1983 that the Reverend Alan Boesak proposed the establishment of the United Democratic Front, which was to become the largest mass organisation in South African history.

The Botha regime tried every means—intimidation as well as inducements—to persuade the Coloured and Indian people to vote in the elections in August 1984, but there was more than an 80 percent boycott.

But the regime went ahead to bring the racist constitution into force on September 3, 1984, and that became the signal for the beginning of the revolutionary upsurge in South Africa—to make South Africa ungovernable by the racist regime and its puppets, to destroy apartheid and to establish a non-racial democratic state.

The unity forged in the long struggle is the guarantee that from now it is, as they used to say in Ghana, "Forward ever, Backward never."

I must pay the highest tribute to the great leaders of the African people for their vision and leadership, which has built this unity. They have seen their struggle not as a conflict between black and white, but as a struggle against a racist system. The liberation of the African people will be the liberation of all the people of South Africa.

That is why even some White people have been risking their lives in that struggle.

There are few instances in history where minority communities have rejected the enticements of ruling powers and joined the oppressed majorities in a common struggle. The solidarity demonstrated by the Coloured and Indian people with the African majority in South Africa is, therefore, remarkable.

Thousands of Indians have risked their lives and comforts in that struggle, ever since Dr. Dadoo and Dr. Naicker led them into an alliance with the African majority.

Suliman Salojee, Ahmed Timol, Hoosen Haffejee are among those tortured to death in racist prisons.

Ahmed Kathrada is serving life imprisonment with Nelson Mandela and others for founding and leading the *Umkhonto We Sizwe*.

Many Indians are in the leadership of the UDF, risking constant harassment, imprisonment and torture.

Mewa Ramgobin, a member of the Gandhi family in Durban, was among those charged with treason for leadership in the UDF.

In the family of the adopted son of Mahatma

Gandhi—the Naidoo family in Johannesburg—every single member of the family for three generations has been in prison.

India's Solidarity with Southern Africa

. . . There has been no World War since 1945 but colonial wars have caused millions of deaths and enormous suffering.

. . . The history of solidarity will need to be written in the near future along with the history of freedom struggles which will end the shameful era of slavery, colonialism, racism and humiliation of the majority of humanity.

The struggles for freedom and acts of solidarity contribute to peace because colonialism and racism are the root causes of war and because they are, in fact, systems of permanent aggression against the oppressed peoples. In no colonial country have the people taken up arms until the rulers began to suppress peaceful protests and resort to massacres. The cause of peace cannot be served by surrender to or appeasement of colonialism, any more than it was served by the appeasement of Hitler in the 1930s, but by the elimination of those evil and inhuman systems.

Upsurge in South Africa

. . . The upsurge in South Africa—which began in 1984 when the apartheid regime imposed a new constitution to dispossess the African people and divide the oppressed people—is nothing less than a revolution of enormous significance. The regime is unable to suppress it despite all its military might and its brutal violence against the black people.

Many African townships have become ungovernable. The police are unable to enter them without large military escorts, the puppet councils in the townships have been destroyed. Several repressive laws have become unenforceable because of mass defiance.

The trade union movement has become a powerful force and has led strikes of unprecedented scope. A million students have been on strike intermittently for two years. The people are no more afraid of death, imprisonment and torture, and those released from prison go back into the struggle without any hesitation.

USA and Britain

. . . The United States and British Governments have been unable to understand the situation in Southern Africa. They cannot believe that the Black majority can defeat the White racist regime despite its monopoly of military and economic power. They have not learnt from their mistake of assuming that the 500-year-old Portuguese colonialism would survive indefinitely.

. . . In August 1984, when that regime imposed a new constitution in the face of opposition by the African majority, as well as the great majority of the Coloured and Indian people, the United States State Department welcomed it as a "step in the right direction." In September 1984, when six African and Indian leaders of the United Democratic Front and the Natal Indian Congress sought refuge in the British Consulate in Durban and appealed to the British Government to prevail upon the Botha regime to stop arbitrary mass detentions of popular leaders, the British Government refused even to meet representatives of the two organisations.

That was a clear indication to the Black people in South Africa that they could not count on any intervention by the major Western powers and that their salvation lay in struggle. African townships erupted in revolt and a million workers went on an unprecedented strike in the Transvaal in November 1984.

International Action

As violence by the regime increased, international action in support of the liberation movement reached new levels. The Free South Africa movement was launched in the United States in November 1984: hundreds of thousands of people joined in demonstrations against the policy of "constructive engagement" and thousands courted arrest in the largest passive resistance movement since the civil rights movement of the 1960s.

Responsibility of Major Western Powers

The South African people had to carry on a long and difficult struggle not only because they had to struggle against a large White settler minority poisoned by racism, but also because their oppressors could count on the friendship and even support of foreign military and economic interests which were deeply involved in that country. They have tried hard and patiently to unite all the oppressed and decent people of that country—Africans, Coloured people, Indians and democratic Whites—in an alliance against racism. This alliance includes people of all religious faiths and diverse ideologies.

The international movement of solidarity with the South African freedom struggle, which has now developed into a powerful force, also includes governments, organisations and individuals of varied ideologies and persuasions.

. . . If only the Governments of the United States, Britain and West Germany stop their obstinate opposition to sanctions against South Africa, and cooperate with the overwhelming majority of States, there will be the prospect of a speedy end to apartheid in South Africa and of the liberation of Namibia. The shameful era of the rape and humiliation of Africa will end, colonialism will be buried and a decisive blow struck at racism.

Indians in South Africa

. . . India can be proud of the important role played by the Indian people in South Africa in promoting unity in the liberation struggle in South Africa. They have always recognised the primacy of the interests of the African majority and the leadership of the African National Congress. They have asked for no special status. In fact, they have rejected the "privileges" offered by the apartheid regime in 1984 and called for a non-racial democratic society.

The leaders of the African Congress deserve great credit for their vision of a free South Africa and for their leadership of the alliance which has destroyed the caste system which the rulers have sought to impose on the oppressed people in order to divide them. India has rightly honoured Nelson Mandela and Oliver Tambo, the twin leaders of the ANC.

But I hope that India will also appropriately honour Dr. Yusuf Dadoo and Dr. G.M. Naicker for their historic contribution, and that Indian public opinion will be better informed of the sacrifices of thousands of other people of Indian origin who have given their lives in the struggle or suffered imprisonment, torture and persecution—people like Babla Saloojee, Dr. Hoosen Haffejee and Ahmed Timol who were tortured to death; Ahmed Kathrada who has been in the struggle since he was eleven years old and is serving life imprisonment with Nelson Mandela; Billy Nair, who is still continuing the struggle after spending nearly twenty years in prison and being tortured in prison a few months ago; of Nana Sita, the Gandhian, who repeatedly went to jail for refusing to obey racist laws; the Naidoo family in which every member for three generations has been in jail; and many others like them. They have not only struggled for justice in their country but, by their sacrifice, helped promote indestructible friendship between India and Africa.

The Indians in South Africa are nationals of South Africa and their destiny is with the African people of South Africa. But India can never stand by if the Indian people anywhere are humiliated or oppressed because of their ancestral origin . . .

India may be separated from South Africa by an ocean but for all practical purposes India should always be in the frontline of those supporting the liberation struggle in that country.

Appendix 1. Homelands, Regions, and Countries

CLAIMING "INDEPENDENCE"
- Bophuthatswana
- Ciskei
- Transkei
- Venda

HOMELANDS WITH LIMITED SELF-GOVERNMENT
- Gazankulu
- KaNgwane
- KwaNdebele
- KwaZulu
- Lebowa
- QwaQwa

SOUTH AFRICAN PROVINCES
- Cape Province
- Natal
- Orange Free State
- Transvaal

COUNTRIES INDEPENDENT OF SOUTH AFRICA (1990)
- Botswana
- Lesotho
- Namibia
- Mozambique
- Swaziland
- Zimbabwe

Appendix 2. Pronunciation Glossary

(syllable in CAPS = emphasis)

Afrikaner	Ahf-ree-KAHN-er
Apartheid	Ah-PAR-tayd
Azania	Ah-ZAYN-ee-ah
AZAPO	Ah-ZAH-poh
Bisho	BEE-show
Bophuthatswana	Boh-pooh-tah-TSWAH-nah
Botswana	Boh-TSWAH-nah (not **Bot**-swana)
Ciskei	Sih-SKY
COSAG	CO-sahg
De Klerk, F. W.	Duh KLAYRK
Gatsha Buthelezi	GAHT-sha Boo-tay-LAY-zee
Oupa Gqozo	OOH-pah GOH-zoh (The G in GOH is pronounced with a glottal click,)
Hani (Chris)	HAH-nee
Inkatha	Een-CAH-tah
KwaZulu	Kwah-ZOO-loo
Mandela (Nelson)	Mahn-DAY-lah
Mangope (Lucas)	Mahng-OPE-ay
Natal	Nah-TAHL
Transkei	Trahn-SKY
Transvaal	Trahnz-VAHL
Umkhonto we Sizwe	Uhm-KOHNTOH-way-SEEZ-way
Verwoerd	Fair-VOORD
Viljoen (Constand)	Fill-YOON
Volksunie	FOLKS-u-nee
Zwelithini (King)	Zway-lih-THEE-nee

Appendix 3. Constitutional Worksheet[1]

PURPOSE AND STRUCTURE OF THIS WORKSHEET
One of the most important things to consider when crafting a constitution is to decide which political institutions will best meet the needs of the nation. This worksheet is designed to aid delegations in this decision by outlining a range of different institutional choices. The four types of institutions considered below are the **executive, electoral system, legislature**, and **degree of federalism**. By no means comprehensive, this worksheet briefly outlines the most common varieties of each institution, provides a few real-world country examples, and considers the advantages and disadvantages of each option. It is then left to the individual delegations to further research the various alternatives before deciding which will most likely advance the needs of their specific constituents.

I. **The Executive.** Traditionally, the executive's primary functions have been to oversee the day-to-day operations of government, administer policy through various bureaucratic agencies, and, increasingly, to set the policy agenda. In this latter role, the executive has been known to wield significant power in initiating legislation and steering the course of public policy. Below are several options for delegations to consider.
   a. **Presidential System**
      - Where. Presidential systems are found throughout Central and South America as well as in a few states in Africa and Asia.
      - How elected. The chief executive (president) is directly elected by eligible voters in a separate election. This provides the president with an independent power base apart from the legislature and makes presidents directly accountable to voters. Most modern democracies have incorporated presidential term limits into their constitutions. In other less democratic systems, it is not uncommon for presidents to attempt to subvert term limits by either disregarding or amending the constitution. Fixed terms give a president substantial stability to move forward with unpopular legislation without the risk of a contentious legislature removing him or her from power.
      - Roles and composition. There is a single executive that acts as both head of state and head of government.
         1. Head of Government. The president is responsible for overseeing the daily functioning of government and enforcing laws
         2. Head of State. The president is the country's chief diplomat and representative.
         3. Cabinet. The cabinet is composed of the heads of all federal bureaucratic departments or ministries (e.g., Secretary of Defense). The president has the power to appoint all members of the cabinet, a feature designed to foster close working relations and a unified agenda. For this reason, presidential systems may be quite durable during periods of transition or turmoil since the president can usually count on unified support from his or her hand-picked team when making

1. Prepared by Peter Doerschler, Bloomsburg University of Pennsylvania.

tough decisions. At the same time, one should be wary of the dangers of nepotism when a president opts to appoint to important posts close friends over more seasoned and competent leaders.

- Checks on presidential power. Opponents of presidential systems sometimes counter that presidents wield too much power through fixed terms, one-party cabinets with hand-picked appointees, and the ability to veto legislation. Under the right circumstances, this may lead to corruption and an abuse of power. For this reason, presidential systems are often designed with a built-in separation of powers between the different branches of government. When adopting a presidential system, delegations should therefore consider instituting various checks on presidential power (e.g., limited use of the veto, veto override by the legislature, federal constraints such as greater autonomy to regional governments, impeachment, etc.).

- Relationship to the legislature. Separate elections for the executive and legislature can result in divided government with different parties holding a majority of power in each branch of government. At its worst, this can result in gridlock, halting legislation and rendering government largely ineffective. In times of greater consensus between the executive and legislature, divided government can offer another check on presidential power. When choosing institutions, delegations should assess the tradeoffs of divided government.

b. **Parliamentary System**
- Where. Parliamentary systems are common throughout Europe and in former British colonies belonging to the British Commonwealth.

- How elected. Instead of a separate direct election, typical of presidential systems, the executive in parliamentary systems is formed after parliamentary elections. Traditionally, the leader of the party with the most seats in Parliament after a recent election is charged to form government.

- Building the executive. The basic requirement needed to form government is the support of a majority of Members of Parliament (MPs). This majority can be formed from either a single party or a coalition of parties (i.e., two or more). Delegations should be aware that majority governments are a rare breed. Especially in multiparty systems, election results usually necessitate the coalescing of multiple parties to form the needed majority. Therefore, when choosing a Parliamentary system, delegations should consider the feasibility of different parties engaging in shared governance. Old wounds, bitter rivalries, or strong ideological differences may render some coalitions untenable, thereby undermining the credibility and effectiveness of government. On the other hand, willing coalition partners can provide a strong foundation for shared governance around a working policy agenda. Moreover, coalition governments are generally thought to be very good for representation since varied constituent interests are represented by the coalition partners. For example, the former coalition of Social Democrats and Greens in Germany gave strong representation in government to both mainstream leftists and those with stronger environmental interests. Once a majority is consolidated and government formed, the leader of the strongest party usually assumes the role of head of government and is designated as prime minister.

- Roles. Under a Parliamentary system, separate individuals occupy the roles of head of government and head of state. There are many names for the head of government, including Prime Minister (PM), Chancellor, or (in Ireland) the Taoiseach. There are also noteworthy differences in the composition of the head of state. In the Scandinavian countries, for example, a monarch serves as head of state. These constitutional monarchies have preserved a role for the reigning monarch, though one that is usually ceremonial without any real political power. In other Republican forms of government, monarchs have been replaced by civilian heads of state either voted in via separate elections or appointed by the legislature.[1] Deciding between a constitutional monarchy and a republic often comes down to the symbolic importance of having a monarch as head of state. In making this decision, delegations should consider whether a vestige of the old regime is worth preserving that might unite the country.
- Cabinet composition. An important aspect of coalition negotiations is to determine the composition of the cabinet. In contrast to presidential systems where cabinet members are presidential appointees loyal above all to the president, cabinet posts in Parliamentary systems are divided among all parties in power and are generally loyal to their parties. As coalition governments are often the most likely outcome in Parliamentary systems, it will be crucial for delegations to consider how the various cabinet posts are to be divided among coalition partners. Reflective of its relative power, the senior coalition partner, in addition to occupying the chief executive, usually takes a majority of cabinet seats. Though a weaker player in the legislature, junior coalition partners often hold considerable leverage in claiming cabinet posts since their support is needed to form government.
- Relationship between executive and legislature. Once a stable majority has formed and is anchored in place, Parliamentary governments are usually highly effective at passing legislation and getting things done. This has a lot to do with the relationship between government and Parliament. Since the same party or group of parties controls both branches of government, the Parliament often acts as a "Rubber Stamp" for bills initiated in the executive.
- Checks and balances. The close-knit relationship between government and Parliament effectively concentrates power in the hands of the prime minister and the ruling parties. While a stable majority can produce a high level of effectiveness under this system, it can also severely limit the ability of the opposition to contest government actions. Concerned delegations should therefore consider ways to check majority power such as a powerful upper house or strong federal system (see below). Without these constraints, opposition groups are exposed to tyranny by the majority. Delegations

1. The head of state in many republics is also called a president.

should also be aware of a built-in check against an abusive majority, the vote of no confidence. In cases where a particular individual or party in government is advancing a radical agenda, coalition partners may defect from the coalition by calling a vote of no confidence. Under this scenario, a vote is taken in the Parliament to assess majority support for the government. If the vote fails to garner a majority of MPs, then government collapses and new elections are called.[1]

c. **Semi-Parliamentary Systems, Semi-Presidential Systems, Mixed Systems.**

- Where. A third option for delegations to consider is a mixed system that attempts to combine the best of presidential and Parliamentary systems. Mixed systems are fewer in number though prominent examples are found in France (Fifth Republic), Russia, and Ukraine.
- How elected. Separate elections take place as in presidential systems with a directly elected president and a prime minister that enters power via Parliamentary elections.
- Roles. Under a mixed system, the dual roles of the executive (head of government and head of state) are split as in Parliamentary systems. The principle difference here is that the directly elected president has substantial political powers far beyond that of a symbolic figurehead. Among the various powers held by the president are the ability to dissolve Parliament and call for new elections, appoint the prime minister, chair cabinet meetings and

veto legislation (with veto override possible). Furthermore, the president and not the prime minister may usually represent the country in important international affairs though this role, like the others, is subject to negotiation.

- Advantages and disadvantages. Hybrid systems attempt to combine the best of Parliamentary and presidential systems. With a Parliament elected from proportional representation and multimember districts, hybrids garner strong representation and consensus-building in the executive and legislature. To this, the directly elected president adds an element of stability as well as potentially another check on the power of the ruling parties and the prime minister. One problem with hybrid systems exists when substantial disagreement arises between members of the dual executive. Known as cohabitation, sharp ideological (usually represented by different parties) or personality differences between the prime minister and president can force gridlock and greatly diminish government's effectiveness.

d. **Consociationalism.** Another option for delegations to consider in this state-building exercise is a power-sharing agreement among major societal groups (i.e., ethnic, religious, cultural, linguistic, ideological etc.) known as consociationalism (see Lijphart 1977). The central goal of consociational democracy is to reduce existing tensions between major segments in a plural society by assimilating them into a power-sharing arrangement. Elements of consociationalism have been adopted in the Netherlands, where it first appeared; in Switzerland, in the so-called Swiss Model; and in Lebanon and Northern Ireland. There are four core features that distinguish consociational democracy:

1. Under an alternative scenario called a constructive vote of no confidence, a new majority is assembled to step in for the fallen government without calling for new elections.

- Grand coalition. Major societal groups together build a governing coalition that consists either of major party groups (aka a Parliamentary system) or elite figures (aka a presidential system). This brand of elite cooperation aims to permanently include groups in the decision-making process that would otherwise be relegated to the opposition and, depending on existing power structures, be hard pressed to ever gain power. Instead of being subject to the whim of the majority, minority groups are incorporated into what is intended to be a stable, consensual power base.
- Mutual veto. To protect from any abuses resulting from majority rule and to guarantee minority freedoms, all segments represented in the power-sharing arrangement are given an unconditional veto.
- Proportionality. Another core feature of consociational democracy consistent with the idea of power sharing is the allocation of civil service positions (e.g., police, teachers) among all major segments proportional to their relative power standing. For example, a segment with a 25 percent standing in the coalition would receive a 25 percent stake throughout the various civil service sectors. This arrangement makes it very difficult for a single actor or grouping to dominate any part of the public sphere, a problem that can easily spawn corruption and abuses by public officials in systems of majority rule.
- Segmental autonomy. In addition to power sharing at the national level, consociational democracy also calls for a well-defined federalist structure with considerable regional autonomy given to plural groups. This division of power between levels of government allows specific segments to prioritize and advance some of their common interests without first seeking the consent of the grand coalition. Obviously, before deciding to advance consociational democracy, delegations must determine whether regional and/or territorial interests are present and, consequently, whether regional autonomy would unnecessarily create new tensions at the local or regional levels.

Delegations should also consider some of the potential disadvantages of consociational democracy. First, the broad power-sharing arrangement emblematic of consociationalism reduces the voice and effectiveness of the opposition. And without a strong opposition, the democratic process may stagnate. Second, delegations should weigh whether regional autonomy would come at the cost of national unity. In other words, would major segments abandon the project of building national unity in favor of consolidating their power regionally? Finally, is it realistic to ask a number of divergent social groups with a history of animosity and mistrust toward one another to coexist peacefully in this consensus-building experiment? What incentive do they have to enter into this agreement? Moreover, how great is the risk that a consensus cannot be reached, leading to the kind of gridlock that perpetuates rather than reduces tensions?

e. **Direct Democracy.** All of the executive options outlined thus far are based on the principle of representative government. While all modern democracies have found some form of representative government to be a necessary vehicle for efficient policy-making, delegations should also consider whether any new political system would also be well served by direct citizen involvement in the policy-making process. A handful of modern democracies, most notably the Swiss, incorporate aspects of direct democracy into their policy-making process in the form of the citizen referendum. In the Swiss case, citizens can bring any issue to a national vote with a mere 50,000 signatures.[1] Consequently, the Swiss have made frequent use of the referendum on everything from EU membership to women's suffrage. Though not as embedded as a regular part of their political process, other states, as per their constitutions, have put critical issues to a national vote. Delegations should consider the relative merits of the referendum: While it empowers ordinary citizens by giving them a decisive voice in particular areas of policy making, its value to the political process relies on the ability of ordinary citizens to make informed decisions based on limited information. Are ordinary South Africans up to the task?

f. **Partition (aka The Balkanization of South Africa).** History is full of examples where a contentious and sometimes bloody struggle to preserve national unity is shown not to be the best option. Instead, in the interest of peace and prosperity for a majority of those concerned, the best option may simply be to let things fall apart and forge a new beginning. Delegations should ask themselves whether the prospect of a united South Africa is really better than the alternative of a number of smaller, independent political units.

II. **Electoral Systems.** Electoral systems are essential for translating votes into seats in the legislature after an election. In this way, they help to determine the level of representation and stability in a country's political system. Delegations should consider the following two options:

a. **Single-Member District (SMD).** As the name implies, each electoral district under an SMD system sends only one representative to the legislature. Representatives are elected based on either a plurality (i.e., winner-takes-all or first-past-the-post) or a majority (50 percent +1) of votes. In the latter case, a runoff election between top contenders is often needed to secure a majority of the vote (for example, France's double-ballot system). Because of strategic voting, SMD tends to produce two-party systems, which offer poor representation (think of the US example where third parties are essentially shut out of the political process) coupled with significant stability. There is also a high level of accountability with SMD since voters know exactly who their representative is and can punish or reward him/her accordingly at the next election. Besides providing poor representation, SMD electoral systems also tend to magnify majorities. This has been particularly common in the British system where mainstream parties like the Conservatives or Labour can acquire a much higher percentage of seats in Parliament than their actual vote total would otherwise dictate.

b. **Proportional Representation (PR).** PR employs multimember districts with anywhere from several MPs per district (e.g., Sweden, Finland, and Luxembourg all have a district magnitude of more than 10, while Greece has 56 districts for 300 seats) to the entire country representing one supersized district (e.g., the Netherlands). Under PR the percentage of

---

1. Consider that Switzerland has approximately 7.5 million citizens (CIA Factbook).

votes approximates the number of seats for each party in the legislature. The table below shows one example:

Party	%Vote	# Seats
Party A	40	4
Party B	30	3
Party C	20	2
Party D	16	2
Party E	4	0

As this example illustrates, PR advantages smaller parties that are able to pick up seats despite not winning the election. Under SMD Plurality, the same results would have provided just a single winner (Party A) while excluding all other parties from representation in that district. While PR obviously bodes well for representation, it can also produce highly fragmented party systems whose members have difficulty forming and sustaining coalition governments.

Most PR systems also include a threshold clause that sets a minimum percentage needed by parties to gain seats in the legislature. A common threshold is around 5 percent (Germany), although other countries employ smaller ones (e.g., Denmark 2 percent, Netherlands 0.67 percent). In the example above, Party E fails to gain representation with the threshold set at 5 percent. A lower threshold therefore advantages smaller parties that can secure seats with a relatively small share of the vote: here again, Party E would have been guaranteed representation with a 4 percent or lower threshold. In selecting an electoral system, delegations should consider the potential tradeoffs of expanded representation. While PR may serve to give a needed voice to smaller parties and less mainstream opposition groups, it may unwittingly empower more radical antisystemic groups that wish to undermine democracy from within or, at the very least, attempt to subvert government efficiency and stability. Therefore, in selecting an electoral system, delegations must weigh the tradeoff between representation and stability.

c. **Mixed Systems.** A handful of countries (e.g., Germany, Italy) have instituted a hybrid system that combines SMD and PR.

III. **Legislative Systems.** Delegations must also decide on the form of the legislature. Though bills are often initiated in the executive as part of that branch's agenda-setting function, much of the actual work happens in the legislature, where bills are fine-tuned in committees before being brought to the floor for debate and a vote. Delegations should consider either a unicameral (one chamber) or bicameral (two chambers) system.

a. **Unicameral.** In unicameral systems, legislative power is concentrated in a single chamber, with members usually elected from national party lists. This setup is particularly advantageous for majoritarian rule with power concentrated in the hands of the strongest party or parties in Parliament. With only a single chamber in play under unicameralism, the legislative process is comparatively efficient and legislators are able to push forward reforms and controversial measures with relative ease, especially with a prime minister backing the agenda. Some examples of unicameral systems are Israel, Portugal, and Greece.

b. **Bicameral.** In bicameral systems, the first chamber or lower house is traditionally composed of national-level representatives elected from national party lists. In contrast, the second chamber or upper house is usually composed of representatives of regional entities (i.e., states, cantons, Länder, departments, etc.). Bicameral systems differ in the distribution of power between the two houses. In some bicameral systems (e.g., Britain, Botswana), the upper house holds little formal power and thus fails to serve as an effective counterweight to the lower house. Such systems maintain their bicameralism out of tradition and are de facto unicameral. Other bicameral systems (e.g., Columbia, US, Germany) have a much more symmetrical distribution of power in which the upper house is endowed with real powers such as voting on legislation; this serves to protect regional interests. While greater legislative symmetry can greatly complicate the electoral process by requiring a majority from both houses to pass legislation, it can also be quite valuable in protecting certain minority interests from an unchecked majority. In determining the need for greater minority representation, delegations may wish to consider bicameralism with a set of formal powers (e.g., the right to vote on bills, veto power).

IV. **Degree of Federalism.** Framers of the new constitution should also consider the distribution of power between national and regional political governments. Should power be concentrated in a federal government that essentially delegates authority to lower levels, or is a more equitable distribution of power among local, state, and national governments representing varied interests more desirable?

a. Federalism vs. centralization. To some extent, regional interests may already be well represented in the form of proportional representation or a strong upper house in the legislature. A federal system would take this one step further by granting a degree of autonomy and decision-making power to regional and/or local governments. Deciding on the degree of federalism and the different issue areas (e.g., education, control of police forces) that would come under the jurisdiction of regional governments is no easy task. Here delegations should consider which interests are in need of additional representation, what specific powers to grant them (e.g., jurisdiction in a particular issue area), and how to resolve discrepancies between national and regional interests (e.g., the existence of a supremacy clause whereby national laws trump regional ones). The implications of a federal system are substantial. On the one hand, instituting a federal structure may be necessary to placate volatile regional interests that under a more centralist structure would be prone to protest, violence, or even secession. On the other hand, delegations should also consider the implications of federalism for national unity such that diffuse power sharing may undermine any effort at building consensus around a shared identity or set of values. In an effort to build greater national unity, a centralized government may therefore be the better option.

ADDITIONAL READING AND REFERENCES

CIA. "The World Factbook." https://www.cia.gov/library/publications/the-world-factbook/.

Gallagher, Michael, Michael Laver, and Peter Mair. *Representative Government in Modern Europe: Institutions, Parties and Governments.* 4th ed. New York: McGraw-Hill, 2006.

Lijphart, Arend. *Democracy in Plural Societies.* New Haven: Yale University Press, 1977.

———. *Patterns of Democracy: Government Forms and Performance in Thirty-Six Countries.* New Haven: Yale University Press, 1999.

Norris, Pippa. *Electoral Engineering: Voting Rules and Political Behavior.* Cambridge: Cambridge University Press, 2004.

Sartori, Giovanni. *Comparative Constitutional Engineering.* 2nd ed. New York: New York University Press, 1997.

Shively, W. Phillips. *Power and Choice: An Introduction to Political Science.* 11th ed. New York: McGraw-Hill, 2008.

Bibliography

GENERAL

African National Congress. "The Freedom Charter." Adopted at the Congress of the People, Kliptown, 26 June 1955.

Amandla! A Revolution in Four-Party Harmony. Directed by Lee Hirsch. ATO Pictures, Kwela Productions LTS, 2002.

Apartheid, Part III. PBS Frontline, 1987. Videocassette (VHS).

Azanian Peoples' Organization (AZAPO). "Our Constitution." Accessed 16 December 2016. http://azapo.org.za/about-azapo/our-constitution/.

Beinart, William. *Twentieth-Century South Africa.* Oxford: Oxford University Press, 2001.

Biko, Steve. *I Write What I Like.* Johannesburg: Picador Africa, 2004 [1978].

Clark, Nancy L., and William H. Worger. *South Africa: The Rise and Fall of Apartheid.* Harlow: Pearson Longman, 2004.

Davenport, T. R. H., and Christopher Saunders. *South Africa: A Modern History.* London: Macmillan, 2000.

"Document 18: The Pretoria Minute, 6 August 1990." South African History Online. Accessed 26 November 2016. http://www.sahistory.org.za/archive/document-18-pretoria-minute.

"Document 17: The Groote Schuur Minute, 4 May 1990." South African History Online. Accessed 26 November 2016. http://www.sahistory.org.za/archive/document-17-groote-schuur-minute.

Frederickson, George M. *Black Liberation: A Comparative History of Black Ideologies in the United States and South Africa.* New York: Oxford University Press, 1995.

Giliomee, Hermann. *The Afrikaners: Biography of a People.* Charlottesville: University of Virginia Press, 2003.

Johns, Sheridan, and R. Hunt Davis Jr. *Mandela, Tambo, and the African National Congress: The Struggle against Apartheid, 1948–1990.* New York: Oxford University Press, 1991.

Kairos Theologians. *Kairos Document: Challenge to the Church; A Theological Comment on the Political Crisis in South Africa.* Braamfontein: Skotaville Publishers, 1985. http://www.sahistory.org.za/archive/challenge-church-theological-comment-political-crisis-south-africa-kairos-document-1985.

Lodge, Tom, Bill Nasson, Steven Mufson, Khehla Shubane, and Nokwanda Sithole. *All, Here, and Now: Black Politics in South Africa in the 1980s.* London: Hurst, 1992.

MacKinnon, Aran S. *The Making of South Africa: Culture and Politics.* Upper Saddle River, NJ: Pearson Prentice Hall, 2004.

Mandela, Nelson. "I am Prepared to Die." Statement from the dock at the opening of the defense case in the Rivonia Trial. Pretoria: Palace of Justice, Pretoria Supreme Court, 20 April 1964.

———. "Verwoerd's Grim Plot." *Liberation: A Journal of Democratic Discussion*, no. 36 (May 1959). http://v1.sahistory.org.za/pages/library-resources/articles_papers/1959_verwoerds_plot_mandela.htm.

Mason, David. *A Traveller's History of South Africa.* New York: Interlink Books, 2004.

Meli, Francis. *A History of the ANC: South Africa Belongs to Us.* Bloomington: Indiana University Press, 1989.

Reddy, Enuga S. "The Significance of the Indian and South African Joint Struggle." Enuga S Reddy Papers, University of Witwatersrand,

Historical Papers Research Archives, A2094, item Ab2.6.

Seekings, Jeremy. *The UDF: A History of the United Democratic Front in South Africa, 1983–1991.* Cape Town: David Philip, 2000.

Sontonga, Enoch. "Nkosi Sikelel' iAfrika." 1897. Accessed 16 December 2016. https://en .wikisource.org/wiki/National_Anthem_of _South_Africa.

Thompson, Leonard. *A History of South Africa.* 3rd ed. New Haven: Yale University Press, 2001.

United Democratic Front. "Statement by the UDF National Executive Committee on National Launching of the UDF." 1983. Accessed 16 December 2016. https://www.nelsonmandela .org/omalley/index.php/site/q/03lvo2424 /04lvo2730/05lvo3176/06lvo3185.htm.

United Nations. "Universal Declaration on Human Rights." 10 December 1948. http://www.un.org /en/universal-declaration-human-rights/.

Van Kessel, Ineke. *"Beyond Our Wildest Dreams": The United Democratic Front and the Transformation of South Africa.* Charlottesville: University of Virginia Press, 2000.

Verwoerd, Hendrik. "Apartheid" Speech to Parliament, 1950.

Worden, Nigel. *The Making of Modern South Africa.* 3rd ed. Malden, Mass.: Blackwell Publishing, 2000.

BIOGRAPHY, AUTOBIOGRAPHY

Bezdrob, Anné Mariè du Preez. *Winnie Mandela: A Life.* Cape Town: Zebra Press, 2003.

de Klerk, F. W. *The Last Trek—A New Beginning. The Autobiography.* London: Macmillan, 1998.

Mandela, Nelson. *Long Walk to Freedom: The Autobiography of Nelson Mandela.* Boston: Little, Brown, 1994.

Sampson, Anthony. *Mandela: The Authorized Biography.* New York: Alfred A. Knopf, 1999.

Slovo, Joe. *Slovo: The Unfinished Autobiography.* Johannesburg: Ravan Press, 1995.

1989–1994 TRANSITION

African National Congress. "ANC Constitution." 1991. Accessed 27 November 2016. http://www .anc.org.za/content/anc-constitution-adopted -december-1991.

African National Congress National Conference. "Ready to Govern: ANC Policy Guidelines for a Democratic South Africa Adopted at the National Conference, 28–31 May 1992." Johannesburg: Policy Unit of the African National Congress, 1992.

Barber, James. "South Africa: The Search for Identity." *International Affairs* 70, no. 1 (1994): 67–82.

Barnes, Catherine, and Edlred De Klerk. 2002. "South Africa's Multi-Party Constitutional Negotiation Process." Conciliation Resources (South Africa), http://www.c-r.org/accord/peace /accord13/samul.shtml.

Baskin, Jeremy. *Striking Back.* New York: Routledge, 1991.

Beresford, David. "Judge Condemns SA Riot Police." *Guardian (UK),* 9 September 1990.

———. "SA Alliance Endangered By 'Iron Fist.'" *Guardian (UK),* 9 September 1990.

Buthelezi, Mangosuthu G. "The Future of South Africa Should Be Determined By All Its Citizens." *New York Times,* 13 February 1988.

———. *South Africa: My Vision of the Future.* New York: St. Martin's Press, 1990.

Davenport, T. R. H. *The Birth of a New South Africa: The 1995 Joanne Goodman Lectures.* Toronto: University of Toronto Press, 1998.

De Haas, Mary, and Paulus Zulu. "Ethnicity and Federalism: The Case of Kwazulu-Natal." *Journal of Southern African Studies.* 20, no. 3 (September 1994): 433–46.

de Klerk, F. W. "F. W. de Klerk's Speech at the Opening of Parliament, 2 February 1990." https://www.nelsonmandela.org/omalley/index .php/site/q/03lvo2039/04lvo2103/05lvo2104 /06lvo2105.htm.

———. "Meeting between the State President of the Republic of South Africa and the President of the African National Congress." 26 September 1992. Accessed 26 February 2017. http://ucdp.uu .se/downloads/fullpeace/SyA%2019920926.pdf.

"Document 22: CODESA I Declaration of Intent, December 1991." South African History Online. Accessed 26 November 2016. http://www .sahistory.org.za/archive/document-22-codesa-i -declaration-intent.

Ellis, Stephen. "The Historical Significance of South Africa's Third Force." *Journal of Southern African Studies* 24, no. 2 (June 1998): 261–99.

Friedman, Steven, ed. *The Long Journey: South Africa's Quest for a Negotiated Settlement.* Johannesburg: Ravan Press, 1993.

Friedman, Steven, and Doreen Atkinson, eds. *South African Review 7. The Small Miracle: South Africa's Negotiated Settlement.* Johannesburg: Ravan Press, 1994.

Giliomee, Hermann. "Surrender Without Defeat: Afrikaners and the South African 'Miracle.'" *South African Institute of Race Relations Spotlight* 2, no. 97 (October 1997): 5–30.

———. "'Survival in Justice': An Afrikaner Debate over Apartheid." *Comparative Studies of Society and History* 36, no. 3 (July 1994): 527–48.

Ginwala, Frene. "Into and Out of CODESA Negotiations: The View from the ANC." In *Peace, Politics and Violence in the New South Africa*, edited by Norman Etherington, 1–27. London: Hanz Zell Publishers, 1992.

Inkatha Freedom Party. "The Birth of the Inkatha Freedom Party." 1990. http://www.ifp.org.za/.

Johnson, R. W., and Lawrence Schlemmer. *Launching Democracy in South Africa: The First Open Election, April 1994.* New Haven: Yale University Press, 1996.

Johnston, Alexander. "South Africa: The Election and the Emerging Party System." *International Affairs* 70, no. 4 (1994): 721–36.

Lawrence, Michael, and Andrew Manson. "The 'Dog of the Boers': The Rise and Fall of Mangope in Bophuthatswana." *Journal of Southern African Studies* 20, no. 3 (September 1994): 447–61.

Mallaby, Sebastian. *After Apartheid: The Future of South Africa.* New York: Times Books, 1992.

Mandela, Nelson. "Address to Rally in Durban, 25 February, 1990." Nelson Mandela Foundation. http://db.nelsonmandela.org/speeches/pub_view .asp?pg=item&ItemID=NMS020&txtstr=durban.

———. "On Release from Prison." Delivered to the Grand Parade, Cape Town, 11 February 1990. http://db.nelsonmandela.org/speeches/pub _view.asp?pg=item&ItemID=NMS016.

Maphai, Vincent. "Prospects for a Democratic South Africa." *International Affairs* 69, no. 2 (1993): 223–37.

Meer, Fatima, ed. *The Codesa File.* Durban: Madiba Publishers, 1993.

Murray, Martin J. *The Revolution Deferred: The Painful Birth of Post-apartheid South Africa.* London: Verso, 1994.

"National Peace Accord." 14 September 1991. http://www.incore.ulst.ac.uk/services/cds /agreements/pdf/sa4.pdf.

Pauw, Jacques. "Violence: The Role of the Security Forces." Speech given at the University of the Witswatersrand, 27 May 1992, http://www.csvr .org.za/wits/papers/pappauw.htm.

"Record of Understanding between ANC and NP. Statement by Nelson Mandela, President of the ANC, at the Opening of the ANC/NP Government Summit, 26 September 1992." South African History Online. http://www.sahistory.org .za/archive/record-understanding-between-anc -and-np-statement-nelson-mandela-president -anc-opening-ancnp.

Reynolds, Andrew, ed. *Election '94 South Africa: The Campaigns, Results and Future Prospects.* London: James Currey, 1994.

Schrire, Robert. *Adapt or Die: The End of White Politics in South Africa.* New York: Ford Foundation, 1991.

Slovo, Joe. "Has Socialism Failed?" Paper submitted to the South African Communist Party, January, 1990. http://www.sacp.org.za /docs/history/failed.html.

South African Communist Party. "Constitution of

the SACP." 1991. http://www.sacp.org.za/main.php ?include=docs/history/1991/constitution7.html.

Southall, Roger. "The South African Elections of 1994: The Remaking of a Dominant-Party State." *Journal of Modern African Studies* 32, no. 4 (1994): 629–55.

Sparks, Allister. "South African Police Criticized in Natal Violence." *Washington Post*, 8 September 1990.

———. *Tomorrow is Another Country: The Inside Story of South Africa's Road to Change.* Chicago: University of Chicago Press, 1996.

Spence, J. E., ed. *Change in South Africa.* London: Royal Institute of International Affairs, 1994.

Waldmeir, Patti. *Anatomy of a Miracle: The End of Apartheid and the Birth of a New South Africa.* New York: Norton, 1997.

Welsh, David. "The Making of the Constitution." In *The Bold Experiment: South Africa's New Democracy,* edited by Hermann Giliomee and Lawrence Schlemmer, with Sarita Hauptfleisch, 81–97. Johannesburg: Southern Book Publishers, 1994.

Acknowledgments

We wish to express our gratitude to the many people who have supported and aided the development of this project, though any errors we claim only as our own. First of all, to Peter Doerschler (Bloomsburg University), who composed the "Constitutional Worksheet"; to Nancy Jacobs (Brown University), for her expert and detailed commentary on historical details and feedback on playability; to Nick Proctor (Simpson College), who provided deep insight and important suggestions as he guided this work through the publication process; to Jace Weaver (University of Georgia), for his gracious and invaluable help in the publication process; to Jon Truitt (Central Michigan University), for helpful comments and conversations on game mechanics; and to Ian McNeely (University of Oregon), for outstanding editorial suggestions.

Our gratitude extends also to our colleagues at Loras College, especially Chris Budzisz, who offered comments and suggestions over many years of running this game and who gave it the experiential longevity that allows these games to grow into maturity. We also thank Mark Carnes, for his transformative vision that generated the Reacting Consortium and his enduring support for the creation of this game.

And finally, to the very many people who have contributed comments, suggestions, and criticisms at Reacting to the Past conferences at Barnard College and Drake University, most especially Donna Scimeca of the College of Staten Island and John Burney of Doane College.

Made in the USA
Middletown, DE
12 November 2017